The
GRAND DUKE
from
BOYS RANCH

Eugenia & Hugh M. Stewart '26 Series

The

GRAND DUKE

from

BOYS RANCH

Bill Sarpalius

Foreword by Bill Hobby

Texas A&M University Press
College Station

This paper meets the requirements of ANSI/NISO Z39.48-1992
(Permanence of Paper).
Binding materials have been chosen for durability.
Manufactured in the United States of America
♻ ∞

Library of Congress Cataloging-in-Publication Data

Names: Sarpalius, Bill, 1948– author.
   Title: The Grand Duke from Boys Ranch / Bill Sarpalius; foreword
by Bill Hobby.
   Description: First edition. | College Station: Texas A&M
University Press, [2018] | Series: Eugenia & Hugh M. Stewart '26
series | Includes index.
   Identifiers: LCCN 2017054328 (print) | LCCN 2017056329 (ebook)
| ISBN 9781623496586 (ebook) | ISBN 9781623496579 | ISBN
9781623496579 (cloth : alk. paper)
   Subjects: LCSH: Sarpalius, Bill, 1948– | Legislators—United
States—Biography. | Lithuanian Americans—Biography. | Cal
Farley's Boys Ranch (Tascosa, Tex.)—History. | Future Farmers of
America—History. | LCGFT: Autobiographies.
   Classification: LCC E840.8.S27 (ebook) | LCC E840.8.S27 A3
2018 (print) | DDC 328.73/092 [B]—dc23
   LC record available at https://lccn.loc.gov/2017054328

To Cal and Mimi Farley and Boys Ranch;

To my grandparents, Clarence and Ruby Maxwell;

To my mother, Honey; my brothers, Bobby and Karl; and my son, David;

And to my wife, Jenny, my true inspiration.

CONTENTS

FOREWORD

This is an American story, but don't think that it's just another inspiring story of an aspiring boy making good—it's so much more.

Bill's mother was an alcoholic at a time when treatment options were few and far between. Abandoned by her husband and unable to hold a job, she moved her three boys from apartments to vacant houses. At one time, Bill was a delivery boy for the *Houston Post*, my family newspaper, and what he earned from two paper routes was nearly all that supported the family. Not much later, a Houston judge took charge of a desperate situation and referred the boys to Cal Farley's Boys Ranch when Bill was thirteen.

At Boys Ranch, still a well-respected Panhandle home for boys, it seemed like the solution to every problem at that time was a good beating, but to Bill it was the first stable home he had ever had. It was a tough environment; however, Bill credits Boys Ranch with teaching him the work ethic that made him a success.

But success did not come easily. Bill was determined to go to college and worked several jobs—including one milking cows and feeding hogs at 4:00 a.m.—to pay for a degree in vocational agriculture. He started at Clarendon Junior College and graduated from Texas Tech University. Determined to seize opportunities that came his way, he parlayed a membership in Future Farmers of America into becoming state president of that organization.

And when the chance came to run for the Senate, he ignored the odds against him and worked harder than anyone else to get the votes.

I first met him when he was on the campaign trail, and then, after he was elected, he came to talk to me about committee assignments.

He told me that his goal was to create more treatment options for alcohol and mental problems. I put him on the Human Services Committee, and since he was a likely lad and well qualified, I also made him chair of the Agriculture Subcommittee.

Bill remembers that when it came time to pass his first major bill, to raise the drinking age from eighteen to nineteen, he was confronted by Senator "Mad Dog" Mengden, a Houston Republican with a bad temper. Mengden informed him that the bill was his property since he had been in the Senate longer. Bill refused to back down, and the two of them ended up in my office.

Bill remembers that I tossed a coin to determine whose bill came to the floor. The coin rolled behind my desk. What happened from there? Well, you have to read this book!

As a senator, Bill did what good senators do and represented his constituents well. He also took advice from many others. He picked his share of controversial issues, including one that resulted in a death threat, and when he carried a bill, he was well prepared and resourceful.

We did not always agree on all issues, but I respected his hard work, his determination, and his ability to tell a good story.

No surprise then that when a US congressional seat opened, he was ready to campaign for that, and when he won, he headed for Washington, where he served for six years in Congress helping with the breakup of the Communist Party of the Soviet Union. For his efforts, the country of Lithuania gave him the highest award they can give a noncitizen and named him their Grand Duke.

Bill is now a successful lobbyist in Washington, DC, and is a highly respected motivational speaker. Most importantly, Bill is my friend.

This is not just another book about politics. It is the inspiring, motivational, compelling story of my friend's life—and politics happened to be a part of it. You will enjoy Bill's story. I know it because I know Bill and I know his story. I am proud to say I was a part of it.

Bill Hobby
Lieutenant Governor of Texas, 1973–91

ACKNOWLEDGMENTS

T his book would never have become a reality if it had not been for my wife, Jenny, and my friends who encouraged me to tell my story. It took me thirteen years to put it on paper. Jenny has never lost faith, convinced that my story should be told to inspire and motivate others. She has spent endless hours editing and helping me with this book, and she is both my greatest blessing and my best friend. Many of the alumni of Boys Ranch have shared experiences like mine, and I must thank those who have enriched my life. Special thanks to Aaron Alejandro, who is like a brother, and to Rick Smith, who has always supported me. I will be eternally grateful to them.

A special thanks to the members of both the Texas legislature and the US Congress with whom I served for many years. Many of them are lifelong friends—there are too many to name. I also greatly appreciate current and former members of the Congressional Prayer Breakfast, who meet every Thursday morning to pray for divine guidance to make the right decisions for our country. Many of them have also encouraged me to write this book.

A special thanks to my friend Bettye Speed for the countless hours that she spent editing this book.

I can't speak of the past without thanking some of the staff and teachers at Boys Ranch who gave me that proverbial "shirttail to hang on to." Many of my teachers never gave up on helping me overcome my learning disabilities. They taught me how to read and write. Mr. and Mrs. Peggram, my dormitory parents, never lost faith in me. There were so many at Boys Ranch who positively influenced my life, and I will never forget what they did for me. I am who I am today because of the influence of many at Cal Farley's Boys Ranch.

David, my loving and devoted son, and my granddaughter, Katy, have enriched my life tremendously. They are my pride and joy.

Finally and most importantly, I want to thank my brothers, Bobby and Karl, who traveled this journey with me. The experiences we shared brought us closer than most brothers. Words cannot express how much I love them.

The
GRAND DUKE
from
BOYS RANCH

PART I
Cal Farley's Boys Ranch

CHAPTER 1

Abandoned

On the day after Christmas in 1960, everything my two younger brothers and I owned was packed into a small cardboard box and put in the back of a white Chevy station wagon. Painted in black on the wagon's front doors was a logo of a young boy wearing a cowboy hat and riding a bucking horse with another boy behind him holding on to the cowboy's shirttail. "Cal Farley's Boys Ranch" was printed across the top and below were the words "Amarillo, Texas."

Looking out the car window, I watched the fast-falling snow and a small herd of antelope running across the rugged mesquite-covered prairie. My brothers and I grew excited, having seen the pictures on the Boys Ranch's Christmas stamps. These stamps were mailed out twice a year to people across the country to solicit money for the ranch. One stamp showed a boy about eight years old wearing a blue cap and holding a puppy. The puppy was licking the boy's face. Another showed two boys in cowboy hats riding horses through the snow. They both rode with their chins down, a Christmas tree tied behind the saddle on one of the horses. I longed to be the boy holding that puppy or the cowboy riding the horse with the Christmas tree tied to the back of his saddle.

While we were excited, Bobby, Karl, and I were also frightened. We were moving to this strange new place hundreds of miles from our mother, whom we'd been taken away from. My mother, whom we called "Honey," was an alcoholic and suicidal. Providing for three children with no help is hard enough without an addiction—she just couldn't handle it alone. She had moved us from one vacant house to another, so we had never attended the same school for an entire year. Our mother's parents didn't have the means to take care of us, and our other grand-father, on my father's side, Karl "Doc" Sarpolis, didn't want us. Nobody wanted my brothers and me except for Boys Ranch.

Paul Stuart was our driver. My brothers and I kept asking him questions about what Boys Ranch was like. After driving thirty-six miles northwest of Amarillo, Texas, which seemed to us like it was in the middle of nowhere, Paul Stuart pointed out to us a hill in the shape of a saddle. He told us that the hill was known as Saddleback Hill, which was on the edge of the Canadian River and served as a marker for the Native Americans. He told us it was a shallow bed of the river for the buffalo to cross and that the Native Americans would make arrow-heads on top of the hill and wait for the buffalo. The western town of Tascosa sprung up alongside the river. Ever since I was a small boy, I loved Native American artifacts and stories of Buffalo Bill, Kit Carson, and Wild Bill Cody. In my mind, I couldn't wait for a chance to look for arrowheads at the top of Saddleback Hill.

We entered the arched entrance to Cal Farley's Boys Ranch. I noticed a beautiful white chapel, which Mr. Stuart explained had been moved to Boys Ranch from the air base in Dalhart. It was the focal point of the ranch. We parked in front of the Boys Center, an old white building with two large cottonwood trees in front. The Boys Center was the center of operations at the ranch. The post office, bank, and snack store were located in the Boys Center. This was also where visitors registered and where new residents were processed upon arrival. We were now new residents.

Three men in cowboy boots and jeans shook our hands and invited us to sit in the chairs along the wall. One of the men told us that we would do fine at the ranch if we followed the rules. He explained that we could go to Amarillo every third Saturday if we were not on "restriction." If we were on restriction, we would be assigned extra chores after school and on weekends.

We could not carry cash, he said. If we wanted to buy anything, we'd write a check from a Boys Ranch bank account. All checks had to be initialed by our dorm parents. We would each be provided new clothes. After that we would buy our own clothes from a monthly allowance, which was based on each boy's age. Church and Sunday school atten-dance was required. Most importantly, each boy was required to report at every roll call, which was called "muster," several times a day. We were

Boys Ranch Chapel and Tascosa Courthouse. Courtesy of Boys Ranch.

to follow all orders from our dorm parents or be punished. If we did not earn passing grades in school, we would be placed on restriction.

"Finally," he said with a smile, "the older boys will help you adjust and learn the rules."

Then a man with a limp came in, also wearing a cowboy hat and cowboy boots. He was about twenty-five years old and a little overweight. He had a big smile, and somehow he reminded me of Santa Claus.

He stuck out his hand and said, "I'm Gene Peggram, your dorm parent." He shook our hands and picked up our cardboard box. "I'll show you your dormitory." We followed him to his pickup, and he put our box in the back as Bobby, Karl, and I jumped into the front seat. As we drove away from the headquarters, Mr. Peggram said our dorm was named "Jim Hill," after a man who had donated money to build it. He added that thirty-six boys were living in Jim Hill.

We drove up a small hill and approached the dorm, built with Colorado red stone. A porch stretched across the front. Apartments for the dorm parents anchored each end of the building. Between them was the living room, or "big room," furnished with couches, a coffee table, and a TV set. Full-time dorm parents lived in one apartment, while alternate dorm parents, usually schoolteachers, lived in the other.

Jim Hill was one of a group of four dorm buildings known as the "Hilltop dorms," while the dorms on the other side of the dining hall and around a big hill were known as the "Valley dorms." We parked in front of Jim Hill, got our box out of the pickup, and went inside.

By the door were two cardboard boxes, one filled with oranges and the other with bananas. Located at each end of the big room was a door that led to a long hall that stretched from room 1 to room 6. Each room had three bunk beds and three closets. Located at each end of the hall was a bathroom with four sinks, four toilets, and four showers. Thirty-six boys shared a bathroom at each end of the hall.

Mr. Peggram explained that each room was numbered. Bobby and I would live in room 2, while Karl would live in another dorm for younger boys. It hadn't occurred to us that we could be separated. I asked Mr. Peggram why Karl couldn't live with us. He said Karl would move to a "big boys" dorm the following year, when he was older. He must have realized how upset this arrangement made us because he relented, saying Karl could stay with Bobby and me for the next five days until all the boys returned from Christmas holiday.

In our room, there was a couch and a desk along with the three bunk beds. The mattresses on the bunk beds were about an inch thick. Each closet was about five feet by four feet. Mr. Peggram said we would share our closet with another boy. He opened one closet door, and I saw that the clothes that took up half of the closet were perfectly folded—the other half of the closet was empty. There were a few family photographs on the first shelf and a few pair of pants and T-shirts on the other two shelves. Mr. Peggram told me that would be my closet and I would be sharing it with a boy named Pete Flack.

Mr. Peggram checked his watch and said it was almost time for dinner and that he'd give us a ride to the dining hall. The dining hall was one large room with about fifty round tables, eight chairs to each table. Hundreds of coat hooks lined the walls. At the center of the front wall was a stage. The kitchen was on one side of the stage, and the dishwashing room was on the other. Mr. Peggram showed us the cafeteria line, where we filled our plates with food, then we followed him to a table where four boys were already seated. They also lived in Jim Hill dorm. Of all thirty-six boys in Jim Hill, these four were the only ones who hadn't gone home for Christmas. As we ate, the four boys introduced themselves and answered the many questions we asked.

As we walked back toward the dorm after dinner, Mr. Peggram pulled up in the same station wagon we rode to Boys Ranch in and asked if we wanted to go bowling or see a movie in Amarillo. All seven of us scrambled in, and Mr. Peggram drove us the thirty-six miles to the bowling alley in Amarillo. We bowled for hours and then slept in the station wagon on the way back. We had a great first day, and I thought this was the beginning of something very special in our lives. As I dozed off to sleep, I could see myself riding a horse with a new pair of boots and a cowboy hat.

The next morning after breakfast, Mr. Peggram took us to a country store to get our new clothes. All I could think about was a pair of cowboy boots and a cowboy hat. The country store was a small white building behind the dining hall. Our "new clothes" were khaki army fatigues that had been donated from the air base in Amarillo. They were too big and didn't fit well, but they were free. Each of us was given two pairs of pants and two shirts. We also got one pair of dress slacks, a dress shirt, and dress shoes to wear only to church or trips to Amarillo. Then we were fitted with army brogans: brown high-top shoes with leather laces. We were each issued four pairs of socks and underwear and two T-shirts.

When I asked Mr. Peggram when we'd get a cowboy hat and a pair of cowboy boots, he chuckled and answered, "When you have the money to buy them."

He labeled all our clothes in red ink with our own laundry numbers, explaining that this was to identify our clothes from the other 350 boys at the ranch when the clothes came back from the laundry. My number was JH83. Bobby and Karl each had their own numbers.

I asked Mr. Peggram when I would get to ride a horse. He laughed and said that later that afternoon, I could go to the horse barn and wait in line to ride a horse. That was all I could think about the entire day. I wanted to ride that horse and pretend I was a cowboy. At 1:00 p.m., I hurried down a dirt road flanked by cottonwood trees to a cinder-block building. There were horse stalls on one side and dairy cow pens on the other side. Standing in line behind several boys, I waited for my turn to pick a horse to ride. A clipboard had a list of the horses' names with a blank line next to each one. I had to select a horse and sign my name on the line. Turning to the boy behind me, I asked which horse to pick. He said to choose the horse named Sleepy because he was slow. Sleepy was the horse they used to teach boys to ride. Another boy helped me pick out a bridle and saddle, showing me how to strap it on the horse. I mounted Sleepy, rode for more than an hour, and fell in love.

I returned to my dorm that afternoon, fell into my bunk bed, and thought about how wonderful it was to be at Boys Ranch. I had a bed, new clothes, and fresh fruit by the door. We went bowling, and I got to ride a horse for the first time. Life could not be any better. Although I missed my mother, Boys Ranch was perfect for my brothers and me. I fell to sleep wondering if my mother was OK. I was twelve years old and had gone to sleep many times worrying about my mother. I had seen her drinking get worse each night for years. She had become very depressed and had tried several times to take her own life. She was my mother, and to me she was the best mother in the world. I knew deep inside she was struggling and that her sons were her life—it must have been so painful knowing she had to give us up and that she could not provide for us. That must have made her feel like a complete failure.

Two days later our lives at Boys Ranch changed when more than two hundred boys returned to the ranch. The dorm parents searched everyone's luggage and clothes, looking for cigarettes, cash, and other contraband.

Before dinner, some boys started walking throughout the dorm yelling, "Muster!" I reported immediately to the living room. Mr. Peggram stood in the center of the big room as all the boys hurried to grab a seat on the couches along the walls.

As Mr. Peggram read the names of each boy in the dorm in alphabetical order, each boy responded, "Here, sir!" After he read all the names, he asked Bobby and me to stand. He introduced us to the group, and the boys clapped to make us feel welcome. We were referred to as the "new boys," a nickname for boys who were new to the ranch.

After muster we walked to the dining hall, where we were assigned permanent seats at a table. Bobby's table was next to mine, and we searched for Karl. He had just moved into the dorm for younger boys and knew no one. At least Bobby and I had each other. When I spotted my little brother, I hurried to his table to ask how he was doing. A man yelled at me, ordering me back to my seat. Karl began to cry.

Karl, Me, and Bobby, taken in our first week at Boys Ranch. Courtesy of Boys Ranch

That man told Karl to shut up and sit down. As I walked back to my chair, I began to realize we were now living in a different Boys Ranch.

On the dining hall stage, four boys sat at a table at the center, right beside a microphone. A boy next to me whispered that it was the head table and one of them would be picked to say grace before the meal. One boy took the microphone, made an announcement, and then said, "We have three new boys, Bill, Bobby, and Karl," and then he asked us to stand. Three hundred fifty boys and a hundred staff members all clapped. It made us feel special to be recognized for the first time in front of all those people.

After supper, Bobby, Karl, and I headed back to our dorms. One of the older boys caught up with me. He said the older boys had another set of rules for us to follow. I didn't understand what he meant, but he told me that I would find out later that night. He snickered and ran off. I became very uneasy.

When we got to the dorm, Mr. Peggram called another muster (this was to ensure that if a boy had run away, he wouldn't get far before the staff would begin searching for him). At bedtime, Mr. Peggram walked down the hall and called lights out. I climbed into my bunk and listened to about twenty radio broadcasts throughout the dorm. If a boy could afford it or got one as a gift, he could have a radio. They were all tuned to the same station, KIXZ in Amarillo, which played popular music of the time. Elvis Presley was at the top of the charts, but Del Shannon's "Runaway" was the song I soon identified with.

I fell asleep, but not for long. An older boy shook me awake, ordering me to follow him. We went outside to find four older boys waiting under the lights of the back porch. They were all smoking short cigarettes they called "snipes." One said that if I wanted to survive at Boys Ranch, I'd better follow their rules. I was never to tell on anyone. If I did, I was a "fink." A second guy shoved me and said that I was to give them any money I had, that everything I had belonged to them, and that I would steal for them if they told me to. A third grabbed my shoulder, saying I was to do whatever they told me to and asked if I understood. I was so scared I could hardly speak, but I nodded that I understood.

The fourth boy shoved me up against the brick wall, grabbed me by the throat, and punched me in the face. They all took turns hitting and kicking me. I cried, but they kept it up while ordering me to shut up. They finally stopped. The boy who woke me up told me to go back to bed. They said to me that this was a test and that if anybody asked what happened to me and I "finked" on them, then they would beat me again as soon as they got the chance. They also threatened to beat Bobby even worse. I went to bed hurt and crying. Now I missed my mother.

At six the next morning, a man named Roger Waldrip came down the hall, turned on the lights, and told us to get up. Lamont and Roger Waldrip both worked at Boys Ranch. Lamont, the older brother, was big, about six foot two, with a deep booming voice. We were terrified of him. Roger, the younger Waldrip, was not nearly as physically imposing as Lamont. He was a schoolteacher and coach, having graduated from college only a few years earlier. Roger would become a positive influence in my life.

When I awoke, I could barely get out of bed. My badly swollen face throbbed. No one—neither my roommates nor the boys I passed in the hall and the bathroom—said a word. They had probably been through the same thing. In the mirror, I saw that my right eye was black and swollen. I was terrified, not knowing what I would tell anyone who might ask about what had happened.

When a staff member asked me at breakfast, I looked down at my plate.

"I fell out of bed," I lied.

The staff member called another colleague over. They told me to get up and led me to the rear of the dining hall. I could feel the eyes of every boy on the back of my neck. My face felt hot. In the back of the dining hall was a large storage room stacked with boxes of food. The two men looked down at me and ordered me to tell them who had attacked me. They threatened to spank me with a belt if I did not confess. When I did not tell them, they pulled off their leather belts and folded them into a loop. Getting hit with the belt was known as "getting your licks." They yelled at me to tell them the names of the boys who had beaten me. I couldn't tell them their names because I didn't know who they were. I thought that might be my saving grace, but I was not so lucky.

One of the men told me to bend over and hold onto some boxes. He raised his belt and swung it hard and fast and struck me on my butt. Pain ripped through my body. I fell to the floor, but I was yanked back to my feet and told to tell them the names. I pleaded with him not to hit me.

He shouted at me again, "Give us the names!" They took turns giving me licks. When they finally stopped, I was told I was on three weeks' restriction. They ordered me back to my table.

I walked back to my chair and held my head down to hide my tears as every boy stared at me. I felt so ashamed. As I walked past one of the boys who had beaten me, he stared me down and smiled as if to say I had done the right thing. I lowered myself carefully onto my chair. I was so embarrassed, and the pain in my thighs and buttocks was unbearable. I wiped the tears from my face as I sat there, feeling so afraid and alone.

Before I knew it, breakfast was over, and I had eaten nothing; my stomach was in knots. Deep-blue bruises appeared later that night. This was not what I was expecting in my first week at Boys Ranch.

CHAPTER 2

Cal Farley

Cal Farley masterminded the entire organization of Boys Ranch. He never requested government funds for his work because he did not want the government telling him how to raise his boys. He did not affiliate with any religious group, though he made certain that Bible teachings undergirded the principles of the ranch, and though he lived and worked in Amarillo, he rarely missed a Sunday at the ranch. After church, he had lunch with all of us in the dining hall, then walked around to each table talking with the boys. After lunch, many of the boys gathered around him. He was our hero.

I never will forget the first time I saw Cal. I had expected a big, tall, powerful man. Instead, I saw a graying, short, stocky older man wearing wire-rimmed glasses. When he came to our table, I stood and shook his hand. He welcomed me to Boys Ranch, though I was disappointed when he called me "Dale." I understood that he couldn't have known my name yet. After all, there were more than 350 boys at the ranch, and that number grew nearly every month. *Eventually*, I thought, *he'll know my name.*

Cal made sure there was enough money in the bank to feed, clothe, and take care of a boy until he graduated from Boys Ranch. His goal was to help the bottom rung of boys, the lowest 10 percent that nobody wanted. Most of the boys had been moved around all their lives, just like my brothers and me. One boy, for example, was ten years old and had lived in twenty-two foster homes before coming to Boys Ranch. Cal was committed to each child equally. He believed they needed a permanent place to grow up. He knew that most of these kids would never finish high school, but he believed that if he could teach them

Cal and Mimi Farley. Courtesy of Boys Ranch.

how to read, write, and balance a checkbook, and if they could learn a vocational skill, they could become productive citizens. Boys Ranch was accredited by the state of Texas, so state funds contributed to teachers' salaries and the cost of running the elementary, junior high, and high school. Almost every boy was behind in his studies, so Cal made sure the student-teacher ratios were low, allowing the teachers to spend more time helping their students.

When my brothers and I arrived at Boys Ranch, there were thirteen vocational programs—among them you could learn to be a cook, painter, plumber, bricklayer, barber, auto mechanic, or electrician. In the vocational program, each student received a small stipend for his work. If a boy wanted to be a painter, he apprenticed to an adult hired to paint buildings at the ranch. Then when he graduated with his vocational skills, the goal was that he would have no problem finding a job.

Upon graduation from Boys Ranch, graduates received one of two certificates: a high school diploma or a vocational certificate. Every boy walked across the stage in the same cap and gown, so nobody knew which certificate the graduate earned. A boy stayed until he turned eighteen or graduated with a diploma or a certificate. Cal Farley knew that most of the boys had never received any recognition or accomplished anything in their lives. To that end, he set up a competitive sports program in which ribbons and trophies were awarded to just about every boy. Dorms competed against each other in volleyball, baseball, basketball, track, and wrestling. The competitions were organized on an elimination basis, so ultimately the champion of the Hilltop dorms competed against the champion from the Valley dorms. Trophies were presented on the dining room stage, and all the winners were recognized. The first ribbon I won was for track, after I had been at the ranch three months. It was a green ribbon. I came in fifth place in a race, and I was so proud of my ribbon. I hung it in my closet so it was the first thing I saw when I got dressed in the morning. For many of the boys, this would be the first time they would receive any type of recognition, even for trying. This motivated a boy to try harder in whatever he was doing.

Many of the boys at the ranch were violent juvenile offenders. At that time, Texas had a prison for juveniles in Gatesville. Judges had the option of sending boys to detention in Gatesville or relinquishing custody to Boys Ranch. Cal and the judges across Texas had an arrangement. If Cal thought he could help a juvenile offender, he would attend the boy's trial and ask the judge from the back of the courtroom if he could take the boy to Boys Ranch. Then the judge asked the delinquent boy what he wanted: Boys Ranch or prison. Of course he'd choose Boys Ranch. The judge would warn the boy that the first time he did something wrong at the ranch, he'd be off to Gatesville. Many times, this was planned in advance of the hearing.

Cal Farley never said no to a boy in trouble. The environment I grew up in at Boys Ranch was made up of boys who had no family, boys whose families could not care for them, or boys who had committed violent crimes. When you put those backgrounds together, it was volatile.

Buddy Fesmier and Jimmy May were good examples. Buddy had come to Boys Ranch as a juvenile delinquent who had stolen anything and everything he wanted. Jimmy, on the other hand, came to Boys Ranch because he had no family and no place to go. He was an unwanted boy who was behind in school and a loner. One night, Buddy convinced Jimmy to run away from Boys Ranch with him, but not before breaking into a staff apartment to steal a gun. Then they went to a ranch house nearby; tied up an old couple; stole their rifles, pistols, and pickup truck; and took off for Amarillo. When the police found them, a high-speed chase ensued. The boys shot at the police car chasing them. Either Buddy or Jimmy shot and killed an officer. At this point, the situation became uncontrollably violent, and the police responded by shooting out all the tires and opening fire on the pickup. Jimmy May was killed, and Buddy was shot four times. This type of tragedy was unusual but not completely shocking for the boys at Boys Ranch.

I remember when it happened. We all saw it on the news on the living room television. A reporter and a cameraman were standing out in front of the ranch trying to reach Cal Farley for comment. Sherman "Sherm" Harriman, Cal's son-in-law and assistant at the ranch, stayed at the town office all night. Sherm had married Cal and Mimi's only daughter, Genie.

Sherm asked Cal, "What are we going to do now?"

Cal stood up from behind his desk and declared that they would continue to help boys like Buddy and Jimmy. "If we don't help them, no one else will." Nonetheless, it was a dark day for Cal Farley and his Boys Ranch.

We all attended Jimmy May's funeral. Boys Ranch had been his only family. He was buried next to a pond in a cemetery in Amarillo. Jimmy was just fourteen years old. When Buddy went to trial, he claimed that Jimmy had held a gun on him and forced him to shoot at the police. I never believed his story; I knew Buddy was lying. A few character witnesses from Oklahoma testified on his behalf. Buddy spent time in jail.

Two years later Buddy was released to his father in Oklahoma. While out with a girl, he said he wanted to stop by his house to check on his father. While she waited in the car, Buddy went inside. When he returned, he was covered with blood. Then he took the girl inside to show her the dead bodies of his father, his brother, and his brother's friend. He had stabbed, shot, and beaten them to death as they slept.

Buddy was found guilty on three counts of murder and sentenced to death. Although Buddy's execution date was suspended when the state of Oklahoma eliminated the death penalty, Buddy Fesmier would spend the rest of his life in prison being punished for his despicable crimes.

After the tragedy, Boys Ranch significantly modified the intake process regarding the acceptance of boys who had been convicted of acts of violence. Based on my experiences, the violent boys became bullies and were abusive to the weaker boys. This decision over time would eliminate a lot of the abuse that came from the violent boys. Even though Cal Farley's goal was to help that bottom 10 percent, he realized that even Boys Ranch had limits.

One time, before this specific tragedy forced Cal to make the changes, I picked up a bar of soap in the shower, and just as I started to wash, I noticed a razor blade embedded in the bar. No one knew who had put it there. I was constantly struggling to survive in two different worlds of fear: fear of the staff and fear of the violent boys. The older boys would force younger boys to do things for them, such as look for snipes along the side of the streets or steal money. And staff members who didn't like certain children would spank them for no apparent reason. At that time, childcare facilities were not regulated, licensed, or inspected.

After living at the ranch for almost two weeks, on January 10, I celebrated my thirteenth birthday. I was excited and thought about how Honey tried to make my birthday special when we were living on the streets since it was so close to Christmas. She used to split my gifts in twos. One year, for instance, I got a pair of roller skates: one skate for Christmas and the other for my birthday. Another year, I got a pair of shoes: one for Christmas and the other for my birthday.

For my birthday at the ranch, during the lunchtime announcements, the boy at the microphone called my name and told me to stand while the others applauded. This was another way of giving every boy some recognition. I was still tender and hurt from the spanking I had received in the back of the dining hall several days earlier, but I stood up with my head down. I was very shy and not accustomed to being recognized in a crowd. When the applause stopped, I sat down in my chair.

After the dorm muster that evening, Mr. Peggram called me to the center of the living room. He had a large sheet cake with white icing decorated with blue letters that said, "Happy Birthday, Bill." There was

My first birthday at Boys Ranch with my new shirt. I was thirteen years old, in the fifth grade, and couldn't read. Courtesy of the Sarpalius family.

one wrapped present by the cake. My birthday gift was a shirt with a brown paisley design, the fad at that time.

My laundry number, JH83, was already written inside the collar. It was amazing what a small act of kindness could do for my sense of worth. The cake was cut into squares so each boy would get a piece. There was ice cream too. To many of the boys, the recognition was very important; birthdays became special days. In addition to the cake and the present, Mr. Peggram also asked, "Who do you want to give you your licks?"

I told him that I did not understand what he meant. "You have to pick a boy to spank you thirteen times with his belt" was his response.

Helpless, I looked around at the thirty-six boys who lived in our dorm. I hardly knew any of them. My only true friend was my brother. I said I wanted Bobby because I knew he would not intentionally hurt me.

Mr. Peggram told me to bend over and grab hold of the oak coffee table. He instructed Bobby to take off his belt, fold it in half, and hit me as hard as he could.

Bobby raised his belt high but hit me very softly, even though I had never told him my butt was already bruised from the licks the previous day. All the boys taunted him to hit me harder and harder. I tried my best not to cry as I counted every swat.

"OK, boys! Now let's sing 'Happy Birthday'!"

When we went to bed, Bobby came into my room and asked if I was OK. I showed him my bruised butt and thighs. They were solid dark purple. My brother was horrified. We knew then that we would some-how have to find a way to survive at Boys Ranch.

The next day at muster, Mr. Peggram read the names of the boys who had received mail. Getting mail was a big deal because it meant that someone cared about you. He called my name. Proudly, I walked up to get my letter.

I knew it was from Honey when I saw the envelope. Written in black ink with large letters across the front were the words "Bill, Bobby, and Karl Sarpalius." The envelope had been opened already, which was policy. I was so overcome with joy when I saw her name on the envelope. Pulling the letter out, I saw that many of the sentences had been marked through with a blue marker. Boys Ranch had its own post office, and every letter received or sent was censored. The staff wanted to know if a boy was making plans to run away or communicating about any mis-treatment at Boys Ranch. Some letters were never sent.

Bobby and I ran to my room and sat on my bunk bed. Bobby read the letter aloud. In Mom's childlike block handwriting, it read,

I am doing well and miss my boys very much. I am making plans to move to Amarillo so I can see you every chance I have.

I love you, and you are always in my prayers.
Honey

At the end of the letter in red lipstick was an impression of Honey's lips. Written across the kiss was, "I love you boys."

After reading the letter, I was homesick. I also worried constantly about my mother. At dinner, I gave the letter to Karl. We took turns carrying it in our pockets, keeping Honey close.

Cal Farley once told a story about a boy who lived with his mother on the streets of Dallas. They slept in a cardboard box and had nothing. Eventually, he wound up at the ranch. One Sunday, the boy ran up to Cal after church services and asked when he could go home. Cal said that he had taken that boy out of a terrible environment and given him three meals a day, a warm bed, a good school, and a horse to ride, but all that boy wanted was to return to his mother in that cardboard box. Cal said that it took him years to understand the bond between a boy and his mother.

~

I wanted to learn how to milk a cow, so they assigned me to work at the dairy barn. It was that same barn where I learned to ride a horse. I was supposed to report to the barn at 5:00 a.m., so I set my alarm to get there early. But when I arrived, there were already about thirty boys on the job. The dairy barn was a cinder-block building with a large room where the cows entered through a large door into separate stalls. The boys each took a stall; we could milk about thirty cows at a time.

When I reported to the staffer in charge, he turned me over to an older boy who steered me to the center of the barn, introducing me as the new milker. He told me to grab a stool and bucket. In the corner of the milking room was a stack of tree stumps that we used as stools. One of the older boys ordered me to sit on the opposite side of the cow that he was milking. I put my metal bucket under the cow and sat down on the stool. When I touched her, she kicked me, knocking me off the stool. I slammed onto the wet cement floor, and all the boys howled with laughter. Every new boy to the dairy barn got the same initiation. I realized that every cow had two boys milking her, one on each side. The cow that I was asked to help milk would only allow us to milk one side at a time. After the embarrassment, I was paired up with a boy and slowly and steadily learned how to milk a cow. I enjoyed working at the dairy barn and worked there for years.

A few months later, two of the older boys told me to sneak up to the ranch's headquarters and look for snipes along the sidewalk and curbs. I ran up to the Boys Center and started looking as fast as I could, but I could not find any. My heart was racing; I knew if I got back to the barn with nothing, they would beat me. I had no choice; I had to get back to the dairy barn before someone noticed that I was missing.

I returned with nothing. The two older boys hauled me to the back of the dairy barn into a room that was used to store grain for the cows. I was sexually abused. I never cried so hard. I felt so ashamed, humiliated, and violated. And I was terrified. All I wanted was to go home and be with Honey, my mother. I never said a word because I was scared of what they might do to my brothers. I kept this to myself for years. I later learn that this happened to other boys at the ranch.

~ CHAPTER 3 ~

A Schooling

When I was five years old, my legs and arms began to shrink, and I would fall a lot. I became very skinny. It got so bad my parents took me to St. Joseph Medical Center in the heart of Houston, Texas. After several tests, I was diagnosed with polio. In the 1950s, polio had become one of the most serious communicable diseases among children in the United States. In 1952, alone, nearly sixty thousand children were infected with the virus; thousands were paralyzed, and more than three thousand died. In 1955, the National Health Service began widespread vaccinations. By 1979 the virus had been eliminated across the country. The Catholic nuns at St. Joseph's Medical Center massaged my legs and arms for hours several times a day, and I was convinced that God had sent them to me as angels. I saw many kids get worse and many become well. I was blessed, and I slowly got better. Because of polio, I was behind in my studies, to the point that my younger brother Bobby started school before me. It was not until my senior year in high school that I caught up with him, and we graduated together. We moved around so often, we never finished a year in the same school until we came to Boys Ranch. When I arrived at the ranch, I was thirteen and in the fifth grade. It was embarrassing to have my younger brother a year ahead of me. My teacher was Pat Stuart, wife of Paul Stuart, the man who'd driven us to the ranch our first day. She was a petite brunette with a kind, soft voice.

My desk was in the back of the classroom. Mrs. Stuart introduced me to the other boys in the class, who were much smaller and younger. I felt so awkward and out of place. A few days later, Mrs. Stuart asked each student to stand up and read out of our textbook. She started with the first row of boys and went back until she reached my row. When it was my turn to read, I stood beside my desk. Everyone stared at me. I was so ashamed and embarrassed because I couldn't read. I didn't know how. They all laughed. I fought back tears. I was tall, skinny, and older than every boy in my class. I withdrew and became very shy.

Mrs. Stuart took me to the hall, closing the classroom door behind her. "Don't worry," she said gently. She was compassionate. "I will teach you to read. We'll check with Mr. Peggram so you can stay after school. I'll help you."

She received permission for me to work on my reading comprehension after school every day. She stayed and helped me; she was dedicated. Nobody made her do it. I will never forget her for that. But the best teacher I had at that time was my brother Bobby. He understood my struggles and helped me with my spelling and reading. He also understood about survival at Boys Ranch.

The teachers would distribute report cards as school dismissed, and each boy had to take his report card to his dorm parent for his signature. I had three Fs on my report card, in reading, math, and spelling. I was so disappointed because I had been trying very hard. I gave the report card to Mr. Peggram and told him I would do better. On the way to the dining hall, some of the boys told me that I would get a spanking after dinner because of my grades. I was too scared to eat. After the meal, I went back to my room, opened my schoolbooks, and pretended to study.

I saw Mr. Peggram and Mr. Waldrip walk toward the bathroom, with one of the boys between them. They closed the door. In a few minutes, I heard the belt as it hit the boy. The boy was screaming and begged them to stop. Later he came out crying. When the boy left the bathroom, he would go tell the next boy that it was his turn to go to the bathroom. Every time the bathroom door opened, as I waited my turn, my heart stopped. Finally, a boy with a swollen, tear-stained face told me it was my turn.

I walked down that long hallway and slowly opened the door. The bathroom had four sinks with a long mirror extending the length of the wall above the sinks. Mr. Peggram and Mr. Waldrip leaned against the sinks, their backs to the mirror. I stood in front of them. Mr. Peggram asked me why I had failed three subjects. I said I was trying very hard and promised to do better. Mr. Peggram told me that the punishment for an F was a spanking and restriction for three weeks, which meant that I could not go on the town trips to Amarillo on Saturdays and that I would not be able to see my mother. Instead, I would have to work moving rocks, chopping weeds, sweeping streets, and other labor, as assigned. I started to shake. They already had their belts off and folded in two. Mr. Peggram told me to bend over and grab hold of a sink. They took turns spanking me. I focused on my reflection in the mirror and tried my best not to cry, but I could not withstand the pain. I returned to my room in tears. The next day I hurt when I had to sit in a chair. I was purple and black again. The bruises from the previous licks had barely healed. I could hardly sit. It even hurt to walk.

One of the older boys, Dean Warren, was very kind to me, and I idolized him. Dean was always smiling, and he always had the best ride in the annual Boys Ranch rodeo, where he earned the title of "All-Around Cowboy." He was respected and well liked by most of the boys and staff. Dean and I walked together to the dining hall and to work at the dairy barn, and we became good friends. As he described his experiences with his alcoholic father, I realized we had a lot in common. Dean was also very far behind in school and was trying his best to catch up so he could graduate with his age group. He became like a big brother to me, and he kept the other older boys from picking on me.

Bobby and I wrote to Honey making it sound like we were doing fine. Since our mail was censored, we would never write anything bad about Boys Ranch. Bobby wrote the letter, and I asked him to tell her about my new friend, Dean. We told her about riding a horse, learning to milk a cow, and working at the dairy barn. Bobby ended the letter with how much we missed her and how we couldn't wait to see her. And I asked Bobby to tell her I was learning how to read.

Honey had moved to Amarillo during our first year at the ranch. She started working for a florist and wedding shop. She was a good artist and drew sketches of wedding dresses for advertisements in the newspaper. She would cut them out of the paper and send them to us. She wanted us to be proud of her. When we finally had three letters from Honey, we each carried one of her letters with us all the time.

One Saturday, Bobby and Karl boarded the Boys Ranch school bus bound for Amarillo. They were going to see our mother. I was on restriction, so I had to stay to do chores at the ranch. I was chopping weeds and moving rocks as the bus drove off. It hurt deeply that I could not go with them.

When my brothers returned that evening, they told me how much fun they had visiting our mom at her new apartment. She had cooked eggs for them. I was envious but glad they had seen her. I remember one time, on a visit to Amarillo, Honey asked us what we wanted to eat. All three of us asked for eggs. Bobby and I each ate a dozen, and Karl ate eight! We didn't have eggs at that time when we lived at the ranch.

My brothers also brought me some candy bars, but I had to give them to the older boys, or they would beat me up. When I handed the candy to one of the big boys, he smiled and gave one back. I saved that candy bar because it was from my mother. Although the first year was difficult, sometimes to the point where I cannot imagine how I survived it, life at Boys Ranch became easier over time. I improved my reading skills and began to make friends.

It was a sad day for me when Dean graduated from Boys Ranch. The Vietnam War was reaching its peak, and two-thirds of the senior class enlisted in the military. Dean enlisted in the army and was eventually sent to Vietnam to fight in the war. Dean became a medic and was killed trying to help a wounded soldier. Dean had run up a hill under fire and was shot trying to drag the soldier back down the hill. His devotion to helping anyone in need had a major impact on my life. He will always remain a hero to me.

∽

Mr. Peggram married Tommy Sue, the secretary at the ranch. Many of the boys thought she was the most beautiful woman at the ranch. They were married in the Boys Ranch Chapel, and all the Jim Hill dorm boys went to their wedding. We were proud to have Tommy Sue as our dorm mother. The dorm parents always kept their apartment door open to the living room because Cal Farley believed that dorm parents should be like family, with their home always open to the boys.

One afternoon, several boys sat on the couches in our living room watching TV. Mr. Peggram was lying on the couch in his apartment with his head in Tommy Sue's lap. We could see into their apartment. Tommy Sue had a small white poodle with a pink bow on her collar. The dog was lying on the top of the couch.

We took school exams every six weeks, and report cards would come out the following day. Even though I was trying my best, I always got Fs and would be spanked for my grades and would get a restriction for another three weeks. It seemed like I would never get off restriction, so I was mad at Mr. Peggram. I was upset because I was trying to learn to read and spell, so school was very difficult for me. I became very frustrated with myself.

One time, when the Peggrams' white poodle went outside, I followed her out the front door, caught her, and gave her a suppository that another guy had stolen from the infirmary. The dog went back in the apartment and jumped on the couch. I had a clear view of the poodle lounging above Mr. Peggram, who was once again resting his head in Tommy Sue's lap. About thirty minutes later, the dog arched like a cat, yelped, and the suppository did its work—all over Mr. Peggram and the couch! The Peggrams jumped up off the couch and carried the dog outside. Mr. Peggram yelled at Tommy Sue about her sick dog while we all laughed hysterically. I finally had gotten even with him!

The academic year ended, and the school counselor talked to me about being placed in a "special education" class for kids with learning disabilities who were not expected to finish high school. Those students were ridiculed and considered slow achievers. I begged not to be placed in special education and promised to work harder in school.

To avoid being placed in special education classes, the teachers told me I could attend summer school, so I did. I went to school while the other boys did chores. During the summer months, each boy was assigned a morning job. In the afternoon, we signed up for activities such as swimming, horseback riding, playing ball, or fishing in one of the ranch's lakes. Summers there were wonderful, but we still had responsibilities. We worked hard and we played hard; by the end of the day, we were thoroughly exhausted. Cal believed that if you kept a boy busy, he would be too tired to get into mischief. Even now I believe he was right.

One night a boy was snoring so loud, I couldn't sleep. I got out of bed and put some shaving cream on his hand and piled it as high as I could. Then I got a mop string and tickled his nose. He went to scratch his nose and had shaving cream all over his face. Another night I put an Alka-Seltzer tablet in his mouth, and foam started coming out. The next morning Mr. Peggram came up to me at breakfast and asked me if

I had done that. I lied, but he saw right through me; he took me by the collar and dragged me into the hallway leading to the kitchen. There he grabbed me by the throat and started slamming my head up against the cinder-block wall until I passed out. I had always wondered how he knew it was me, because all the boys were asleep when I did it.

When my brothers and I arrived at Boys Ranch, the food we were served and ate was called "train-wreck food," which had been donated to Boys Ranch by a corporation following a train or truck wreck; the business deducted the loss on its taxes, and Boys Ranch got the food. One "train wreck" landed Boys Ranch a boxcar full of lemon drops. When we first got to the ranch, every boy got a bag of lemon drops weekly. Seven years later, when I left the ranch, boys were still eating those lemon drops.

Mr. Jenkins was in charge of the dining hall. He was a short, old, retired Army cook who drank cheap whiskey regularly. We always knew Jenkins had been hitting the bottle hard when we got cookies after supper. The cookies were also "train-wreck" food, and they were so hard, we could not eat them.

We had toast and cereal. We very seldom had meat—either at lunch or supper. And we never had eggs, except when we went on town trips to Amarillo.

During my years at Boys Ranch, the quality of the food improved a lot because of Guy Finstad. Guy was hired as farm director and advisor for the Future Farmers of America. Guy was a tall, slim man, and he and his wife, Geneva, had four children: a girl and three boys. Their names were Sherry, Gary, Terry, and Berry. The Finstad family would play a major role in my life.

While he was at the ranch, Guy built an incredible agricultural program, complete with a slaughterhouse, meat-processing plant, and cannery. By the time I left, Guy's program was producing all the beef and pork for the ranch. He taught the boys to plant a vegetable garden, and we canned all the produce we grew. The ranch also had a dairy, where the milk was pasteurized and transferred to half-pint cartons with the Boys Ranch logo on them. In just a few years, Guy's farm program produced 80 percent of the ranch's food, and the ranch's Future Farmers of America chapter grew to be the largest in Texas. This is when I first saw, up close and personal, the importance of everyday farmers and the farms they worked their whole lives to till and grow.

CHAPTER 4

The Rodeo

T he biggest event of the year was the annual Boys Ranch Rodeo. The rodeo, always held over the Labor Day weekend, drew thousands of spectators. The younger boys rode small calves. The older boys rode bulls and bareback horses. Animals were assigned based on age, and I was old enough to ride a steer, or a young bull. I was petrified, but if a boy didn't ride, he would be called a coward.

Rodeo practice was three days a week during the summer. The better, more advanced riders were selected to ride in the two-day event and were eligible to compete for the highest honors: Junior and Senior All-Around Cowboy. The winners received awards, and their pictures appeared on the front page of the *Amarillo Globe-News*. The top three contestants in each event won cowboy belt buckles. The top twelve best riders in the rodeo became members of the Honor Patrol, and there were two alternates, so fourteen in total.

Members of the Honor Patrol rode twelve beautiful palomino horses, all direct descendants of Roy Rogers's famous horse, Trigger. One of Trigger's sons was in a train wreck, and one of his front hooves had been cut in half, so Roy Rogers donated the injured horse as a stud to Boys Ranch. Over time we had some beautiful palomino horses to ride.

The Honor Patrol dressed alike, wearing shiny dark-blue shirts, new white cowboy hats, and white chaps with a "BR" (Boys Ranch) brand in blue stitched in the middle of the chaps. Our saddles were alike, and the horse blankets were blue with the BR symbol on each corner.

The Honor Patrol rode in parades and the grand entry of rodeos every weekend across the Texas Panhandle. It was one of the highest honors at the ranch. In those days, nearly every town in the Panhandle had a parade and rodeo.

The highlight of that first summer at the ranch was when we found out that Honey and our grandparents were coming to see us for the Boys Ranch Rodeo. Honey's mother and father were like parents to my brothers and me.

I had ridden only five steers that summer, but somehow I made the cut. I would ride on rodeo day, with my grandparents and Honey in the stands. Finally, I'd be able to see my whole family at the same time. On Saturday of the rodeo weekend, my brothers and I raced to the ranch office. Honey and my grandparents were waiting for us. Honey wore a long green dress and high heels and looked so beautiful; I ran up and hugged her, and we both cried.

We all piled into her green Ford to give her and my grandparents a tour of the ranch. She asked us if we were happy and if they were treating us OK. We told her we were fine. If we told her the truth, she would complain to the staffers and we'd get in trouble. We showed them everything: our dorm rooms, where we ate, the chapel, and where I milked the cows. I was so excited to show her the green ribbon I had won in track. At the end of the day, my grandparents and Honey had to leave just before dinner—we would not see them until the next day. We all cried as they drove off. I went to bed that night holding my prized possession: a picture of Honey. None of the older boys were going to take that from me.

The next day they all came back to Boys Ranch for the rodeo. We were so excited to have them there for our big event. Hoping it would make Honey proud, I wanted to do well in the competition. When the time came for me to ride, I climbed up on the chute. A staffer lifted me by my belt and placed me on the back of the steer. Then the chute gate opened. Keeping one hand in the air and one on the rope, I had to hang on for eight seconds. I surprised myself by placing second in steer riding and winning a place on the Honor Patrol.

I was so pleased about placing in the rodeo. I knew it was only luck, but it sure felt good when other boys would come up and slap me on the back for doing a good job. As one of only two boys in Jim Hill dorm who'd placed in the rodeo, I felt I'd finally begun to fit in. It was a bittersweet day as we watched Honey and my grandparents drive off into the sunset for the second day in a row—this time knowing they would not be returning for a while. I wished deeply that I could go with them.

CHAPTER 5

Homeless

My mother, Joyce Ardys Maxwell (Honey), was born to Clarence and Ruby Maxwell in Bogalusa, Louisiana, on May 24, 1926. My granddad, whose name I bear as my middle name, grew up in Mississippi and, at the age of six, worked for the railroad as a water boy, carrying buckets of water to the men who laid the railroad tracks. He worked for the Gulf, Mobile and Ohio Railroad until he retired at sixty-five. When he was young, my grandfather's goal was to become a locomotive engineer. One day, as a fireman (the person who threw coal or wood into the steam engine) in his early twenties, he was fueling the train engine when the engineer stuck his head out the window. A large bird slammed right into the engineer's face, totally blinding him. He staggered back into the locomotive and yelled to my granddad that he would have to steer the train by himself. My granddad took over the controls and drove the train in safely. After that, he was promoted to engineer, a job he held until he retired. Being a train engineer at that time was like being an astronaut in our time. Everyone respected and loved him. He was my hero. I loved to sit in his backyard under the tall pine trees listening to his stories.

My grandmother, Ruby Maxwell, grew up in Louisiana with four older brothers and a sister. My grandmother was more of a mother to me than Honey could be and was my inspiration throughout my life. Their small house in Jackson, Mississippi, was the only real home I ever knew. At one point, my brothers, Honey, and I lived with them for nearly a year, but we were too much for them to handle after Granddad retired.

*My mother, Honey, at age eighteen, and my father on their wedding day in 1945.
Courtesy of the Sarpalius family.*

My grandmother told me that when Honey was three years old, she got very sick, running a high fever. Following the custom at that time, my grandparents put her in a bathtub packed with ice to try to reduce her fever. She recovered, but over time she became extremely hyperactive and easily agitated. My grandmother always thought that the high fever had affected Honey's mind.

As years passed, Honey grew tall and beautiful. She had black hair and liquid brown eyes. Growing up in Jackson, Mississippi, she was a typical southern belle: popular, smart, and talented as both a cook and an artist. To me she looked like Ava Gardner. When she was a senior in high school, she attended a dance where she met my father, Robert William Sarpalius, who was in town for basic training for the US Army Air Force. They fell in love instantly. My father was six foot two and very handsome. He had black hair and a killer smile, plus he was in uniform, a big turn-on for teenage girls. They married eight days later.

My father had joined the US Army Air Force at age nineteen. He quickly became a navigator for the B-29 bomber and was promoted to lieutenant. He and his crew had flown to Mississippi from Chicago for a few weeks of training. Following their marriage, my father's crew had taken off without him so he could drive back to Chicago with his bride. On their way, the plane developed mechanical problems and crashed. Tragically, all the other men in his crew were killed. Bill Farell, the pilot, was my father's friend. I was named in his honor.

Honey and Bob Sarpalius had three children. I was the oldest, born in Los Angeles; Bobby, named after Dad, was born in Sacramento; and Karl, named after my father's dad, was born in Houston. Honey also gave birth to three stillborn boys.

When I was about eight years old, we were living in La Porte, Texas, in an old green house with a large screened-in porch that overlooked a bayou. By this time my father had been promoted to captain. One day my mother had been drinking heavily, and because he was late getting home, she was convinced my father was out with another woman. She had cooked a big pot of lima beans and ham for dinner. When he finally drove in the driveway, Honey grabbed that pot of lima beans and headed for the door. Just as he opened it, Honey threw the entire pot at him. Ham and lima beans dripped off his blue cap and down his uniform. Honey gasped in horror as she saw my father's commanding officer and his wife standing beside him. They were just as shocked as my father. Honey stood up straight, threw her shoulders back, and invited them in for a cocktail.

Because my father was in the Air Force, we relocated constantly, and we rarely stayed in the same location long enough to finish a grade in the same school. We lived in Texas, Florida, California, Mississippi, and Japan. We crossed the ocean in a warship, the USS *Breckinridge*, in 1956. After living in Japan for about a year, Honey developed a serious drinking problem, which led to a nervous breakdown. We returned to the states on a medical airplane with several patients on board—my father having been transferred to Panama City, Florida. We worried about our mother, but we were too young to understand what was wrong with her and why she was strapped to a stretcher.

Honey tried her best to be a good mother. She was proud of us, and when she could afford it, she dressed my brothers and me alike. When people remarked about how cute we were, she'd swell with pride. But then she would get drunk and lose her temper, and sometimes she got violent. One time in Florida, she attacked our father with our small toy guitar. I handed her a baseball bat, begging her not to break our guitar. After she broke the guitar on him, she went after him with our baseball bat.

I guess my father was exhausted by these constant battles when Honey had been drinking. There were so many nights my brothers and I would lie in our beds listening to them fight. It seemed as if they loved and hated each other at the same time. Eventually, my father's love for her wore out, but I always felt she never stopped loving him. She had no job skills and was completely dependent on him. She was a stay-at-home housewife and mother, which is a full-time job. In those days, very few mothers worked outside the home.

One night, when we were living in Houston, my father came home late and told Honey that he was leaving her and filing for a divorce. Lamps and furniture were thrown around the house. My brothers and I cried and begged my father not to leave. He packed his clothes and walked out the door. I cannot describe the pain of watching him leave. I felt my heart sink into my stomach.

A few hours later, I was in bed when someone knocked on my window. When I opened it, Dad was standing in the flower bed. Everyone else was asleep. He said not to worry, that everything would be OK.

Promising he would be back and that he would see us every chance he had, he asked me to be sure to take care of my brothers and Honey. That made me feel like a grown-up. I listened to his car drive away, but I wasn't worried. I was certain he would not be gone for long.

Twenty-five years passed before I ever laid eyes on my father again. My father left my mother with three young boys, no money, and no job. My parents divorced in Texas, and under Texas law, he was required to pay child support. Instead of being responsible, he abandoned us and moved out of the state, which we would not learn until much later. A lot of the boys I grew up with experienced the same thing my brothers and I did. Divorces were not common in the fifties, and if a parent failed to pay child support, it was frowned upon but not enforced. It was not until 1988, when the federal government passed the Family Support Act, that fathers who avoided their responsibilities and failed to pay child support were held accountable. I always blamed my father for destroying my mother's life.

Soon after my father left us, we were broke and homeless. Honey was at a very low point in her life. She was extremely depressed and drank all the time, and as I mentioned, my father never sent any support. We lived in vacant houses and got food from the local Catholic Church. I had two paper routes with the *Houston Post*, and the money I made was what we lived on. I rode my bike by restaurants when delivering the newspapers, and I can still remember the smell of the food that came from within those walls. Living in vacant houses seemed normal. Late one afternoon while I was delivering newspapers, a wheel broke on my bike just as it had begun to rain. We didn't have a phone, and I knew if it became too late, Honey would start looking for me. It grew darker, and I began dragging my bike from house to house. I knew that my mother would come take me home in the "Honeybug"—that's what we called her old Pontiac station wagon. But when I finally got home, soaking wet and exhausted, there was Honey passed out drunk on her bed. Those were terrible times.

I remember one vacant house we stayed at by Trinity Bay in La Porte, Texas. It was an old, dirty two-story house filled with cobwebs. I will never forget the sight of the kitchen sink, full of large cockroaches. At one time, it must have been a nice home, but not when we lived in it.

We went next door and, without asking, ran the neighbors' garden hose through a window to spray down the kitchen. We got rid of the

Bobby, Honey, Karl, and me in Houston before going to Boys Ranch. Courtesy of the Sarpalius family.

cockroaches and cobwebs and filled the sinks and bathtubs up with water. The neighbors knew the house was vacant and complained to the local judge, a man named Calder Ewing. The judge came to our house, and after he saw the conditions we were living in and realized he had no place to send us, he decided to find a way to help us. He contacted the owners and got permission for us to stay there. The judge told us to return the garden hose, so we rolled it up to look the best we could and gave it back to the neighbors. I remember the judge being very kind and helping us find both food and clothes. He also brought us a big black dog we named Mitsy. Judge Ewing was a good man who cared about us. He brought us some old used furniture and checked on us almost every day.

A bayou ran alongside the house, and the front of the house faced the bay. The front yard had eroded, so we had to climb down a short cliff to get to the sandy beach leading to the water. Large trees surrounded the house, and all the plants and shrubs were overgrown. The old circular drive was covered with weeds.

Despite its appearance, that abandoned house was heaven for us. Every room had large windows, and there was a big living room with a fireplace. It had a dining room and four upstairs bedrooms. The wood floors had rotted in many places, so we were very careful about where we walked. The windows in my room overlooked the bay, so I could watch the big oil tankers in the Houston ship channel, and I often dreamed of sailing away to a wonderful place on one of those big ships.

We had no running water, so Karl, who was about six years old, took a big bowl and went to the house next door. He knocked on the door, held out the empty bowl, and asked for some water. The neighbors felt sorry for us and let us run their garden hose from their outside faucet to "our" house. We used the hose to take care of our needs. Our neighbors had two boys about our age, and occasionally they invited us out on their Sunfish sailboat. I was so envious. They were kind to us, but I don't think they approved of us living in the empty house next door.

Honey was beautiful, and she would land jobs from time to time, selling makeup or clothing in stores, but she never kept a job for long. Either she would not show up for the job or she would be caught drinking on the job and be let go immediately. I know she spent a lot of time at a bar down the dirt road from us. She started dating a man named Al Merkel. He was a short, thin-haired man who tried to make us like him by bringing us candy bars. One time he and Honey had been drinking and got into an argument. Honey lost her temper and told him to leave. When he refused, she pushed Al right through the closed living room window. Glass was everywhere. He landed in the flower bed, got up, and staggered to his car. We never saw Al Merkel again.

Meanwhile, we three boys were enjoying our bayou home. Judge Ewing, who'd been keeping tabs on us, gave us a casting net to catch fish. I got good at throwing that net. Sometimes I'd catch as many as ten mud mullets per throw! We often had them for supper or fed them to Mitsy. They didn't taste that good. One day after school I headed to the bayou with my casting net. I swung it around my head and cast it. The net hit the water and sank to the bottom. As I pulled on the rope, I felt the net sag. At first it seemed I had thrown it over a stump, but then I felt a lot of movement. With Bobby helping me, we walked backward and dragged out a four-and-a-half-foot alligator gar. That ugly old fish, with its rows of sharp teeth, was scary, but it was the biggest fish we had ever caught. I couldn't wait to show it to Honey. Bobby and I dragged the net with the alligator gar up the hill to the house. Karl came running to see my big catch. We had to figure out how to keep it alive until Honey came home so we could show her what we had caught. We decided to put it in a large metal washtub filled with water.

Knowing Honey would come home late, we moved the fish in the tub by the backdoor step so she could see it when she came home. We were certain that Honey would be proud of us for catching such a giant fish, so we went off to bed. When she came home and walked by the tub, the fish jumped out of the tub. It terrified Honey, who fell over backward, screaming for help. The three of us jumped out of bed and ran outside to find Honey sitting on her rear, shaking with fear, and pointing at the fish.

"What the hell is that?" she shouted as she pointed at the ugly fish flopping all over the backyard. It was so funny! My brothers and I looked at each other, trying not to laugh out loud. I loved that time in my life before going to Boys Ranch. We had no idea how bad our circumstances were.

One day a ten-foot wooden boat washed up to the shore. When Judge Ewing came by to bring some food and check on us, we showed him the boat. We were so thrilled when he told us we could keep it if nobody claimed it in ten days, so we hid it in some trees and waited for the ten days to pass. After the time was up, we were finally the proud owners of the boat. Judge Ewing even brought us a small can of black paint and a brush and told us that it was time to name our boat. We named it the *Honeyboat*. We took the boat out after school each day, using long branches as paddles to push our way through the water. We pretended we were Tom Sawyer and Huckleberry Finn looking for hidden treasures left behind by pirates.

One day, Honey took the three of us out of school to play golf at the Glenbrook Golf Course in Houston. We couldn't believe she would let us skip school. It was so much fun. When we finished playing, she told us to wait outside while she went into the club bar at the golf course. We sat on the front porch of the clubhouse for hours waiting for our mother. As I was sitting on the porch, I looked down the street and saw a big tree in a bend down the road. I had a bad feeling, and somehow I knew that Honey was going to hit that tree. I always rode in the front seat, with Bobby in the middle and Karl in the back seat. But when Honey finally stumbled out of the bar and told us to get in Honeybug, I asked Bobby if he would like to sit in front. He jumped with joy. Then I asked Karl if he would like the middle seat as I climbed into the back—he too took me up on the offer.

Honey accelerated as we drove down that road. As we got closer to the tree, I braced myself, grabbing the seat in front of me. We hit that tree at full speed. Honey broke her nose on the steering wheel, Bobby's head went into the windshield, and Karl hit the dashboard. I escaped with minor injuries.

Two ambulances quickly arrived. Bobby's forehead was bleeding profusely, so the paramedics loaded us into the ambulances and raced us to the hospital, Honey and Karl in one ambulance and Bobby and I in the second. The emergency room staff put Bobby in one room and Honey and Karl in another. They told me to wait in the hall. I prayed to God to help my mother and brothers and felt so guilty for letting Bobby ride in the front seat.

As I sat there, an ambulance brought in a man about sixty years old on a stretcher. I overheard them say that he was having a heart attack. His wife sat next to me in the hall, trying to console me, even though she was distressed about her husband.

Eventually, the doctor asked me to come to the emergency room. He wanted me to distract Bobby while he pulled shards of glass out of his forehead. I'd never seen so much blood, but fortunately Bobby didn't seem to be in much pain.

Meanwhile, an elderly man wearing a white T-shirt was having heart issues. He was sitting on the edge of another bed close to Bobby's bed. As the doctors were examining him, he was comforting me and telling me to be brave. Suddenly, his eyes rolled back in his head, and he collapsed back into the bed. I knew he had died. Running into the hallway, I yelled, "He's dead! He's dead!"

The man's wife grabbed me and held me. She thought my brother had just died. When the doctor came to say her husband had died, she let me go and fell to the floor sobbing. Her family took her away. I sat there and watched the staff roll the body, covered with a sheet, down the hall. They pushed the body next to a wall in the hallway and left it there for several minutes. I sat there staring at that body. Just a few minutes earlier, he had been reassuring me, trying to lift my spirits, and his wife did the same thing when I ran into the hall. That was the first time I remember wondering what heaven would be like. After that, each time I got in a car with Honey, I relived the entire experience.

CHAPTER 6

Tascosa

Judge Ewing was the first person who told me about Cal Farley's Boys Ranch. He told me it was a place where we could live like cowboys and ride horses. He showed me the Boys Ranch stamps with the boy and the puppy.

About two months later, Karl "Doc" Sarpolis, my dad's dad, showed up to take us to the Boys Ranch in Amarillo. Doc Sarpolis was a big, muscular man who always had a cigar in his mouth. He was one of five boys born in Pennsylvania to Lithuanian immigrants. Musically inclined, he had mastered the violin and piano. He also played football at the University of Chicago under famed coach Alonzo Stagg. After serving in World War I, he attended Chicago's Rush Medical College and then earned his medical degree from Loyola in 1926. That same year, instead of starting a practice, he became a professional wrestler, changing the spelling of his last name from Sarpalius to Sarpolis. In 1932, he wrestled Jim Londos in San Francisco with ten thousand in attendance. Promoting his Lithuanian heritage, in 1933 he became the undisputed "champion of Lithuania" by winning a tournament in Cleveland. In 1955, Doc and Dory Funk Sr. became partners in a wrestling promotion company in Amarillo, booking professional wrestling matches throughout West Texas.

Doc was a good friend of Cal Farley, who had also been a professional wrestler as well as a baseball player. Cal had moved to Amarillo to play baseball in the Panhandle–Pecos Valley League. They say he asked his teammates to hit the first ball foul over the fence, so any kid who grabbed the foul ball could use it as his ticket to watch the game.

Cal spent his free time trying to help boys who were on the streets. When he retired from baseball, he opened a small business in Amarillo selling tires. Cal Farley was an amazing businessman and very adept at promoting his own business. One weekend, at a promotional event just outside of Amarillo with hundreds in attendance, he dropped a tire out of an airplane, and whoever guessed how high the tire had bounced got a new set of tires. He sold a lot of tires that day. His talents as a promoter and salesman helped him start his home for boys. He was very active in the community and founded the Maverick Club, where boys gathered to play ball and other sports. Wrestling was at the top of the list. As the club's membership grew, Cal was concerned about the boys who had nowhere to go after dark.

Wanting to make their lives better, he asked Julian Bivins, a wealthy rancher, if he knew of a place in the country where he could take some of these boys for the summer so that they could have a place to stay and maybe grow some food while he tried to help them. Julian told Cal about Old Tascosa, an abandoned cow town thirty-six miles northwest of Amarillo, where he and his family had spent many summers.

Tascosa had been the first true town in the Texas Panhandle. Located near that same shallow crossing on the Canadian River where the migrating buffalo herds used to cross, the area became the favorite buffalo-hunting spot for the Native Americans before the herds were wiped out.

Following the Civil War, many veterans settled in Texas. Eventually some acquired large spreads of land for farming and cattle ranching. When the big cattle drives to market began, the shallow Canadian River was the best place to cross the herds on their way to Dodge City and the Kansas stockyards. By the 1880s Old Tascosa had grown into a wild cowboy town, catering to the cowhands on those cattle drives. With thirteen saloons, gambling, a red-light district, outlaws, fast women, and a cemetery, Tascosa was known for its share of violence. Billy the Kid was jailed in Old Tascosa for rustling. He escaped. The old cow town was also a favorite spot for some of the great western legends: Pat Garrett, Jim East, Bat Masterson, Temple Houston, and Wyatt Earp.

In March 1939, Bivins drove Cal to see Old Tascosa. By that time, it had become a ghost town, but the old brownstone courthouse, built in

Equity Saloon, Old Tascosa, 1897: bartender Jack Cooper, Charlie Myers, Marcello Sandoval, Henry Lyman, Burt Killian, and Mel Armstrong. Courtesy of Boys Ranch.

1884, was still in good condition. There was a lake full of fish, the 1889 schoolhouse, some old barns and corrals, a mule, and a cow. Cal told Julian that the spot was perfect for what he planned, so Bivins gave Cal 120 acres with the stipulation that the land had to be used to help needy boys. That is how Cal Farley's Boys Ranch began, opening with just nine boys. Today, it is one of the largest childcare homes in the country and has educated and raised more than ten thousand kids.

Meanwhile, back in La Porte, Honey had reached rock bottom. She was an alcoholic who couldn't keep a job or provide for us. She didn't want her boys to go hungry, so she finally gave in and called Doc Sarpolis for help. I suppose that Honey had involved Judge Ewing at some point as well. Doc got in touch with Cal, and we were accepted into Boys Ranch. I would always be grateful to him for giving us the opportunity that would change our lives. However, my mother had to give temporary custody of the three of us to the ranch. A few days before Christmas, Doc had driven from Amarillo to Houston to pick up my brothers and me. We spent a wonderful Christmas with Doc and his wife. Each of us had a present under the tree. While Doc played his violin and the piano, we all sang Christmas carols.

The day after Christmas, Doc drove us to the Boys Ranch town office in Amarillo. Mr. Stuart, wearing cowboy boots and a black cowboy hat, met us there. He put the cardboard box containing all our worldly goods in the back of the station wagon. We all gave Doc hugs and said our good-byes. Watching him drive away, I felt we were totally alone.

CHAPTER 7

Back to School

I attended summer school and worked on my reading, writing, and mathematics, but I was still struggling with my grades. More Fs on my report card would mean more lickings and more restriction time. I had no interest in either of those. Despite my efforts, the staff and teachers were still trying to decide if I should be placed in special education classes.

That all changed in my second year of school. Mrs. Gertrude Boatright was the most popular teacher at Boys Ranch. She was Bobby's teacher the year before, and he told me that I would love her. She was an amazing teacher and became one of the most influential people in my life. She was older and was always smiling. When she realized how far behind I was in reading, she asked me to meet her after class, with Mr. Peggram's permission.

The first time we met after school, she told me to bring my notebook and follow her outside. We sat on the steps, and she pointed at objects and asked me to write the item in my notebook. I learned to write *ant, insect, tree, sky, leaf, grass,* and *dirt*—very simple words. Using phonics, she slowly taught me to read.

Mrs. Boatright often read classics like *The Yearling* to us after lunch. But my favorite book was *Big Mutt,* about a family dog that was left behind in a South Dakota blizzard yet somehow survived. I could relate to that dog. I wrote Honey telling her how much I loved that book.

Mrs. Boatright let Mr. Peggram know I was improving and asked him to be patient with me even though I was still getting Fs. I still got spanked each time my report card came out, but I had learned to wear two pairs of pants to absorb the impact of the spankings. And Mr. Peggram seemed to be slowing down on the belt licks.

When Christmas came, we decorated our dorm. We had a Christmas party in the dining hall, and Mr. Farley had the event broadcast live on TV, yet another example of what a great promoter Cal Farley was. The chapel choir sang Christmas carols, and Santa passed out gifts. Each boy got a shirt and a winter coat. For many of the boys, this was the very first gift they had ever received. After the Christmas party, boys could go home for ten days. My brothers and I were going to Jackson, Mississippi, to stay with our grandparents. Honey would meet us there.

The next morning, we boarded a Greyhound bus in Amarillo at 6:00 a.m. It stopped at every town on the way to Dallas, where we changed buses. The next day we finally arrived in Jackson. I was so excited about seeing my family, I didn't sleep all night long. My grandmother had baked brownies and made chocolate fudge candy. We walked around the backyard while my grandfather told us all his stories about his days on the railroad.

Christmas Eve was very special. Honey gave me my present from both herself and my grandparents. I opened it and grinned from ear to ear when I saw a copy of *Big Mutt*. It was the first book I ever read. They could never have topped that gift.

When it came time to get back on the bus, Grandmother gave us each a round tin container full of her homemade brownies. We all cried. I wanted to stay with my family so badly. The ride back to the ranch on the bus was long. I opened the tin of brownies and smelled them, but I never ate one. They reminded me of my grandmother, and I was determined to save them for as long as I could.

When my brothers and I got back to the ranch, the staff searched our suitcases. They searched every boy's suitcase, as they always do. They didn't take our brownies, though, so I hid mine in my closet so the older boys wouldn't take them. That night after we were in bed and lights went out, the big boys made their rounds, telling the younger boys to give them what they had received for Christmas. I didn't tell them about the brownies.

For the next several nights, I got up in the early hours, went to my closet, shut the door, took a small bite of a brownie, and thought about my grandmother. One night when I went to the closet for a bite, the door opened, and one of the big boys stood there. He and two others took me outside and ate the rest of my brownies while I watched. Then they shoved me around and threw the empty container at me. They warned me never to lie to them again. Back inside I lay on my bunk bed wishing I were back in Jackson.

A couple of nights later, two older boys woke me up. They took me outside and told me that the Peggrams had left their apartment door unlocked. They wanted me to sneak into their bedroom and search for Mrs. Peggram's purse. I was ordered to steal her cash and cigarettes and bring them back to the big boys. It was 2:00 a.m., and I prayed that I would not wake them up. I had never been so scared in my life. I had been in their apartment before, so I knew where most of the furniture was. I found the door unlocked just like the boys said, and I went into their apartment and slowly crept toward her purse on the bedroom dresser. As I stuck my hand in her purse, I kept my eyes on the Peggrams, who were sound asleep. My heart was pounding. I felt for the cigarettes and pulled them out very slowly. I then reached in and found some cash. I walked out of the apartment, shaking. I gave the money to those big boys and went to bed. I was horrified when I realized what I had done and what would happen to me if Mr. Peggram found out. But I was more afraid of what the big boys would do to me.

~

Though Mrs. Boatright and I continued working together and my grades improved, I still managed to get at least one F every six weeks on my report card. So again, I went to the bathroom for a beating and received three more weeks of restriction. I spent most of that year doing extra chores as punishment.

Turning fourteen at the ranch was a big deal. Fourteen meant you were old enough to attend dances, one of our few opportunities to meet girls. The ranch hosted four dances a year, and my first dance was two weeks after I turned fourteen. On the day of the dance, all the boys ironed their Levi's with a straight crease down the front and wore white socks and black dress shoes. As I walked to the dining hall for the dance, I hoped to meet the girl of my dreams.

The dining hall was decorated with blue-and-gold streamers. The girls came from the YWCA in Amarillo. They put their names on a posted list and then boarded a yellow school bus for the trip to the ranch. When the bus pulled up in front of the dining hall, all the boys rushed to the glass doors to check out the girls. There were more than a hundred boys, all of us staring at about twenty-five girls stepping off the bus. When I finally saw them walking up the sidewalk to the door, I was devastated. Most of the girls, in my opinion, were not very attractive. I quickly escaped out the back door.

Any boy at the ranch who had a girlfriend was considered special. When one of us got a letter from a girl, we showed it off to other boys. If the stationery was scented with perfume, that meant the girl was in love with him, which gave him bragging rights.

Meanwhile, Honey found another job working at Colbert's, a clothing store. She eventually became a buyer and planned and organized fashion shows. When Bobby, Karl, and I made trips to Amarillo, she paraded us around Colbert's, bragging about her three sons. But as soon as she left work, she started drinking again. I was terrified every time I got in the car with her, remembering our horrible accident in Houston.

~

When summer finally came, I attended my first Honor Patrol meeting. We had to practice riding our palomino horses in formation. Each weekend during the summer, we met early in the morning at the rodeo arena and mounted and lined up on our mounts, two abreast. The two boys riding the lead horses carried the American and Texas flags. As the All-Around Cowboy, Dean Warren carried the American flag. The only time we wore our Honor Patrol outfits was on parade day. That was when I finally got to pull on a pair of cowboy boots. I strutted around, pretending I was Roy Rogers. We were loaned cowboy boots only when we suited up for the Honor Patrol. I could not wait for the day when I would have my very own pair of cowboy boots.

Our first event was the Saint Patrick's Day Parade in Shamrock, Texas. We got into formation and rode down Main Street while the crowd clapped and cheered. As I rode, I watched Dean carry the American flag and lead the Honor Patrol—I wanted to be just like him. I felt proud to be from Cal Farley's Boys Ranch. Before the parade, we had some time to kill, so I visited the local high school. Posted along the hall were pictures of the football cheerleaders with their names printed underneath. I thought they were beautiful. One girl caught my eye: Phyllis. She had beautiful hair and wide, brown eyes. I saw down the hallway that the cheerleaders all had pom-poms and their names on their lockers. I searched for Phyllis's locker. When I found it, I set about writing her a little note, telling her I thought she was the prettiest girl in the whole Panhandle. I didn't think anything of it at the time, but I figured, "Never hurts to try!" I put my note in her locker with my name and address.

When summer came, each dorm could go on a weekend vacation. Jim Hill would always go to Vernon, Texas, and stay at Lake Kemp, located just south of the town. We would load up in the back of the yellow school bus with our army cots and sleeping bags. We would leave on Friday after lunch and then drive the 150 miles to the lake. When we got there, we swam and did different activities for hours at Lake Kemp—I even learned how to water ski there. We slept in army cots at night and watched the stars and ate steaks around a campfire. I remember going into town to see the movie *Bye Bye Birdie*. We all fell in love with Ann Margret. Summer trips were a blast and gave us a chance to get away for a long weekend.

In addition to the trip, every weekend in the summer, a different dorm would go on an overnight camp-out to a windmill several miles from Saddleback Hill. We would all gather in the living room, Mr. Peggram would put the names of the horses in his white straw cowboy hat, and we would draw the name of the horse we would have for the weekend. Two boys would be assigned to ride on the green chuck wagon, which was pulled by two large mules named Pat and Mike. The chuck wagon was built to scale to look like Colonel Charles Goodnight's chuck wagon. Goodnight was the first white man to settle in the Texas Panhandle and was the designer and inventor of the chuck wagon. The wagon was designed to carry supplies and food for the cowboys who worked cattle on the plains of the Panhandle.

We all gathered at the barn after lunch on Friday, saddled up our horses, and prepared for the five-hour ride to a windmill on the adjoining ranch. I was given a beautiful palomino horse named Candy, another descendent of Trigger. She was a beautiful blonde horse with a white mane and tail. Candy had a reputation for being a wild and difficult horse. She spooked easily and would take off on a dead run without warning. As I was putting my saddle on her, several of the boys commented that I would be the first one to get to the windmill but that if I wasn't, they would come looking for me. I soon learned that one of Candy's problems was that she always had to be in the lead.

We all mounted our horses and started on the path; it was exciting to see forty boys and staff riding down the street toward the large archway sign I saw when I first came to Boys Ranch. The sound of the horse hooves clicking on the street was unforgettable. I thought that every boy most surely dreams of being a cowboy in Old Tascosa. As we rode past the old Boot Hill Cemetery, we saw many graves of cowboys. The citizens of Old Tascosa had established Boot Hill Cemetery on top of a hill just outside Tascosa, much like that of the famed "Old West" town of Dodge City, with its cemetery just a few hundred miles down the trail from Tascosa. Only cowboys who had died with their boots on could be buried on Boot Hill. Some of the cowboys had died from falling off their horses, but most died from a bullet in a gunfight. Many cowboys—like Cactus Jack, Big Fish, and many others—were buried on top of Boot Hill Cemetery.

As we approached the bridge to cross the Canadian River, there was a highway patrol car on each side. The Texas Department of Public Safety officers stopped all traffic and let the chuck wagon and horses cross. Our horses walked at a fast pace, and of course my horse was in the lead. I felt so proud and excited. When we crossed the bridge, we took our horses off the highway and rode on the shoulder to Saddleback Hill until we came to a gate. We all went through the gate and gathered for our instructions. Mr. Peggram told us that they would start serving dinner at 6:00 p.m. at the windmill, which was several miles away. Most boys knew to keep the chuck wagon, which was at the windmill, in sight, as it contained all our food! We all scattered in different directions. I rode to the top of Saddleback Hill, got off my horse, and started looking for arrowheads. I was always looking for arrowheads at the top of the hills because of what Paul Stuart had told us about the Native Americans making arrowheads out of Alibates flint as they hunted buffalo. The Alibates quarries were only a few miles away and were used thirteen thousand years ago—mammoth hunters used the stone at the site for their flint tools. During my time at Boys Ranch, I found nearly a dozen arrowheads. After I found several arrowheads that day, I got

Camp out. Courtesy of Boys Ranch.

back on my horse and took off to catch up with some of the other boys. I saw Bobby and Karl at a distance, and it didn't take long for Candy to catch up with them.

After hours of riding, I was getting saddle sore, and the insides of my thighs were getting blisters. I was ready to find the campsite. My brothers and I rode to the top of a hill, and at a distance in a valley, we could see the green chuck wagon near the windmill, which had a large tin water tank on its side. A fire was burning, and several of the boys had already arrived and were unsaddling their horses. We ran our horses down the hill and rode to the campfire. The smell of the mesquite wood burning was wonderful. I saw a pile of baked potatoes wrapped in aluminum foil next to the fire. We unsaddled our horses and took them to the tank to get a well-deserved drink of water. Then we led our horses to a corral and took their bridles off and let them free.

We grabbed our sleeping bags and army cots out of a bobtail truck that had brought most of the supplies. We were told that we could sleep anywhere just as long as we could see the campsite. Mr. Pegram reminded us to keep an eye open for coyotes and rattlesnakes. I suggested to Bobby that we should stay close to the fire. After everyone arrived, we were introduced to a Boys Ranch camping tradition; it was time for all the younger boys to be thrown into the water tank. The older boys would pick up the smaller boys and throw them into the tank. We just jumped in, and the water felt great on that hot summer day. We all had fun in the tank until it was time for dinner.

I was starving and got in line at the chuck wagon. On my paper plate, I was given a large steak, a huge baked potato, and some beans. I still consider that one of the best meals ever! We gathered around the big bonfire, Mr. Peggram called on one of the boys to say grace, and then we ate. As the sun began to set, the staff told us stories, and afterward, we went to our sleeping bags, laid down, and looked up at the wide-open sky filled with bright stars. I thanked God for giving me such a beautiful sky to enjoy at that moment. It was the best day of my life. I was finally thankful that we had come to Boys Ranch.

The next morning, I woke up to the sound of pots and pans and the smell of the mesquite wood burning. I saw skillets around the fire that had biscuits in them. I could see a large pot of coffee, and Mr. Peggram asked me if I would like to have a cup. That was special because I had never tried coffee, and the rule at the ranch was that you had to be at least seventeen years old to drink it. The coffee was very strong, and grounds were floating in it; I was not impressed. But I did feel special walking in front of some of the other boys with the cup of coffee, bragging that Mr. Peggram had given it to me.

After breakfast, we packed the truck and chuck wagon with the sleeping and cooking gear. Then we each saddled up our horses for the trip back to Boys Ranch. The trip back was not nearly as adventurous as the trip out. We didn't ride as hard and fast; thighs and butts were sore from the previous day's ride. We stayed in small groups for the most part and took our time heading back. When we were all together at the gate, we rode as one large group across the bridge and to the barn at the ranch.

One day, Danny Stout, who lived in my room, brought a yellow fiberglass bow and arrow set back from a town trip. Danny would go out to the back pasture looking for jackrabbits to shoot. Danny and I were good friends, and he sometimes let me practice shooting with it. The Texas Panhandle was home to some of the largest rattlesnakes in the world. Hanging on the wall of the old courthouse in the museum at

Boys Ranch is the skin of a rattlesnake that is supposed to be the largest ever killed. The snake was eight feet three inches long and weighed thirty-three pounds. One day I borrowed Danny's bow and arrows and was in the back pasture, which was covered with mesquite bushes. I shot an arrow straight up into the air. I watched the arrow soar high into the sky and descend like a rocket. I saw it stick in the ground about fifty yards from me. I ran over to the arrow, and just as I stooped down to pull the arrow out of the ground, I noticed a rattlesnake as big as the one I had seen on the wall in the Boys Ranch museum. My heart stopped; I was so scared. I was only a foot away from the snake. I jumped back and did what anyone would do: I ran as fast as I could. I told Danny what had happened and said, "I'm not going back to that place again!" Given how sparsely populated the area is, I'd guess that arrow is still sticking out of the ground today.

Finally, I made it to the seventh grade. Fifteen years old and taller than most of my classmates, I was now eligible to play football. Football is a big deal in Texas. The coach had us meet at the gym for football tryouts. He called our names and told us to get our football equipment. In the corner of the gym was a room with a pile of shoes, a pile of shoulder pads, a pile of hip pads, and another pile of uniforms. All the equipment had been worn out and donated by West Texas State University in Canyon, Texas. We dug through the piles to find equipment that fit. Most of the shoes were too big, but I finally found a shoe for my left foot, and after I rummaged for a little longer, I found one for my right foot. Next, we searched through the pile of shoulder pads. Again, they were all too big; we seldom found something that fit properly. Finally came the helmets. I got lucky; I found one with a face guard. Those who were not so lucky had scabs on their noses all season. We put on our assorted mismatched uniforms and ran out to the field. Coach told us to start running around the football field and not to stop until he told us to. If we stopped running, we were off the team. I wanted to make that football team so badly, so I happily ran. Since I was tall, Coach started me playing tight end.

One day when the mail came, my name was called. The return address said it was from Phyllis, the Shamrock High cheerleader! I couldn't believe she answered me! I wrote her, saying that I looked forward to meeting her. When our football team played Shamrock High

Boys Ranch football team—nothing matched. Courtesy of Boys Ranch.

School later that season, I'd get my opportunity. We continued to write each other, and the day finally arrived. I got permission from our coach and Mr. Peggram to meet Phyllis after the game. I played my heart out in the first half, but we were still behind. At halftime in the locker room, Coach yelled at the team that I was the only one playing in this game. The entire team knew the only reason I was playing so hard was because I wanted to impress Phyllis.

When the second half started, I ran to the Shamrock sideline to say hello to Phyllis. She was so pretty with her beautiful brown hair and big dark eyes. She also looked good in her cheerleader uniform. I asked if we were still going to meet after the game. She smiled and said she was looking forward to it.

Late in the third quarter, a Shamrock running back swept around the end, and I charged to tackle him on the sideline. When I tackled him, we both flew out of bounds. The two of us landed right on top of Phyllis! We broke her leg. I was devastated. She was crying as the medics lifted her on the stretcher to take her to the ambulance. I remember the streams of mascara running down her cheeks. I repeatedly wrote to apologize, but I never heard from Phyllis again.

In one game, I intercepted a pass and ran it back for a touchdown. This play helped me make the starting varsity team, beating out a senior named Frankie. That made Frankie mad.

One day during practice, as I was running downfield, Frankie ran up behind me and slammed into the back of my knees. He purposely broke my right knee, and I went to the Amarillo hospital. After my surgery, I woke to find Honey beside my bed. Standing next to her was Mr. Farley, holding a chocolate milkshake out to me and saying, "Can you drink a milkshake?" I never felt so special in my life. Here was Cal Farley standing by my bed and talking to me. He didn't have to come to the hospital late at night, but I was one of his boys, and he cared about me. That was the kind of man he was. All the boys respected him and knew he was doing his best to help us.

After they left, the nurse gave me a painkiller, and I fell sound asleep. My leg was in a cast from my thigh down to my toes. During the night, another nurse came in to check on me and forgot to secure the side bed-rail. My elevated leg slid off several pillows, and I crashed to the floor. The nurses put me back in bed and secured the bedrail. But when the medication wore off the next morning, the pain was horrible. I screamed for the nurse. My leg had broken again inside the cast, so I was rushed back into surgery. This time I woke up in a full body cast, from my armpits to my toes. Only my left leg, arms, and head were free to move. I was transported to the ranch infirmary.

I could only lie on my back and had to use a bedpan. My entire body itched inside the cast, but there was no way to scratch. It was miserable. I was totally incapacitated and helpless—I felt just like I did when I had polio. All I could do was watch TV or look out the window, coveting the freedom all the other boys had as they walked to the dining hall.

While I was laid up, Governor John Connally visited me. Cal Farley, being politically savvy, invited the governor to the ranch annually. It was always good publicity for Boys Ranch. I shook the governor's hand, and he signed my cast on my chest. I was probably the only boy in Texas with the governor's autograph on his cast. I was still in the infirmary three weeks later when the TV program I was watching was interrupted. The announcer said President Kennedy and Governor Connally had been shot in Dallas while riding in the same car. Lying in that infirmary bed, I watched history being made. Two days later, I saw Jack Ruby shoot Lee Harvey Oswald in the Dallas Police Station live on TV. Then days later, I watched President Kennedy's long, emotional funeral and saw the shining light of a great man become an eternal flame.

CHAPTER 8

Growing Up

When Karl was twelve, one day he got very sick, and his temperature went up to 104. He was rushed from Boys Ranch to a hospital in Amarillo. While in the hospital, Honey asked him if there was anything he wanted. Karl said he wanted to see his brothers. That was all it took for Honey to head to Boys Ranch to pick us up and take us to see Karl. When she got to the ranch, we were all in the dining hall at supper. She was told that it was against the rules for her to visit and certainly for her to take us off the ranch to see Karl. That didn't slow her down. She headed for the dining hall. Someone from the kitchen came to our table and directed Bobby and me to follow him to the office in the back of the dining hall. We knew nothing about what was going on while we were in the office. We were finally told to go to the Boys Center, and as we were walking there, several of the boys told us about the scene our mother had made. She went into the dining room announcing that she was taking her boys to Amarillo to see Karl. We knew Honey had a temper, but she got so mad, she slapped our football coach's glasses off his face in front of all the boys and staff! When we got to the Boys Center, Mr. Peggram met us and took us into an office. He told us we were going with our mother to Amarillo to see Karl. Honey showed up shortly after with the car to take us to the hospital.

Honey was admired by many of the boys at the ranch because of the way she stood up for us. At the same time, she was a significant problem for many of the staff and for me and my brothers. When I was a junior, I got into serious trouble. We had been on a town trip to Amarillo to visit Honey. At the end of every visit, Honey would drive us back to the ranch's town office in Amarillo, where we would board the bus to head back to Boys Ranch. Honey was driving us while she was drunk, and several of the Boys Ranch staff witnessed this.

After this incident, one of the staff members, who didn't like me, went from dorm to dorm at muster and told the boys that they were not allowed to be seen with Honey because she was an unfit mother and a bad example. Another boy, Roy Dormire, ran to my dorm and told me what was going on. When I saw that staff member walking out of the dorm, I ran up to him and coldcocked him. Several other staff grabbed me and tried to stop me. Another boy, Mike Gower, jumped in to help me. We both got into a fight with the staff. I just lost my temper, and that didn't turn out well for us. Two staff members took me and Mike Gower to the back of the school and tied our wrists and hands, side by side, to the chin-up bars. They removed their belts and took turns beating us. It was the worst beating I ever had at Boys Ranch. And then I was placed on restriction again.

Mr. Peggram was off duty that day. When he found out what happened, he was furious. I was told that at the next day's staff meeting, Peggram made it clear that no one would harm his boys like that. Even though I was still on restriction, Mr. Peggram was very light on me.

~

Yet we still could not wait for our weekend town trips to Amarillo. Honey usually took us to lunch at our favorite restaurant, where they served crispy fried chicken. Then we would visit her at her small apartment.

On one trip, we walked into her apartment to find an entire car transmission disassembled on the living room floor. Engine parts were scattered all over the kitchen and living room. She had enrolled in a course at Amarillo College to learn how to rebuild automatic transmissions. We never quite knew what to expect with Honey—except, of course, her drinking.

On another town trip, Honey was drinking vodka from a bottle like it was water. I found all the other bottles when she wasn't looking, poured all the vodka down the sink, refilled the bottles with water, and put them back where I had found them. After she finished the first one, Honey grabbed one of the other bottles and took a drink. When she realized it was water, she flew into one of her rages and came after me. She knew I had done it. She chased me out the front door, screaming and yelling. I ran to the ranch's town office in Amarillo and sat in the park across the street for several hours, hoping that Honey wouldn't come looking for me.

At 9:00 p.m., it was time to board the bus to go back to the ranch. I got on the bus and took my seat. When Bobby and Karl were not on the bus, I started to worry. Then Honey pulled up with Bobby and Karl. She was very drunk and stood outside, yelling at me to get off the bus. Everyone was silent. I pretended not to hear her, but one of the boys told me my mother was calling me. I didn't move.

When Mr. Peggram rounded the corner of the building to drive us back to the ranch, Honey was beating on the bus. He climbed in the bus and told me I'd better go talk to my mother. Everyone was staring at me as I walked down the aisle. Mr. Peggram started the engine. As soon as I stepped off the bus, Honey grabbed me and started slapping me in the face and pounding me with her fists. She was drunk and hysterical. I was mortified knowing everyone on the bus was watching, but Mr. Peggram stepped out and positioned himself between Honey and me, saying it was time to leave. She kept trying to hit me until I made it to the door of the bus and got in. Again, no one said a word. I was so humiliated—I looked out the window at Honey, still yelling as the bus drove away. I just wanted my mother to stop drinking. On the way back to the ranch, I thought about how much I loved her despite everything she did. And I also knew I would always forgive her.

∿

Boys Ranch did not win many awards in sports, but we had the best wrestling team in the state. On one trip to Amarillo, I went to see my grandfather Doc Sarpolis, who had been a champion professional wrestler. I asked him to teach me a few wrestling holds. Doc was so pleased and proud of my interest in wrestling. He taught me how to gain control of an opponent's wrist in addition to showing me several takedown tricks. He advised me to always practice with bigger boys. Because of his advice, I did well and made the starting varsity wrestling team my freshman year.

I was later chosen to compete in the finals for the Amarillo city championship tournament. The four Amarillo high schools and Boys Ranch would compete for the city championship. The tournament lasted for two days, and the finals were held on a Saturday, with hundreds of spectators packed into the Tascosa High School gymnasium. As it turned out, four boys from Boys Ranch made it to the finals, and I was one of the four boys. Each one of us would have to pin our opponent to have enough points to win the tournament, so the pressure was on. My opponent was a boy from Caprock High School. When it was my turn, I was nervous, thinking how embarrassed I would be if I was responsible for Boys Ranch losing the city championship. I walked onto the mat in my blue-and-gold uniform with the ranch logo on the center of my jersey. The referee blew the whistle, and I focused on gaining control of my opponent's wrist, just as Doc had taught me.

My opponent shot low at my ankles and tripped me, and instantly I was facedown on the mat. As I struggled to get to my knees, I saw Honey out of the corner of my eye coming toward the mat, screaming at my opponent to get off me. She was drunk, of course. She walked right onto the mat and grabbed the boy. The crowd went silent. The referee blew his whistle to stop the match. As he told her to leave, my coach, Carroll Powell, hurried out to the mat.

I got on my feet and asked the ref if I could take my mother outside and come right back. My opponent nodded and told me to go ahead; he would wait. The referee nodded as well. I wrapped my arms around Honey and slowly walked her across the gym toward the door. I was mortified. Coach Powell followed us while hundreds of people watched in silence. When we got outside, I begged Honey to stay put so I could go back and win my wrestling match. My coach agreed to stay with her. I walked back into the gym and went directly to the mat. I stared at the floor, completely embarrassed and unsure of what to do next. Someone in the crowd clapped for me, and then the entire crowd applauded. I approached the referee and my opponent and apologized. The referee told me to resume the same position we were in before we had been disrupted. He blew the whistle. Somehow I managed to wrestle my opponent onto his back and won the match! The crowd stood and clapped and cheered as I walked off the mat.

The best match of that tournament was between a boy named Mike Matheson from Boys Ranch and an opponent who had pinned him in every previous match. Mike was a fighter—like all of us from Boys Ranch—and he knew we were counting on him. The match went into three overtimes, and everyone in the stands cheered and hollered. Mike wore his opponent down and pinned him with seconds left on the clock. We won all four matches and the city championship.

PART II
Farming, My Future

CHAPTER 9

Future Farmers
of America

When I first came to the ranch, I noticed a lot of boys wearing dark-blue corduroy jackets with the emblem of the Future Farmers of America (FFA) on the back and their names stitched on the front. I asked a boy what the jackets meant and how I could get one. I was told that when I got to the ninth grade, I could take the FFA as a class in school, and I would get to raise a farm animal like a pig, steer, or dairy heifer. I knew right then I wanted to have one of those dark-blue corduroy jackets with my name on it.

When I finally reached the ninth grade, I enrolled in the FFA. First-year members spent two hours in class every day learning about agriculture, metalworking, and woodworking. Most towns across rural America had FFA programs in their local high schools. To become an FFA member, each student was required to stand in front of the class and recite the FFA creed from memory. When we became members, we would receive the FFA jacket. The FFA logo was the same then as it is today: an owl perched on a hand plow, the sun rising in the back over a grassy field. My heart swells with pride just remembering the first time I saw it.

Guy Finstad taught my freshmen class. We were called "Green-hands," which is the name given to a first-year FFA member. Being shy and unsure of myself, I begged Mr. Finstad to let me recite the creed to him in the privacy of his office. He refused and explained that standing in front of my class would help teach me self-confidence. When the day came, I stood in front of the class, but I could not open my mouth. I completely froze. Guy finally asked me to follow him to his office. Behind closed doors, I recited the FFA creed to an audience of one. Over the course of that year, he helped me build my self-confidence until the time came when I finally spoke in front of my class. Without his help and guidance, I would not have become the man I am today.

The day finally came when we were given our dark-blue corduroy jackets. I was so proud of it. I checked to see if they spelled my name right, which they had. Little did I know how that corduroy jacket would open the doors for my future.

That year, the Greenhands of the Boys Ranch FFA chapter won first place in the district competition in chapter conducting, which is a competition in parliamentary procedure, like Robert's Rules of Order. There were two divisions within the FFA, the Junior Division for Greenhands and the Senior Division. Within each division, there were multiple teams composed of five students. Teams competed against other schools within the district; six schools were in our district. Within the FFA, the various chapters competed at three different levels: district, area, and state.

The officers within each FFA chapter included a president, vice president, secretary, treasurer, reporter, sentinel, and advisor. It was an honor to be an FFA officer. We didn't campaign for offices; we were nominated, and then the chapter members voted by ballot. It was the first time I had ever been elected to any office. I was the vice president of our Boys Ranch FFA chapter.

During the competition, the officers of each chapter had to recite the opening and closing ceremonies as well as conduct a mock meeting under parliamentary procedure. There were three judges who presided over the competition and provided instructions regarding business to conduct, including passing or amending motions. We practiced for hours, and this helped build self-confidence. It helped me more than I could appreciate at that time. The competition was nerve-racking, but I was never so proud to be a member of a winning team; I had never been part of anything that had won first place in my life.

After the district competition, we competed in the area contest, composed of all the district winners in the Texas Panhandle. Again, we won first place, which meant we then advanced to the state finals and competed against all the ten area winners in the state of Texas. The state competition was in Huntsville, Texas, and we placed second in the state. We returned to the ranch as champions.

As members of the Greenhands, we were required to raise a farm animal. Most boys raised pigs. I was no exception. I never thought I could get so attached to a pig. I named the pig Caesar, and he followed me around like a dog. My big goal, though, was to buy a dairy heifer. After learning to feed and care for heifers when I worked at the dairy barn, I knew it was expensive, but I was determined to buy a Holstein heifer. It would just be a matter of time and hard work.

Caesar and I, along with all the other boys and their pigs from the ranch, were entered into the annual Houston Livestock Show and Rodeo, the world's largest livestock show. We loaded our pigs in a truck, and all the boys followed in a school bus—destination Houston, Texas. I just knew I had the grand champion hog in Caesar. Every other boy on that bus felt the same about his pig. I was so proud of my pig when I ran him into the show ring alongside hundreds of other pigs. I was devastated when Caesar and I walked away with no ribbon and then came to the realization that Caesar was not headed back to the ranch with me. I cried when I saw my pig being led up a ramp into a truck packed with hundreds of other hogs headed for the slaughterhouse. I was depressed for weeks. I did finally receive a check for the sale of Caesar, and I made thirty-six dollars profit, more money than I had ever had in my life. That money would be used toward my next major purchase: a dairy heifer.

After nearly three years at Boys Ranch, I was finally passing my courses in summer school with Cs, so Mr. Peggram let me buy my Holstein dairy heifer. I named her Marion, after a girl I had met and was writing to. I fell in love with my heifer and spent hours working with her.

Just like my trip with Caesar, Marion and I later headed to Houston for the Livestock Show and Rodeo. She had to compete against eighty-six heifers in her class. We stayed in a dorm with bunk beds stacked three high in the new Houston Astrodome. It was so noisy in the dorm, I just slept in the straw with Marion every night.

The next day, I was ready for the dairy heifer competition. I had spent hours with Marion cleaning and combing her hair. The time finally came for me to walk her to the show ring. Wearing a white shirt, dark-blue tie, and my blue corduroy FFA jacket, I proudly led Marion into the ring.

The judge asked us to walk our heifers in a circle. With eighty-six heifers, it was a big circle. The judge looked us all over and then pointed at me to start a line. He began pulling heifers out at random to form a long line. As I looked down the line of eighty-six heifers, I just knew, once again, that I had the grand champion. My heart was pounding. I brushed Marion and was so proud of her. The judge approached the microphone to announce the winners. I knew Marion would be first on the list, but it was the heifer on the other end of the line, so Marion and I were last in place. I was so disappointed, but I loved Marion, and in my eyes, she was my champion. After that, Marion was sold.

Back at Boys Ranch, I had made another F. When it was my turn for my spanking, I entered the bathroom and shut the door behind me. Mr. Peggram stood there. "Look at yourself," he said. "You are seventeen years old and in the tenth grade. There is not another person at Boys Ranch who thinks you will ever graduate from high school, but I do, so don't let me down." Then he walked out of the bathroom and closed the door behind him. I stood there by myself, shocked at his words and the fact that he didn't give me a licking. I went to my bunk and got in bed and kept thinking about what he said, and he was right. I couldn't sleep. That was the last time I made an F at Boys Ranch.

Boys Ranch had become my home, and I loved living there and started taking advantage of everything they had to offer. Time went by fast, and before I knew it, I was a nineteen-year-old senior.

I had finally caught up with my brother in school and was active in everything. I got pretty good at riding bulls and broncs at the rodeo and had made the Honor Patrol every year I lived at Boys Ranch. At my last rodeo, I was in competition with one of my good friends, Soapy Dollar.

Soapy had been born to an Apache mother who abandoned him. He drifted from one family to another, sixteen in all, before finally finding his real home at Boys Ranch. At a young age, he came to the dining hall with soap behind his ears; hence the nickname "Soapy." His real first name was Newman. He was a natural, gifted athlete and a close friend. He was the quarterback of our football team, the All-Around Cowboy at the rodeo, and also very smart.

Even though I tried hard, I could never compete against Soapy in the rodeo. Throughout the rodeo, we alternated between bulls and bareback

Riding a bareback bronc on rodeo day. Courtesy of Boys Ranch.

broncs. Over the years, my rides had improved greatly, but I always came in second to Soapy.

~

The third week in February was FFA week, and every year our Boys Ranch chapter conducted the entire Sunday church service. I was chosen to deliver the sermon. Mr. Kenneth Quaid was the full-time chaplain at Boys Ranch, and only on special occasions, a boy would stand in for Mr. Quaid to deliver the Sunday sermon. This would be my first public speech before a real audience. On ruled notebook paper, I had written my sermon, titled "Are You Prepared for Death?"

I had read it through so many times that I had it memorized. On Sunday, February 19, 1967, we all gathered in the Boys Ranch Chapel. The members of the FFA all wore their blue jackets. Mr. Farley had driven out to the ranch to attend the services, as he did every Sunday.

I was petrified. All I could think about was standing on that stage behind that podium to speak to all those boys and staff members, but most especially to Mr. Farley.

A boy came up to me and told me Mr. Farley wanted to see me before the service. He wore a dark-gray suit and stood on the steps of the church, shaking hands and talking to some boys as they entered the chapel. It was a big deal if Mr. Farley shook your hand.

He put his hand on my shoulder and told me he was looking forward to hearing what I had to say. I admitted to him I was nervous, but he assured me I would do just fine. He told me to look over the top of everyone's head and not focus on any one person. Then he shook my hand and said he would see me after the service. He asked me to save him a chair next to me in the dining hall. To sit beside Mr. Farley was special. The pressure was on for me to do my best.

As the church filled up, Mr. Farley came in and sat in a pew near the back. I prayed that my sermon would be good enough for him. He was talking to one of the boys sitting next to him in the pew when he pulled out a paper and pen and began writing something. Suddenly, Cal Farley closed his eyes and slumped sideways.

Some of the staff hurriedly took him out of the pew and into the chaplain's office at the rear of the church. Efforts were made to revive him. They quickly loaded him into the ranch ambulance and rushed him to Northwest Texas Hospital.

Sitting at the front of the church, facing the congregation, I had seen what had happened. It all seemed like a bad dream. The pastor walked to the podium and asked us to bow our heads and pray for Mr. Farley. As I did, I realized I could not possibly deliver my sermon on being prepared for death, so I didn't know what I could say that would be appropriate. Everyone there was thinking of Mr. Farley.

When the time came for my sermon, I prayed to find just the right words. Beginning with a prayer for Mr. Farley, words just flowed through me. I talked about Cal Farley's life and how he began as a successful athlete and then became a successful businessman and finally a caring man through his work with Boys Ranch. I also talked about his achievements as a husband and father. I pointed out that Cal Farley was a great salesman who could have chosen a different path in life and said, "Instead, Cal Farley chose to devote himself to helping unfortunate children." I added that when each of us came before God to be judged, He wouldn't be impressed by how much money we had or the material things we owned. "I think He will judge us based on just two things: first, what we did with our lives to serve Him and, second, what we did to serve others. What we give of ourselves in service to God and in helping other people is what matters. I believe that our Lord will judge Cal Farley as a man who devoted everything he knew to making life better for the bottom 10 percent of boys in America."

I had never given a speech in public and certainly never thought that when I did, it would be unrehearsed. I just spoke from my heart. I will never be able to explain where or how I found the right words, but everyone in that congregation was listening. We were all hoping and praying that Mr. Farley was alive.

After the service, we all went to the dining hall for lunch as we always did after church. But this time, no one said a word. You could have heard a pin drop. At my table at the back of the dining hall, I tilted the chair next to me against the table to save a seat for Mr. Farley. One of the boys went to the microphone, and we all lowered our heads and prayed.

We all sat down, but no one could eat. More than five hundred people, boys and staff, sat in silence. We all heard the phone ring in the kitchen office. Minutes later Mr. Quaid took the microphone to tell us that Mr. Farley had been pronounced dead on arrival at the hospital. He had suffered a massive brain hemorrhage.

I stared at the empty chair next to me, and I could not hold back tears. Walking back to my dorm, I could not believe Mr. Farley was dead. The more I thought about losing him, the more devastated I became. I sat down on my bed and cried my heart out.

I thought of how God had led Mr. Farley to help so many boys. If a boy was hungry, Cal Farley fed him; thirsty, he bought him a milkshake;

homeless, he took him in; without clothes, he clothed him; sick, he took care of him.

Like a good father, he had provided us with a warm bed, three meals a day, horses to ride, a church to attend, and a good education. Mr. Farley prepared us for life. He had cared for boys who lived in cardboard boxes, took boys out of prison, and rescued youngsters from places where they had been abused or were failing in school. He took in the kids that nobody else wanted. Not only did he spend his life helping others; he was also a smart businessman who had built a thriving community at Boys Ranch to help kids indefinitely.

My thoughts turned inward. What was I going to do with *my* life? I would be leaving Boys Ranch in three months. I had no plans and no ideas about what I was going to do. I had few skills, and no one had encouraged me to try college. All I knew was that I wanted to help those who needed a hand.

I thought about Mr. Farley and how he had built this home for unfortunate boys. I thought about how other people probably thought he would never succeed and how he asked for money through mail campaigns and took in any boy with a promise to educate, feed, and clothe him until he turned eighteen or graduated.

On my knees and in tears beside my bed, I asked God to please show me the way. I knew I wanted to help people but didn't know how. I just prayed. A Bible verse I memorized from Isaiah repeated over and over in my head: *Then I heard the voice of the Lord saying, "Whom shall I send? And who will go for us?" And I said, "Here I am. Send me."*

I felt a sense of calm, faithfully believing that God would lead me down a path in life on which I could make a difference in others' lives.

My life changed on Sunday, February 19, 1967, the day that Cal Farley died. His funeral was one of the most well attended in the city of Amarillo. A month later, on Sunday, March 19, 1967, his wife, Mimi Farley, died. Together they had given their lives to help so many unfortunate kids from across America, those who were in the "bottom 10 percent."

The Farleys are both buried in front of the Tascosa Courthouse, where their Boys Ranch began. Engraved on their headstone: "If you want to know what Cal and Mimi Farley did, just look around."

~

During the years we lived at Boys Ranch, childcare homes were not regulated or licensed. Abuse and bullying were prevalent at that ranch at that time, both from the staff and the boys at the ranch. I witnessed it and was a victim of it. My little brother Karl had to cover both of his thighs with bandages when he played against Dalhart High School on the varsity basketball team to hide the awful bruises he got from being whipped. That was a different time.

In 1973, parents of residents in the Lester Roloff Girl's Home contacted authorities regarding widespread abuse. The documented abuse of the girls at the home included beatings with leather straps, girls handcuffed to drainpipes, and girls locked in isolation cells. This incident ultimately led to the Texas Child Care and Licensing Act, which was passed in 1975 by the Texas legislature and regulated childcare institutions like Boys Ranch.

When this legislation was enacted, many other homes did not meet the required standards and were ultimately closed. Today, all homes are now licensed, inspected, and regulated by the state government. My friend Bill Hobby was the lieutenant governor of Texas when this legislation was passed.

We were fortunate at Boys Ranch to have an ethical, compassionate, and spiritual man in Cal Farley. He ran a tight ship. When we were at the ranch, if Cal Farley ever became aware of any instances of staff mistreating a boy, the staff member was immediately terminated. That said, many boys were often so intimidated, they were afraid to report the incident, knowing full well there would be retribution from some of the staffers. Additionally, the abuse at Boys Ranch did not come from just the staff—it also came from the other boys. So Cal was kept in the dark about much of the abuse at the ranch.

Despite the abuse at that time, everything I have accomplished in my life I owe to Boys Ranch. If not for caring teachers and hardworking staff, I don't know where I would be today. When I went to Boys Ranch, everything my brothers and I had was in that one small cardboard box, and when I left, I had only one suitcase of belongings—but those were only material things. When I left Boys Ranch, I had self-confidence. I had a strong faith. I had friends who would be like brothers for life, and I had a work ethic that trained me to never quit and to give it my all. It was at Boys Ranch where I learned how to dream and make those dreams come true.

~

When I told Mr. Peggram I wanted to go to college, he did not laugh at the idea. He offered to put in a good word for me with the school counselor and the scholarship board of the ranch. When I was able to stand before the scholarship board, I told them that when I started at the ranch, I couldn't even read and was so far behind in school that nobody except my dorm parent believed I could even graduate from high school. So although my grades weren't good, I wanted to go to college. The board noted my SAT scores were not high enough to be accepted into college. I told them, "No test can measure my determination to succeed."

FFA was still a major part of my life. Bobby was the president of our local chapter, I was vice president, and Roy Dormire was treasurer.

In the spring, the competition began again for the FFA area and state officers. Within the FFA, there was also a state sweetheart competition and a state talent competition at the district, area, and state levels. Each FFA chapter elected a nominee to compete at the district level, which was hosted by one of the schools in the competition. In my senior year, the Boys Ranch FFA chapter was selected to host the district convention. It was a highlight of the year.

Each school was represented by two voting delegates who selected the winning candidate for area and state president and the winners of the sweetheart and talent competition. The contestants remained sequestered in a separate room until called before the voting delegates to give a three-minute speech and respond to three preselected questions. The final winners would be called upon to speak on behalf of the FFA, so polish, poise, and speaking skills were important. The FFA wanted someone to represent them well. I had none of the above.

A few weeks before the district convention, our FFA chapter met in the evening at our monthly meeting to nominate candidates to compete for area and state president. Bobby had been competing in public speaking contests for several years, and Mr. Finstad was already working with him for a run at state president, so Bobby was our nominee.

When Mr. Finstad left the room to answer a phone call, Roy Dormire grinned and nominated me for area president. I stood up and told him to forget it and that nobody would vote for me. Everyone started laughing. Mr. Finstad returned, and Roy reported that he had nominated me. Another boy seconded the nomination, and within minutes, I was the Boys Ranch nominee! I'd had no intention of seriously running for area office.

A week later, Mr. Finstad said he wanted to hear my speech. I didn't have a speech. I told him the whole thing was a joke! He got mad, telling me I would give a speech or be on restriction. Back then I was crazy about a girl I planned to see in town on Saturday, so I sure didn't want to be on restriction. I agreed to give a speech.

Buses from other schools arrived at Boys Ranch for the FFA district convention. Everyone at the ranch came to the dining hall to watch the talent contest and the pretty girls competing for district sweetheart. The FFA building was packed with delegates from every chapter in the district. I had not written a speech, so when my turn came, I walked into the room, stood in front of the podium, and spoke from the heart. I answered all three questions and was asked to leave the room. After the election, we gathered in the dining hall and awaited the results.

After the winners of the sweetheart and talent contests were announced, the candidates for area and state competition were announced. The candidate for state president was Lowell Catlett from Dalhart, who was already serving as the area vice president. Then Lowell announced my name as the candidate for area president! I was in shock. I was the first Boys Rancher ever to become a candidate for an area officer of the FFA. Everyone congratulated me.

A few weeks later, the FFA area convention was held in the Texas Tech University auditorium in Lubbock. The same process was repeated. I was terrified when it was time to give my speech. I again responded to the three preselected questions and then returned to the sequestered room to await my fate. I thought I had done OK.

As the FFA area convention ended, the winners were announced. Lowell Catlett won again for the area nomination for state president. And I became area president of FFA. I could not believe I had won. Now I would give speeches at banquets all over the Texas Panhandle and would preside over the FFA area convention the following year. My picture appeared in the Amarillo newspaper. Honey was so proud of me when she saw it.

Just three short months before, I had been physically shaking when I stood before an audience in the Boys Ranch Chapel on the day that Cal Farley died. On my knees in my room, I had asked God to use me in some way to help people. Now I had been elected area president of an organization representing thousands of members. I could not wait to see what God had in store for me next.

The day I got my senior ring, Mr. Peggram sat next to me at lunch. He asked me to show him my ring. I proudly placed it in his palm. The ring was gold with the "BR" brand on one side and a cowboy riding a bucking bronco on the other. In the center was a blue stone. He handed my ring back to me and told me he was proud of me. I told him I wouldn't be where I was if he hadn't believed in me. I told him he opened my eyes, and I thanked him for not giving up on me. He smiled and asked me if I knew what I was going to do when I graduated. I didn't have any plans. College seemed to be impossible. My grade record was dismal, and now at nineteen years old, I would finish near the bottom of my class.

He told me that he wanted me to meet again with the school counselor for advice. Over the years, Mr. Peggram and I had developed a very strong bond. He seemed to care about my brothers and me. He was the only staffer at the ranch who believed in me, so I agreed to go.

When I met with the school counselor, she asked me what I would be if I had my choice. I told her I wanted to be a schoolteacher. She asked why, and I told her I wanted to help kids like the teachers and coaches at the ranch had helped me. She explained that in order for me to become a schoolteacher, I had to attend college and that with my grades at Boys Ranch, it was unlikely that I could pass the college courses. She told me that if I was interested in helping people, that I might consider becoming a nurse, but that required schooling as well.

It was clear to me the school counselor didn't understand what was in my heart and how hard I was willing to work to become successful. I knew God had a plan for me to help people, and I would just follow His guidance.

CHAPTER 10

The Free World

M ost kids' goal in high school is to graduate, and most achieve that. But when you're thirteen years old and can't read or write, it seems like an impossible dream. For me, that dream was about to come true. On graduation day in May of 1967, I put on my blue cap and gown and looked at myself in the mirror, feeling very proud of what I had accomplished through my years at Boys Ranch.

It was beginning to sink in: I was leaving some close friends who had become like brothers. These were boys I had gone to school and church with and ate every meal with. We had grown up together, like family. I had spent as much of my life at the ranch with them as I had with Bobby and Karl.

It was at that moment Karl found me standing in front of the mirror. The look on his face told me that he already missed me. I promised I would come see him and would always be there for him. Karl had adjusted very well to the ranch; he was the football quarterback and was active in all sports. He was by far a better athlete than Bobby and I. He was popular and served as his class president. He would be fine, but both of his older brothers were leaving the ranch in a few days, so his pain was understandable. I hugged him and told him to make the best of what Boys Ranch had to offer.

Commencement ceremonies were on a Friday night, and graduates could sign their release papers and leave the ranch after the ceremony to enter what we called "the free world." We had already been living in the free world but didn't realize how blessed we were. We had a free place to sleep and three free meals a day.

Class of '67 from Boys Ranch, a band of brothers. Courtesy of Boys Ranch.

The graduation ceremony was held in the dining hall. There were twenty-nine seniors in my class. Soapy Dollar was the valedictorian, and Bobby was the salutatorian. I ranked near the bottom of my class, but I had earned my diploma and had come the furthest in the shortest amount of time of any of the boys there.

After the families and guests were seated, the seniors entered from the back and marched up the center aisle to our seats at the front of the room. Soapy and Bobby gave their speeches. Then the senior class stood and turned around to face the audience, and we sang "You'll Never Walk Alone" by Gerry and the Pacemakers. Our class was so close, we sang that song to each other as tears rolled down our cheeks.

Garland Rattan, the high school superintendent, walked to the microphone to announce the scholarship recipients. This would be the first time the ranch awarded a Cal Farley Scholarship, worth thousands of dollars, covering all expenses for four years of college. The winner was Soapy Dollar.

Garland Rattan then announced that the next scholarship was the Mimi Farley Scholarship, awarding the same amount of money as the Cal Farley Scholarship. Bobby won this scholarship. We were so proud of him. After about ten other scholarships were given out, I thought for sure I would not make it. My grades were just not good enough. Garland Rattan then said the final scholarship would go to me. I walked to the stage and accepted my envelope and returned to my seat. I hoped my scholarship would be worth a lot to help pay for college. I quickly opened the envelope and pulled out a certificate for sixty-five dollars, to apply toward my first semester's tuition. I couldn't complain. College was a lot cheaper back then, but sixty-five dollars wouldn't get me far.

The senior class rose and sang "The Impossible Dream (The Quest)" from the 1965 Broadway musical *Man of La Mancha*. Then Rattan called each name, and we walked up to receive our diplomas. When I opened mine, I felt saddened when I noticed that Cal Farley's signature was missing—and would never be on another diploma again.

After the ceremony, Honey came running up and hugged me, saying how proud she was. I thanked God she wasn't drunk. I told her I was proud of her. I will always hold the smile on her face that day near my heart.

I found Bobby and said, "We finally made it." We hugged each other, and I thanked him for all his help. Most graduates would leave that night, but we decided to stay one last night at the ranch and ride the bus to town the next morning.

I continued to thank teachers, staff, and friends for all their help while living at the ranch. Mr. Peggram walked up with a big smile on his face. He shook my hand and then hugged me. That was the only time he had ever hugged me.

"I'm so proud of you, Bill," he whispered. "I knew you would make it."

"If it weren't for you, I would never have graduated," I answered. No words can describe the feelings we had for one another.

I saw Mrs. Boatright. If Mrs. Boatright had not given her extra time teaching me to read back in the sixth grade, I would never have received that diploma. There were tears in her eyes when she asked me to visit her whenever I could. I thanked her once again for all she had done for me and hugged her.

For the first time, as I walked back to the dorm with some of the guys, I felt apprehensive about leaving. For the seven years I had lived at the ranch, I couldn't wait to leave, but now, deep down, I didn't want to go. Boys Ranch was my home.

After that long, emotional day, I climbed into my bunk to spend my last night at the ranch. I felt anxious and fearful, wondering just where I would be sleeping the next night.

In the morning, I finished packing and walked with Bobby to the dining hall for our last free meal as Boys Ranchers. After breakfast, we went to the Boys Center, where Bob Wilson, the Boys Ranch superintendent, handed us our release papers to sign. I was now legally on my own. He gave me a hundred dollars from my bank account, the proceeds from selling Marion, my dairy heifer.

After I put my suitcase on the bus, I turned and saw Karl standing there, crying. Bobby and I assured him we would visit him every chance we had. We hugged him good-bye and boarded the bus. As the bus passed the ranch entrance, I looked back. Karl stood there alone, waving good-bye with tears running down his face. Karl would tell me later that 1967 was the worst year of his life, when he lost both Cal Farley and his brothers.

Nobody on the bus spoke until the ranch was out of sight. As we rode over the Canadian River bridge, I remembered crossing it on horseback on our way to a camp-out. When we passed Saddleback Hill, I recalled the first time I had seen it the day we came to the ranch. The Native American arrowheads I found there were packed in my suitcase.

I was scared the day my brothers and I went to the ranch, but seven years later, during that thirty-six-mile drive back to Amarillo, I was terrified. As Amarillo came into view, I didn't know what was in store for me.

The bus pulled up in front of the town office. Soapy, Bobby, and I went inside, into the big room with a TV and enough couches to seat about eighty boys. None of us knew where to go. Bobby and Soapy decided to move in with an ex–Boys Rancher who was looking for potential roommates to share expenses. I picked up my suitcase, walked out the office door, and went to the edge of the street. I had one suitcase, a little more than a hundred dollars in my pocket, and no place to go. I looked in one direction up the street and the other way down the street, trying to figure out what to do next. I prayed to God to help and lead me in a direction to help people. The one person who came to mind who needed help was Honey.

I walked to her apartment to see if I could sleep on her couch until I came up with a plan. When I arrived at her apartment, she was drunk.

Her car had broken down, she had lost her job, and she was at another low point in her life. I tried to talk to her, but when she was drunk, that was impossible. She went into her bedroom and passed out. When she woke up, she cooked dinner, and we had a long conversation. She asked me what I was going to do next. I asked her the same question. Honey would never admit she was an alcoholic and that she desperately needed help.

I told her that she needed treatment to get cured. I had heard of a treatment center in Vernon, Texas, about 150 miles away. After more convincing, she agreed to talk to them. I knew I had to act quickly; this was the very first time I had seen Honey admit she had a problem. Apparently, I was getting through to my mother for the very first time.

But I had no way to get her there. We agreed to hitchhike to Vernon. Hitchhiking was common back in the sixties. The next morning, we walked to Route 66, and we were in Vernon in a few hours. We walked to the treatment center and spoke with the administrator. After he listened to us, he asked if he could talk to me alone. Honey waited in the hall.

He explained that his facility was a mental hospital, certainly not what my mother needed. He thought there was a more suitable place in Stephenville, Texas.

We hitchhiked to Stephenville, and when we got there, they suggested we go to Tyler, Texas. After two long and frustrating weeks on the road, we hitchhiked back to Amarillo. We were exhausted and broke. Naïvely, I had assumed that if we showed up at a rehabilitation center, they would take her in, just as Mr. Farley had never turned a boy away. It was on this journey that I first learned that Texas ranked last in the nation for alcohol treatment programs. When we finally got home, I realized that while we were trying to find help for her, she had never taken a drink.

This experience was extremely valuable to me. I began to see how bad alcoholism was in Texas. I saw many people just like Honey who had reached rock bottom and wanted help. I knew something had to be done. At that time, I had no idea what.

I had to find work as soon as possible. I applied for a construction job at a company named Page and Wertz. When they saw that I was a Boys Ranch graduate, I was hired. Boys Ranchers had a reputation for being dependable and hard workers. I was told to report to Northwest Texas Hospital, where they were building an addition.

My job was to climb on scaffolding to the third floor and use a jackhammer to pound out a six-inch concrete ledge. I stood on a board about eighteen inches wide, positioned between two buildings. The noise of that jackhammer reverberated off the building walls, making my ears ring. That job left me with permanent hearing damage; I still suffer from tinnitus, a constant ringing in the ears. But I earned a paycheck.

When I got that first paycheck, I couldn't believe I had made so much money: $3.65 an hour! In my eyes, I was rich, so I went to Sears to buy a shotgun. I didn't know much about guns, but I thought I would enjoy hunting quail, since other guys I was working with did that. I will never forget the look on the salesman's face when I asked him how much it would cost to put a scope on the shotgun; I had no idea that scopes only go on rifles!

I continued my effort to help Honey, but it wasn't easy. When she was drunk, she said that she was tired and had nothing to live for. I told her that Bobby, Karl, and I needed her. She was our mother and the center of our world.

I knew that Honey was depressed enough to be suicidal. One evening when I came home from work, I was exhausted and flopped on the couch to watch TV. She started yelling at me. I kept watching television. She came into the living room from the kitchen, stood in front of me, and said, "Nobody loves me." Then she stuck her arm out and sliced her wrist wide open with a kitchen knife. Blood gushed everywhere. She sank into a chair, and her head collapsed against her chest. I thought she was dead.

I ran next door and beat on the neighbor's door and asked them to call an ambulance. I raced back to her and grabbed a towel to wrap around her wrist. She looked up at me, kissed me, put her other hand on my head, and pulled me close. As tears ran down her face, she said she loved me.

Blood was everywhere. Finally, the ambulance arrived and took her to the hospital. I stayed with her all night and then went to work early the next morning.

Not long after that, Honey found a job advertised in the newspaper. It involved caring for an elderly man named Bill who was paralyzed from the waist down. We had to move into his large home to look after him.

Honey was good to him. She cooked, washed his clothes, and took him anywhere he wanted to go. The work was also good for Honey. Bill had been a successful attorney who had argued before the US Supreme Court. He had suffered a stroke, which had impaired his speech. It seemed that Honey had found a job where she could help someone else, and I hoped that would bring her peace and satisfaction.

I thought that my mother was on the mend and her situation was improving, so I decided to enroll in a night class in English at Amarillo College. I used my sixty-five-dollar scholarship to pay for the course. I planned to work construction all day, get a ride home, take a shower, and walk or get a ride to campus. This was my opportunity to prove to myself that I could pass a college course and get my first semester of English out of the way.

English had always been difficult for me, and I tried my best. It was hard to study because by the time I got home from class late at night, I was so exhausted that I fell into bed. At the end of the summer, the grades were posted on the classroom doors. Just two students in the class had failed. I was one of them. I was so disappointed in myself.

I had been so proud of being a student at Amarillo College. Now I wondered if everyone had been right, that I could never get a college degree. Again, I felt like a failure. I didn't want anyone to know about my grade. Honey continued to encourage me to keep working toward my goal.

I wondered if I might do better at a junior college, which had fewer students in each class. I heard about a small school, Clarendon Junior College, about sixty-five miles east of Amarillo. I took off work the following Monday and hitchhiked to Clarendon.

The college, located next to Clarendon High School, was in an old three-story building. I went to the administration office and asked to speak with someone about enrolling. The receptionist introduced me to a stocky man with very broad shoulders. He introduced himself as Tex Selvidge and invited me into his office. He had a big smile, and I liked him immediately. I explained to him that even though I had no money, I wanted to go to college and that I was willing to work any job and do whatever was required to go. He told me that I could enroll as a student and that the college would give me a loan to cover my first semester. He offered to help me find a job and do whatever he could to ensure that I made my loan payments. I believed him. Clarendon Junior College was my answer. I hitchhiked back to Amarillo.

By that time, I had saved enough money for a down payment on a used blue-and-white Volkswagen Karmann Ghia. It cost nine hundred dollars. I was so proud of my first car. The first chance I had, I drove to Boys Ranch to visit Karl. Then I found Mr. Peggram to show off my car and to tell him that I was planning to attend Clarendon Junior College in the fall.

I finally appeared to have some direction in my life, but Honey's world was not as fine at all; in fact, it was crumbling around her. She got drunk, locked herself in the bathroom, and would not let me in. Through the locked bathroom door, she told me that she was so unhappy and that she wanted to kill herself. Frantic, I begged her to open the door. When she finally did, she lost her balance and fell, hitting her head on the toilet and splitting it open. Once again, blood was everywhere.

I picked her up, pressed a towel to the back of her head, and drove her to the hospital emergency room. A nurse tried to examine her, but Honey was out of control, yelling at everyone. The nurse finally told me to take her home. I said that Honey needed stitches, but the nurse said the staff would do nothing for her in her current condition. I had no choice but to take her home. The bleeding finally stopped, so I put her in bed with an icepack on her head. Finally, she fell asleep.

The next morning when I checked on her, her hair was matted with blood. I helped her wash her hair, then drove her back to the hospital. The doctor who examined her was furious when I told him they wouldn't treat her the night before. He explained that it was too late to stitch up her head, so he cleaned the wound, and I took her home, put her in bed, and went to work. I had been up all night.

I felt so sorry for my mother. She constantly searched for happiness and was good to other people, but she could not help herself. Bill, the man she cared for, told me that no one had ever been as kind to him as my mother. He said he had always wanted to visit the zoo, but none of his other caregivers would ever push him around in his wheelchair. But Honey had; she bought him cotton candy and treated him like a little kid. He loved it.

I was a light sleeper, and the ringing in my ears from my construction job often kept me awake. One night, I had been dozing when I woke to the sound of the car running in the garage. I looked at the clock on my nightstand: 3:00 a.m. I jumped out of bed. In the closed garage, I found my mother unconscious in her car. She had attached the exhaust pipe to the garden hose and pulled it through the car's rear window. When I opened the car door, she slumped into my arms. She was still breathing but was barely conscious. When I carried her outside, she began to cough. At the time, there were no emergency centers or easy-access ambulances. So I put Honey in my car and raced to the hospital. Fortunately, she had not been in the car very long.

Honey would continually get drunk and then try to take her own life. I worried constantly about my mother but had no idea how to help her. She was in bad shape, but I had to leave for Clarendon. I packed my car, gave her a big hug, and told her that I loved her. That was the last time I lived with my mother.

I arrived at Clarendon on Sunday evening and called Mr. Selvidge. He invited me to his home for dinner and introduced me to his wife, Norma, who was the English, speech, and drama teacher at Clarendon College. They both wanted to know all about Boys Ranch. They knew that I had been elected as area president of the FFA, and Norma asked if I was interested in taking her speech and drama class.

Tex arranged for me to live in the athletes' dorm. He said he would introduce me to a local farmer who needed help and suggested that I apply to the high school for a bus driver's job.

The dorm I stayed in was in the middle of Clarendon. It had been converted from an old hotel, and it showed its age. On the first floor was a large living room with worn-out couches and chairs and a pay phone in the corner of the room. At the far end of the room was a large table that served as the dining room. The kitchen was useless. Next to the kitchen was a bedroom for the dorm parents. Upstairs were ten tiny bedrooms.

I carried my stuff upstairs to my room. It was small, with two beds and two small dressers. After unpacking my few things, I went downstairs. Some of the guys were in the living room watching TV. They introduced themselves. Everyone in the dorm was on the basketball team except me. I shook hands with one of the students. At nineteen years old, that was the first time I remember ever shaking hands with an African American. I was the only white person in the dorm. There was only one African American at Boys Ranch, and he'd only arrived a few weeks before I graduated.

I returned to my room and climbed into bed. I wondered if I had done the right thing by coming to Clarendon. I felt alone. I didn't know anyone other than Mr. and Mrs. Selvidge, and I barely knew them. I prayed again for God's strength and guidance and wondered what He planned for me.

All my classes were very informal, very different from the structured teaching environment I was used to at the ranch, but what made class especially different was that there were girls in the classroom. After my first day of classes, I applied for the job driving a school bus and got it.

Tex arranged for me to meet Jay Gould, a local farmer. His primary business was planting grass seed on large ranches, and he needed a tractor driver. He hired me to work on weekends, then told me about another farmer with a large hog farm who was looking for someone to care for his hogs. I got that job too, feeding hogs twice a day, seven days a week. The next weekend, Jay was at the dorm at 5:00 a.m. to take me to the tractor. I worked from sunup until sundown every Saturday and Sunday.

Tex also helped me get a job in the college work-study program, which allowed students to work to help defray some of their tuition expenses. I was assigned to be a teacher's assistant in the local high school. The teacher was Mrs. Palmer, who worked with kids who were behind in school. I certainly could relate to those kids. I was one of them.

Mrs. Palmer and her husband, Lee, lived on a large ranch in Goodnight, Texas, known as the JA Ranch, which had once been the residence of Colonel Charles Goodnight, the first white settler in the Texas Panhandle. A cattle rancher, he brought several head of cattle into Palo Duro Canyon. Many books have been written about the colonel and his ongoing struggles with Chief Quanah Parker, the last chief of the Comanche. The Palmers offered me a part-time job on their ranch.

The job that Lee Palmer gave me was the best I ever had. He had a problem with prairie dogs at his ranch. Prairie dogs dug large holes in the ground all around the ranch, which then developed into "villages" or underground tunnels. This was problematic on a ranch because the cattle would step into those holes and break their legs. Lee Palmer paid me by the hour to shoot prairie dogs. He provided the .22 rifle with a scope and all the shells I needed. It was a great job, and I became a good shot.

One day in speech class, Mrs. Selvidge asked each of us to give a speech. Our grade was based on how well we grabbed everyone's attention with our first sentence. When my turn came, I stood behind the podium and held a rock in my hand. When I had everyone's attention, I hurled the rock through a window. Everyone was shocked and stared at me like I was crazy. I said that the subject of my speech was how to fix a broken window. I had already measured the window and had brought a pane of glass with me. Then I fixed the window. I got an A!

At Clarendon, the students gathered in the school basement to have cold soft drinks and socialize. While talking to several guys and a few girls, I turned to take a drink from one of the two side-by-side water fountains built into the wall. As I bent to get a drink, one of the girls grabbed me.

"Don't use that one!" she told me. "It's for the blacks to drink from."

Confused, I looked at her and then noticed everyone's eyes on me, including some of my African American dorm mates. I bent down and drank from the "colored" fountain. My new African American and Hispanic friends smiled at me.

In 1967, the civil rights movement and the Vietnam War were coming to a head. I didn't see much friction in the small town of Clarendon even though students were rioting in the streets and on university campuses across the country. I had wanted to go to Vietnam like many of my Boys Ranch brothers but failed my physical.

One day in the library, a cute girl with short dark hair caught my attention. There was something I liked about her. I went to the library every day to see her; her name was Donna Ritchie. After several weeks, I found the courage to introduce myself. She was very shy, just like me. She was from the area and had grown up in a small town called Hedley. I asked her out to a basketball game.

~

As the fall semester ended, I had saved enough money from my six jobs to pay for the next semester. And most exciting for me, I passed every course, including English, my most challenging subject. That did wonders for my self-esteem.

Every chance I had, I drove the two-hundred-mile round trip to Boys Ranch to visit Karl and check on Honey in Amarillo. When I spent Christmas with Honey in Amarillo, I told her about Donna. It was not a happy holiday. Boys Ranch would only allow Karl to come home for Christmas if Bobby or I were present due to the continual and justified concerns over Honey's drinking and overall instability. We spent some time with Honey, and then I drove Karl back to Boys Ranch. I drove back to Amarillo and stayed a few more days with Honey. She seemed to be drinking more. The night before I returned to Clarendon, she got drunk and was extremely depressed. She repeatedly said she was tired of living. I had heard this so many times before, but hearing it still worried me. My brothers and I lived in constant fear of getting a phone call informing us that our mother was dead. I got up the next morning and checked on Honey before leaving for Clarendon. She was asleep, but her words haunted me as I drove down Route 287.

Later that week I learned that Honey was spending so much time drinking that Bill's children had become worried about their father and fired Honey. Honey packed her car and headed toward Jackson, Mississippi, to stay with her parents. When she drove through Clarendon, she stopped at the college office, where Tex met her. She said she wanted to see me, and he invited her to wait in his office while he got me out of class.

Walking with Tex to the office, I was so afraid that Honey would again be drunk and embarrass me, but she was surprisingly beautiful. She was wearing a dark-blue dress with her hair perfectly styled. She had a big smile, and at that moment, I was proud that she was my mother. She had gone out of her way to look nice for me. I took Honey on a tour of the college, and then we went to the library to meet Donna, who worked there. I introduced Donna to my mother, and they hit it off right away. On our walk back to the parking lot, I saw that Honey's car was packed with everything she owned for her trip, so we took my car to the drive-in restaurant for lunch. Honey promised me she would try her best to stop drinking. She knew Granddad would not tolerate it and that my grandparents would only allow her to stay with them if she stayed sober.

After lunch, we drove back to my dorm so I could show her my room. We had a wonderful visit, and I prayed she would stay exactly as she was at that moment. I was so proud of her. She cried as she drove out of the parking lot. Honey was so very fragile. I got into my car and drove to the bus barn. During my two-hour school bus route, I asked God to watch over Honey as she returned home to her parents.

As the area president of the Future Farmers of America, I was invited to speak at FFA high school annual banquets. I put a lot of miles on my car and often did not get back to the dorm until two in the morning, then I had to get up a few hours later to feed the hogs and drive the school bus before going to class. But for some of the speaking engagements, I was paid twenty-five dollars, and that was a lot of money for me.

Late one night, I was on my way home from a banquet when one of my tires blew out. I had no spare. I pulled off the road, jacked the car up, and took the tire off. I didn't know what to do. I had no money. I glanced down and saw a dollar bill lying on the side of the road. I picked it up along with my flat tire and hitchhiked to a gas station in the next town. I asked the attendant how much he would charge to fix my tire. He looked at it, then said, "One dollar."

I knew that God was still watching over me, but my troubles continued. A month later I was on my way to Plainview to attend an FFA meeting. I left Clarendon at four thirty in the morning and took the old farm-to-market road. I was going about seventy miles per hour when I approached a stop sign at a T in the road. I put my foot on the brake but nothing happened. I had no brakes and couldn't stop. I tried to turn the wheel, but as I did, the car rolled over three times into a gas station in the small town of Brice, just south of Clarendon. My car was demolished. The roof was caved in on the passenger side all the way to the seat. The driver's side was the only place where the roof was not crushed. I pushed the door open and crawled out. The gas pumps at the gas station were inches from the car.

I walked to the house next to the gas station and knocked on the door. A Hispanic lady answered, speaking to me in Spanish. I did not know Spanish, so I pointed at my car. She nodded and let me use her telephone. I called the police and told them about my accident. The officer asked if I was hurt. That was the first time I considered that. Suddenly I felt a stabbing pain in my back like something sharp was stuck inside me. A few minutes later, an officer arrived and drove me to the hospital in Clarendon. I told the lady in the admissions office that

I had no insurance and no money and asked if I could pay my bill in installments. The pain got worse.

I called Tex. When he got to the hospital, he offered to help pay my bill. After two days in the hospital, I stayed at their house until I could walk. I had damaged my lower back, and it would cause me pain for a long time afterward. My car was totaled, and I had just made my final payment. There was just enough auto insurance money to pay my hospital bill.

I was flat broke, and I had no car to get to and from work or to my speaking engagements, so I walked two miles to class and paid another student for use of his car when I needed one. Everything seemed to be going wrong. I questioned my decision to attend college. I didn't know how I was going to make it. I owed the college money, and I owed Tex money. Without help, I simply could not afford to stay in school.

Just when I thought things couldn't get any worse, Mike Eddins, one of the guys who graduated from the ranch with me, called and asked all about Clarendon Junior College.

"I've been working a construction job since I left the ranch," he explained, "and I'm thinking about going to college."

"Come join me," I said.

Mike moved into the same dorm I was in. I liked having a fellow Boys Rancher around. But soon I began to suspect he had come to meet girls, not attend classes. He was good looking and smart and should have had no difficulty making passing grades, but he spent most of his time partying.

Late one Saturday night, when I came back to my room after work, I was shocked at what I found. Mike had left Clarendon and taken almost everything I owned—all my clothes and most of my personal belongings. The only clothes I had left were those I was wearing.

I went to the men's clothing store across the street and asked if I could buy some clothes on credit, but the owner refused. Mike had run up a big bill, and the owner knew he'd never be paid. He said that no one from Boys Ranch could be trusted. In Mike Eddins's case, he was right.

I was trying so hard to succeed, but everything seemed to be stacking up against me. Thankfully, the boys in the dorm came to my rescue by giving me some of their own clothes and tried to help me through this very difficult period in my life.

Then I began to think. I mean, really think. If I ran for Future Farmers of America Texas state president and was elected, I would receive a full four-year scholarship from the Houston Livestock Show and Rodeo! I didn't think I had much of a chance, but it was certainly worth a shot. At this point I had nothing to lose. During my many hours each weekend on Jay Gould's tractor seeding grass, I planned my FFA state presidential campaign.

Meanwhile, I continued seeing Donna Ritchie. She had become very involved in college life. She was a member of the student council, was elected "Sophomore Class Favorite," and was chosen "Most Courteous." I considered myself lucky to be dating her.

As I planned my campaign strategy for state president of the FFA, I called Guy Finstad to let him know about my ideas. He was very encouraging. "Come to one of our chapter meetings at the ranch and we'll nominate you as our candidate to the district convention," he offered.

I had to borrow a car to drive to the ranch for the chapter FFA meeting, but it was worth it. I was elected the Boys Ranch chapter's FFA state president nominee. A few weeks later, I won the election for the district level. Since I was already the area president and had to preside over the area convention, I had an advantage and won the nomination to compete as one of the ten statewide candidates running for FFA president. The state convention would be held in Lubbock in July.

Meanwhile, I had finished my first year of college, passing all my courses except chemistry, which I would need to repeat the following year. Donna and I discussed getting married. We decided that if I won the election for state president, we would wait a year until my term was over. If I lost, then we would get married and she would work to help cover my school expenses. I was torn. I wanted to marry Donna, but that scholarship money would make life much easier for us.

My odds of winning were slim. I was competing against guys from all over the state who had also served as area presidents—and most of them had money. Each candidate needed a campaign booth, which was usually designed by a professional advertising firm.

Once elected, the new FFA state president would have to take a year off from school to travel across the entire state, speaking each day at high schools and banquets. Therefore, the Texas FFA provided a car and all expenses for the final winner. The state presidency was the highest honor for any member of the Texas FFA.

That year—whether I was driving the school bus, feeding hogs, or driving Jay Gould's tractor—I was constantly planning my speech, my booth design, and my destiny. I visualized myself on a stage, speaking to at least two thousand delegates representing hundreds of schools from across Texas. I was mentally preparing myself for the challenge. This became my goal.

The state convention was held at Texas Tech University in July 1968. I had to design my display booth, where I would greet members in the exhibit hall. I got a piece of plywood and covered it with dark-blue material, the same color as my FFA jacket. I framed some black-and-white eight-by-ten pictures of me wearing my FFA jacket. I had pictures of me with Marion, my dairy heifer; pictures of me at Boys Ranch; and pictures of me giving speeches as the area president of the FFA. It would have to do. I screwed the picture frames to the plywood. It looked great, and I was ready.

Jay owned a house in Eagle Nest, New Mexico. He was at that house at the time of the state FFA convention. I needed transportation and figured Jay would not mind if I borrowed his old farm truck. Since he was not around, I could not ask him, so I tied my booth on the back of Jay's pickup and headed for Lubbock. After only about an hour on the road, it started to rain. I pulled off the road and tried to cover my booth. It seldom rains in the Panhandle. Once again, luck was not on my side. When I arrived at the convention center, my booth was a downright disaster. All my pictures were ruined. I watched the other officers set up their campaign booths—mine could not compare.

I had to start over, so I bought more blue cloth and some shiny gold stick-on letters. Thankfully, some of the other candidates came over to help me. There was little doubt that I was the candidate with no money. The ten booths were in a row. Each of us stood by our booths shaking hands with everyone who passed by, asking for votes, and explaining why we deserved to be elected. Each convention delegate wore his FFA jacket with his name stitched on the front, so I learned to glance at the name and then address each delegate by his first name, thinking how creative I was for this personal touch. While asking for a vote from one delegate, I looked for the next one's name on his jacket. I was impressed with myself.

My booth when running for Texas state FFA president. Courtesy of the Sarpalius family.

The state convention lasted for three days. It was finally time for the competition. The ten state presidential candidates drew numbers to determine the order in which we would speak. I drew number eight. It seemed like forever until my turn. I walked onto the large stage, and the spotlight blinded me. I stood behind the podium, took a deep breath, and gave my speech. I began with "I have a dream, and that dream is to . . ." Then I shared my ideas about how to improve the FFA and how much the FFA meant to me. I said that it was time to allow girls in the FFA (at that time, the term "girl" was commonly used—and in my world, it was "girls and boys"). I felt that I did well in answering my three questions and that I would make the first round of eliminations. The delegates voted and everyone left for the night.

The next morning, all candidates returned, and we stood in one line across the stage. Danny Burns, the then state president, announced the four finalists. I had made the final four, and my heart was beating fast. Each of us then had to give a two-minute speech. The delegates voted again. We had to wait until Friday, the final day, for the results. I could not sleep that Thursday night—tossing and turning and wondering if I would win and get that four-year scholarship.

Friday came. The four finalists stood on the stage again with Danny Burns, once again behind the podium. Two had been eliminated, and there were two finalists remaining. The first name called was Dennis Pharris from Hillsboro. He stepped forward to loud applause. At that point, I was sure they wouldn't call my name, but I was so glad that I had made it this far. Then they called my name! My heart skipped about three beats as I stepped forward to stand next to Dennis—to even more applause.

I stood on that stage, pretending to be confident, but my knees were knocking, and I was trembling. I had dreamed of this moment but never really believed it could become a reality—I might actually have a chance at a full college scholarship. Dennis and I were escorted off the stage for the final ballot count.

After the final ballots were counted, we returned to the stage. Danny Burns explained that the winner would spend all the next year traveling across Texas, speaking on behalf of the FFA. After a dramatic pause, he said, "And your next state FFA president is . . . Bill Sarpalius."

My heart was racing as I walked to the podium. I had won! I thanked all the delegates for believing in me and promised that I would do my very best to represent them throughout the state of Texas.

I received an FFA blanket, an FFA ring, a shotgun (no scope!), and a pair of cowboy boots from the Justin Boot Company. I finally owned my first pair of cowboy boots! Then I was handed the gavel and sworn in as president.

After the FFA closing ceremony, I banged the gavel and announced that the convention was adjourned. I walked off the stage to applause. Then Guy Finstad and his wife, Geneva, came up to congratulate me. Guy told me he was proud of me. I had never felt so good in my life than at that moment.

Now that I was state president of the FFA, the reality of what that meant began to set in . . . I was president of an association with more than sixty thousand members. This was a big job—what if I could not do this job well? I would embarrass Boys Ranch and myself.

I climbed into Jay's truck and tuned the radio to KGNC in Amarillo. The first thing I heard was the interview I had given just a few minutes before. I was impressed with myself and on a serious high note. About an hour later, I was once again humbled. I was driving down a rural farm-to-market road nearing Clarendon, and a patrolman turned his lights on. I pulled to the side of the road and stopped. The police officer approached the pickup and asked to see the title of the vehicle. I dug the paper work from the glove box and gave it to him. I then realized I had not told Jay that I had borrowed his truck. Turns out, Jay had reported his truck stolen when he got back from New Mexico. The officer had the Clarendon dispatcher call Jay for verification. "It's OK," the dispatcher said. "Mr. Gould asks that we convey his congratulations to his young friend." As I drove off in Jay's old pickup, I thought he might have been better off if someone had stolen his piece-of-shit truck so that he could collect the insurance on it.

About twenty miles south of Clarendon, I pulled off the road by a hilltop park with a beautiful view overlooking the valley below. I sat there alone and took in the beauty of the sunset across the prairie. Again, I prayed for guidance, remembering the day Cal Farley died, when I had asked God to show me the way. Even though I had dreamed big dreams and prayed for guidance, I never thought I would be where I was at that moment with this opportunity in front of me.

When I got back to Clarendon I sensed that Donna was proud of me but uncertain about our future together. We both knew the scholarship would be a big financial help to us, but this also meant we would have to wait a year before we could get married. I promised her I would drive to Clarendon every chance I got, no matter how far, to see her. We were very much in love.

Two weeks later I boarded an airplane and flew to Austin. Mr. Scroggins, the state FFA advisor, handed me the keys to a Ford LTD and a credit card for my expenses. He explained to me that most nights I would be staying in someone's home while on the road. I told Mr. Scroggins I would keep everything I owned in the car and take it with me. After all, this was not too difficult for me. He said OK and then asked me what address I wanted printed on my business cards. I had no permanent address, so I called Guy Finstad to ask if I could use the Boys Ranch post office for my business cards, and of course he agreed.

Mr. Scroggins told me I would follow a daily schedule and would speak to about five schools a day and usually a banquet in the evening. Most would be high school assemblies. Then he told me I would start in the morning with my first high school in Austin, and then I would travel to the next school on the schedule. I loaded up my few clothes, shotgun, and fishing pole. I was ready to do the best job I could representing the FFA.

I could not sleep much that night, thinking about what I would say for my first speech as the Texas FFA president. I was very nervous when I showed up at the school at 9:00 a.m. I walked to the principal's office, and he and the agriculture teacher led me to the auditorium. When I walked on the stage, I was standing in front of about four hundred boys and girls, all African American. When I started my talk, only a few students were listening; most students were talking and not paying attention. When I finished, you could hear a pin drop—that is, until they gave me a standing ovation.

Later in the month, I drove to Dallas and spent the next four weeks attending the Texas State Fair, the biggest state fair in the United States. My assignment was to work in the children's barnyard with all the baby farm animals. I spoke to the crowd every fifteen minutes, telling them about the FFA and its purpose. In my free time, I walked all over the fairgrounds, taking in the exhibits.

When the state fair finally ended, all the farmers and farm kids arrived to pick up their baby animals. But no one came for twenty baby turkeys. During the four weeks of the fair, those ten white and ten gray chicks had grown to the size of small turkeys. I would not leave until the owner picked them up. I hung around for several hours waiting. I had to hit the road for the long drive to Clarendon; Donna was expecting me for dinner. I had the farmer's name and phone number, so I finally called him.

"I can't bring them back to my turkey farm," he told me. "Just kill 'em."

I didn't have the heart to do that, so I called Guy Finstad. "Can I raise twenty turkeys at the ranch?" I asked. "I'll pay for their feed and keep." I figured when they were grown, I could sell them and make a little money.

"Bring them on," he said.

All twenty turkeys had climbed out of the boxes inside the car and were perched on the ledge of the back seat and rear window. I almost had a heart attack, realizing there was no way I could keep those turkeys in those boxes. I needed to get them to the ranch as quickly as possible. I stopped one time at a gas station. I got out of the car quickly and slammed the door so none of the turkeys would escape. I looked through the window, and the turkeys were running wild all over the car while I filled the tank. When I paid the attendant, he squinted at me and then noticed the FFA emblem on the door and all those turkeys jumping around in the back. He was grinning from ear to ear as he returned my Texaco gas card. I am sure the news of the young FFA guy with the turkeys in the car traveled faster than I made it to Clarendon.

But I made it in time for supper with Donna. After that, I drove to Boys Ranch, stopped in front of the chicken house, and got the turkeys out of the car. What a mess! I scrubbed the interior of the car, thinking this would all pay off when I sold the turkeys. I planned to check on them whenever I had a chance to stop by the ranch, and I would send Guy a monthly check to cover the cost to care for them.

One day I returned and found the chicken house empty. "What happened to my turkeys?" I asked.

"They made one good meal." Guy grinned.

There went my turkey profit, but Boys Ranch had done so much for me, I didn't mind. "Glad to hear it," I said and left it at that.

In November, I attended the National FFA Convention in Kansas City. I traveled to the convention by train with Lowell Catlett. Over the years we had become good friends. I was one of the two Texas delegates, and the primary issue on the convention's agenda was reapportionment—to change the number of delegates based on each state's enrollment. There had been a heated debate on this issue the previous year, and it was voted down due to the fear that states with the largest enrollment would dominate the convention.

For several weeks, I spoke at FFA banquets in central Texas. Some had been scheduled around my itinerary, as I had started to gain a reputation for motivational speaking. Roy Rogers and his wife, Dale Evans, were the featured guests at the Fort Worth stock show. Like so many boys my age, I grew up watching his movies, always wearing his white cowboy hat and riding his famous horse, Trigger. As I introduced them, I thanked both Roy and Dale for their many contributions in the early 1950s to Cal Farley's Boys Ranch. Roy spoke about the early days of Boys Ranch and the visits he and Dale used to make there. On every visit, they had contributed name-brand cowboy boots to each Boys Ranch kid.

Following Roy's speech, I told him I wished I had been at the ranch when he gave out those boots—I had wanted cowboy boots so badly when I was a kid. It was an honor to meet both Roy and Dale. They reminded me of Cal Farley and how he had helped so many young people. That night I called my grandmother and told her all about the banquet and Roy and Dale.

I continued my travel across Texas speaking to high school assemblies and FFA chapters, and every opportunity I had, I would drive to Clarendon to see Donna. One day as I was speaking, I turned my FFA ring on my finger and noticed a young boy looking at it. I took the ring off, and then it became a speaking prop for me. I held the ring up during my speeches and challenged the students to become active in FFA and told them that one day I would pass this ring on to the next president, hopefully one of them. That ring was passed on from one state president to the next—covering eight state FFA presidents—until Aaron Alejandro, also a Boys Rancher, became president of the FFA. At the end of his year as president, he presented the ring back to me.

In February, I went to Houston to work at the children's barnyard at the Houston Livestock Show and Rodeo. Sponsored by Houston's businesses and citizens, this annual event raises money for college tuitions for deserving youngsters in addition to furthering research at Texas universities and colleges. The champion animals are bought for thousands of dollars. Many young people sell their own farm animals there to earn money to pay for college.

The *Houston Post* had written a feature story about me growing up at Boys Ranch. Because of that newspaper story, I met two very special people. Late one very hot evening, an elderly woman pushing an even older woman in a wheelchair approached me in the children's barnyard. They both looked exhausted.

"Are you Bill Sarpalius?" one asked.

"Yes," I said.

"My mother and I read that story about you in the paper, and we wanted to meet you," she said.

They told me they had been all over the exhibit center looking for me. The exhibit center was next to the Astrodome and was lined with rows of farm animals and had a show ring in the middle. They must have been searching for hours.

I knelt to greet the mother in her wheelchair, and she smiled the biggest smile I had ever seen. She introduced herself and her daughter and told me they both were widows. She was ninety-one, and her daughter was sixty-nine.

"We'd love to hear about Boys Ranch," the daughter said. "We have sent ten dollars to them every month ever since it opened."

"But we've never actually met anyone from Boys Ranch," her mother added.

I was so touched. I described the ranch and told them how much they had done for so many boys like me. As I looked at those two ladies, I realized that my brothers and I had been given a chance due to donations from people like them.

"Every month, Mr. Farley would personally write a thank-you note for our check," the mother said. Dabbing at tears, she added, "Now there are no more thank-you notes from him."

As I traveled all over Texas, I met thousands of people just like those two women who had supported Mr. Farley and donated annually to Boys Ranch. Cal Farley had touched many more lives than just those at Boys Ranch.

I left Houston and drove to Austin to meet Governor Preston Smith, who signed a proclamation for FFA Week in Texas. Photographs were taken with the governor, and then I met my state representative, Bill Clayton, from Spring Lake. Representative Clayton kindly offered his help: "If you ever need anything, just give me a call." I had no idea how valuable that kind offer would be to me in my future.

He took me on a tour of the state capitol, introducing me to Speaker of the House Gus Mutscher and Lieutenant Governor Ben Barnes, and then took me to lunch. Later, from the visitors' gallery in the House and Senate chambers, I was impressed as I watched the members debate several bills. I was also amazed with the size and beauty of the Texas State Capitol.

I left Austin and traveled south to spend three weeks at HemisFair, the 1968 World's Fair in San Antonio. The city spent several years and $156 million preparing to host countries from all over the world. Hosting a world's fair provides any city with a major opportunity for future investments. San Antonio's now famous three-mile River Walk, featuring boat rides, restaurants, clubs, shops, and hotels, was part of Hemis-Fair. They also built the Tower of the Americas, a 750-foot tower topped by a restaurant that rotates every hour, offering a spectacular 360-degree view of the city. After the HemisFair was over, San Antonio became a major tourist attraction and a center for many conventions.

During all my travels, I kept Honey updated. I called her from San Antonio and described the city and how I wished she could see it. She had a new job working in a women's clothing store in Jackson. Most importantly, she told me she had stopped drinking. I prayed that she was cured, but only time would tell. We decided to meet in San Antonio.

We spent two days together. Honey made dinner reservations for us at the Tower of the Americas. I told her that the restaurant was too expensive.

"I want to do this for you," she said.

Honey bought a beautiful black dress for the occasion. She had planned for this event before she left Mississippi.

I was already staying in a hotel, and Honey met me in the lobby. I was so thankful she had not been drinking, and she looked so beautiful.

We walked to the tower, and when we arrived at the hostess stand, Honey said confidently, "Two, please. The name is Sarpalius."

We had a table by the window and admired the incredible view of the city. I sat across the table from Honey, appreciating her beauty as well as the city lights below, wishing that moment would never end.

She reached to take my hand. "I am so proud of you."

I put my hand on top of hers. "I am proud of you too. Everything I have accomplished, I owe to you." I knew Honey felt she had failed as a mother. But before we went to Boys Ranch, she had taught us good manners, compassion, respect, and love.

"I am so proud of you for not drinking," I continued. Honey and I shared a special bond—I think because I was the eldest and she looked to me as her protector and for support. That dinner is my fondest memory of my mother. She was an amazing woman and could be extremely beautiful, poised, and smart. When she was drinking, she was just the opposite. Throughout the dinner, the floor in the tower rotated as the sun was setting. It was an unforgettable moment. When they brought the check for our dinner, Honey grabbed it, and I could tell she was so proud to pay for our beautiful dinner.

As we walked back to the hotel, I thought about how wonderful it would be if Honey could be that way all the time. I cherished this moment as the best ever spent with my mother.

~

Every year the Rural Electric Cooperatives in Texas took a busload of kids to Washington, DC, to visit their congressman. That was my first trip to DC. I couldn't believe I was going to meet Congressman Bob Price, who owned a large ranch just outside Pampa, Texas. One of the few Republicans from Texas at the time, he had been a pilot in Vietnam and was now serving on the Armed Services Committee.

He asked me about Boys Ranch, and we had our picture taken in his congressional office. It was hard to believe that I was standing beside a US congressman. Several weeks later, I received an autographed copy of that photograph.

I returned to Boys Ranch to stay with the Finstads for a weekend break. One of the board members of Boys Ranch, Jay Taylor, arrived to check on the progress of the farm program. Mr. Taylor was a major supporter of Boys Ranch and a millionaire rancher and oilman.

Guy asked me to join them for a tour of the ranch. Settling into the back seat of Mr. Taylor's Jeep, the first thing I noticed was a big,

Meeting my congressman, Bob Price. Courtesy of the Sarpalius family.

bright-yellow Motorola phone between the front two seats. Until then I had never seen a phone in a car.

As we drove around the ranch, Mr. Taylor asked about my year as state FFA president. I told him all about it, adding that our FFA state convention would be held in Fort Worth that year, with about two thousand kids planning to attend.

"I wrote to President Johnson to ask if he would be the keynote speaker, but I haven't heard back from him. Time is running short." I hesitated. "I heard the president is your friend," I continued. "Could you help me get an answer?"

Mr. Taylor turned to Guy. "Where's the tallest hill on the ranch?"

"About ten minutes from here," Guy said.

Soon we were parked on the hilltop. Mr. Taylor picked up that yellow phone and dialed a number. "I'll put the speaker on so you can hear the conversation," he told Guy and me.

We waited until a woman picked up on the other line.

"This is Jay Taylor. I need to speak to the president."

"Just one moment, please," the woman responded.

We waited.

The next voice I heard on the phone was very familiar. It was the president of the United States. "Jay! How're you doing?"

"Just fine. I'm out at Boys Ranch, talking to you on my mobile phone."

The president responded, "Jay, they tell me one of these days, people will carry a phone in their pocket."

Jay responded, "It won't happen in my lifetime."

"So, Jay, what can I do for you?"

"I have the FFA president, Bill Sarpalius, in the back seat of my car here." He told the president about my letter and the dates of the convention. "Now, Lyndon, they need to get their programs printed."

President Johnson hollered to his secretary to bring him his schedule book. Seconds later, I could hear him turning the pages.

"Put Bill on the phone," President Johnson said.

I leaned toward the speakerphone. "I'm right here, Mr. President." I was in total awe; I was speaking to the president of the United States from a phone in a car in Texas!

"Bill, I'm sorry to say I'm already committed to speak at a veterans' convention."

"Bill grew up here on Boys Ranch," Jay said. "He's done a fine job representing the Texas FFA for the past year."

"Congratulations, young man," President Johnson said, and the conversation ended.

Jay turned to me. "Well, I'm sorry you didn't get the answer you wanted, but at least you got an answer."

The FFA state convention was the first meeting to be held in Fort Worth's new convention center. Donna, Honey, Bobby, and Karl were all there. A story ran in the *Fort Worth Star-Telegram* about my year as the FFA president with the headline "State President Exchanges 60,000 Farmers for a Wife." Next to the story was a picture of Donna and me in front of the convention center. We had waited for my year of service to end before getting married. Our wedding was in two weeks.

I was worried about Honey, hoping that she would stay sober at the convention. I thought about the wrestling tournament episode. Bobby promised to take care of her, no matter what.

The convention was a success. I received a four-year scholarship to college from the Houston Livestock Show and Rodeo. The only stipulation was that I had to attend a university in Texas and major in some form of agriculture. I had once thought about becoming a lawyer, but I was so grateful for that scholarship. It truly was a blessing.

The Houston Livestock Show and Rodeo (HLSR) began in 1932 and over the years has spent more than $430 million helping the youth of Texas. Thousands of citizens volunteer for the three weeks of the show. This event includes a livestock show and competition, rodeo, concerts, a carnival, barbecue cook-offs, trail rides, and many other activities. The event was held each year in the Houston Astrodome through 2002. In 2003, the event was moved to the new Reliant Stadium (NRG). In 2017, approximately 2.6 million people attended the combined rodeo events, and the HLSR provided more than $26 million in that year alone for scholarships, grants, and graduate assistance. Over the years, more than seventeen thousand students have benefited from financial assistance from the HLSR. In 1968, at the age of twenty, I was one of those recipients. The scholarship was for $1,000 per semester, or $2,000 per year. For me, that was a lot of money. Without this scholarship, I would have never finished college.

When the ceremony concluded, I gave the FFA ring to the president-elect. My farewell address brought a standing ovation. Serving as president of the Texas FFA was one of the best years of my life. I met thousands of men and women, not only in the FFA, but also future leaders of the state of Texas and the United States. For the most part, I slept in different homes every night with wonderful people who welcomed me. Other times, I slept in my car at roadside parks as I traveled to other parts of the state. I had driven seventy-three thousand miles in nine months, visited almost a thousand high schools, and averaged six speeches a day to thousands of students across Texas. God was using me to help people. For the first time in my life, I felt like I knew my purpose.

CHAPTER 11

Politics

Two weeks after the convention, Donna and I were married in the Boys Ranch Chapel. Bobby, who was now an ordained Baptist minister, officiated the ceremony. Nine FFA vice presidents attended.

That summer I worked as a bricklayer for the construction company working on the Clarendon Junior College campus. I was glad to have that job. In the fall, I drove the school bus again and did everything I could to make money while attending school. It was a relief to have the scholarship money from the HLSR. Donna graduated from Clarendon the following May and joined a carpool to attend West Texas State University, where she was a business major.

As the outgoing president of the FFA, I would be a delegate to the National Convention again. Every state had only two delegates, and the delegates representing Texas were the incoming and outgoing state presidents. Texas did not support the equal two-delegate representation since one-fourth of the national enrollment was from Texas and for years had been trying to change the bylaws in favor of reapportionment so that the number of delegates was based on each state's enrollment.

This was my first big test. Could I find a way to negotiate a compromise that would allow Texas a bigger voice and larger representation at future conventions?

We developed a strategy that I thought would work based on my speech that I had given when I was running for state FFA president. At that time, the FFA had been criticized for excluding girls from membership. I made a motion on the floor to allow girls as members in the

FFA and to modify the number of delegates to the convention based on each state's membership in addition to the existing two delegates from each state.

Delegates from New York, Ohio, Indiana, California, Florida, and other states, aware that their membership would increase, spoke in support of my motion. When the vote was finally called, our motion carried. I was thrilled. This was my first experience negotiating a successful compromise. Allowing female membership in the FFA was a turning point for the organization, increasing the membership significantly and opening doors for women in the field of agriculture, which up until that time, was male dominated.

That December, Representative Bill Clayton called me to ask if I might be interested in running for the Texas state representative seat. The current incumbent, a Republican, had become very unpopular because he wanted to sell his property to the state of Texas for a lot of money. The state planned to construct a major highway through his ranch. The plan eventually drew many protesters. Clayton asked if I would come to Austin to discuss the proposition. I explained that it would have to be a one-day trip, so he said he would make the arrangements.

He set up a meeting for me with Speaker of the House Mutscher and Lieutenant Governor Ben Barnes. We met in Barnes's private dining room in his apartment on the second floor of the state capitol. The state provided a furnished apartment behind the Senate chamber for the lieutenant governor and provided one for the Speaker of the House behind the house chamber. There was a large crystal chandelier over the dining room table, and the Texas state seal was etched on the fine china on the table. I had never seen anything like this and felt completely out of place.

Lieutenant Governor Barnes was a large man with huge hands. He had curly reddish-brown hair, heavy eyebrows, and piercing eyes. When he entered the room, we stood. He walked straight over to me and gripped my hand, pulling me toward him. He looked straight at me, smiled, and said, "Welcome to the state capitol. I'm Ben Barnes."

Ben had been elected to the Texas House at the age of twenty-two and was elected Speaker of the House at twenty-seven. At thirty, he was the state's youngest lieutenant governor. I remembered reading an article in *Newsweek* about Ben that predicted that he was one of the people most likely to become the country's president. Unfortunately, Ben got caught up in a stock fraud scandal, known as the Sharpstown scandal, while he was serving as lieutenant governor, which tainted his political career. He was very impressive and personable. I felt privileged to meet him. As lunch was served, my hosts discussed my political future and told me I could become the youngest state representative in Texas history. My twenty-first birthday was on January 10, 1969. They told me they would help me raise all my campaign funds and offered to endorse me in the district at a press conference. My district had more Democrats than Republicans, which would be a distinct advantage for me.

I was beyond flattered and thought that there was no way I could lose if I had their support and backing. I thought how thrilled Honey would be if I was elected and what a boost it would be for Boys Ranch. Less than two years ago, when Cal Farley died, I'd asked God to direct me toward my goal to help people. I wondered if this was another part of His plan.

On the drive back to Clarendon, reality set in, and I began to wonder how I would finish college and how I would support Donna if I were to run for the state legislature. I got home and told Donna about the meeting and told her that this was a great opportunity for us. She asked the same questions that I had asked myself. I did not have answers.

A few days later, Representative Walter L. Knapp of Amarillo called me and encouraged me to run for the House seat. He offered to help me in any way he could. Less than one hour later, Representative Hudson Moyer, also from Amarillo, called and made the same offer. As soon as I hung up, the phone rang again. It was the much-loved and well-respected state senator Grady Hazelwood. Senator Grady Hazelwood was a legend in Texas and had represented the Texas Panhandle for thirty years. I was floored, but I felt very comfortable talking to him.

"I am concerned about finishing college and being able to make a living," I said.

"Doors will open for you," he assured me. "Just think how wonderful it will be for you to be a college student and a member of the Texas House of Representatives at the same time! Think about the example you will set for the young people of our state."

When our conversation ended, I hoped this could all work out. A few hours later, Representative Clayton called to ask if I had made up my mind. I was aware that he had arranged for the calls from Knapp, Moyer, and Hazelwood.

"Time is running short," Clayton said. "You have to decide. If you don't want to run, we need to find someone else."

That night Donna and I talked. "This is an opportunity of a lifetime," I said.

"What are we going to live on?" she asked.

"The legislature meets for only five months every other year. It'll just take a little longer to finish college."

"What about my education?" she asked. She was very upset. "How will this affect me?" Donna was a junior at West Texas State University. "I think you are making a big mistake."

"If I run, will you support me?"

"You should wait until you finish college."

I thought about it, took a deep breath, and said, "I'm not going to let this opportunity pass me up. I'm going to run."

On Sunday night, I called Representative Clayton, Representative Knapp, and Representative Moyer. I gave them my decision and said I would appreciate any assistance they could provide. Representative Moyer offered to put together a press conference in his office at ten on Tuesday morning.

When I got off the phone, I asked Donna if she would be at my side at the press conference.

"No," she replied. "I can't miss any of my classes."

"It won't look good if you're not there with me," I said. "Your teachers will understand."

She held firm. I hoped that by the day of the press conference, she would change her mind.

On Tuesday morning, I got up and again asked Donna to come with me. She was clear that I was on my own with this decision.

I drove the school bus that morning wearing my only suit, knowing I would be pressed for time to make it to Amarillo after. I felt very alone and confused. All I thought about while driving the bus was how it would look if my wife did not attend the press conference with me. When I finished my bus route, I drove home. The house was empty.

I sat at the kitchen table and wondered what to do. Donna was not home, and I was not going to Amarillo for a press conference by myself.

I got up my nerve and phoned Representative Moyer to tell him I had changed my mind, that I needed to finish college first before running for office. He said I might never get another opportunity like this and said everything he could to get me to change my mind. I thanked him for his help. Then I called Representatives Clayton and Knapp, Senator Hazelwood, and Lieutenant Governor Barnes, telling them each the same thing.

I knew that I was letting a major opportunity pass me by, but without Donna's support, it would have been impossible.

As fate, would have it, I got a phone call a few days later from Max Sherman, an Amarillo attorney. He said he was running for the Texas Senate and wanted to talk to me about his race. A few days later, Max and I had lunch together in the college cafeteria. He was a well-built man with an honest face. He explained he had never held a public office but was very active in the Democratic Party in Amarillo.

"Senator Hazelwood is retiring," he went on, "which will open up a Texas State Senate seat. I expect a lot of people will run for this seat." Then he asked if I would be his campaign manager for Donley County.

Senator Grady Hazelwood was a legend in Texas and had represented the Texas Panhandle for thirty years.

"Max, I'm truly flattered, but I've never been involved in a political campaign," I said.

"That's all right. I want new workers who are committed to me and the party."

I had no idea what I was doing, but I promised I would deliver Donley County to him.

I had been elected student body president of Clarendon College, which gave me a huge advantage for soliciting volunteers. We hung Max Sherman signs in business windows and on utility poles. We covered the county with dark-blue yard signs with *Sherman* emblazoned in fluorescent orange. The contrasting colors stood out from all the other signs.

Max won the primary and the general election. Donley County delivered one of his biggest margins. He became one of the best state senators in the Texas Panhandle, and *Texas Monthly* named him as "Outstanding Legislator" several times. Max Sherman was and still is an inspiration, an advisor, and a good friend to me.

I will always have fond memories of Clarendon. The people were so good to me. I worked as many as six jobs at the same time while going to school. I became involved in my first political campaign. I made very close friends of different ethnicities and races. And I received another honor before I left: the students elected me "Mr. Clarendon College," the highest honor elected by the student body.

Donna and I moved to Canyon, Texas, so she could finish her last year at West Texas State University. I got a job working at the school dairy barn and went to work at four in the morning.

School was still a struggle for me, so I had to study much more than other students, but I was determined to succeed. I passed every course. In May, Donna graduated with a business degree, and we stayed in Canyon for the summer.

I was invited to speak at Fort Worth's July Fourth patriotic rally in a football stadium. It was estimated that twenty thousand people would attend. I would be paid five thousand dollars for my speech, and I could not believe my good fortune. It was a major opportunity to prove myself as a professional public speaker. This speech needed to be special—I needed to leave a lasting impression.

I bought a reel-to-reel recorder and recorded some patriotic music that I planned to play in the background. Donna and I drove to Fort Worth, arriving at the stadium several hours early. I found the audio technician, explained that I wanted to play background music during my speech, and asked if he could connect my recorder to the stadium's speaker system.

"I've never done anything like that," he said, "but I'll give it a try."

The recorder had been bounced around in the trunk of the car, so it was bent when we lifted it out, but we decided to try it anyway. The technician and I discovered that if we tilted the recorder forward, sometimes it would play. Donna's job was to tilt the player and turn it on when I gave her the signal.

It was time for my speech. The stadium was full. I took my seat on the platform. Looking out at the thousands of people, I was so nervous. *You can do this,* I kept telling myself. *You'll do a great job.* Then I thought, *What if the recorder doesn't work? What if it doesn't go as planned? What if my speech is not good?*

I had prepared an outline of some points that I planned to cover, even though I always spoke off the cuff, but I had never been the keynote speaker for twenty thousand people on the Fourth of July.

A very distinguished man sat next to me. He had heavy eyebrows, and his eyes sparkled. He smiled, extended his hand, and said, "I'm Congressman Jim Wright." As we shook hands, he said, "I'm looking forward to hearing what you have to say."

The program began with a performance by the local high school bands. During the presentation of the flag by an honor guard, the program chairwoman asked if I could make my speech a little shorter than the thirty minutes they had allotted. I had no choice but to agree.

I knew I was in trouble, and my mind started spinning, trying to think of how I would shorten my speech, which stories I could cut, and how I would sync this with my music.

Congressman Wright was the first to speak. When he finished, everyone stood to sing "God Bless America." As we were singing, the chairwoman approached me again.

"Would you make your speech a little longer?" she asked sweetly.

"Sure. How long?"

"Until the sun goes down. After your speech, we'll start the fireworks display."

I looked at the sun; it was a long way from setting. Now I was in trouble trying to figure out how to improvise. Before I had completely organized my thoughts, she introduced me to the crowd.

I stood, smiled, and walked to the podium. I have no memory of my speech or what I said that day, but the background music worked perfectly, and the standing ovation I received lasted a long time. I do remember watching that sun set in front of me. That was the most beautiful sunset ever.

Congressman Wright approached me after my speech and said, "When you're ready to run for Congress, give me a call."

~

At this point in time, Honey had fallen in love with a man named Cecil Hopkins, a home builder from Foley, Alabama. She seemed very happy and bragged about her new home with a big yard full of azaleas. I was thrilled for her. I hoped she had stopped drinking and had finally found happiness.

My brothers were doing well too. Bobby, after becoming ordained as a Baptist minister, continued his education and earned his doctorate in ministry from Southwestern Baptist Theological Seminary. Karl, after graduating from Boys Ranch, worked in Amarillo for the summer prior to starting college at West Texas State University.

Donna and I drove to Foley to spend Thanksgiving with Honey. When we arrived, Honey was drunk. I held her hand as we walked around the backyard, and she told me how unhappy she was.

"I'm going to end it all," she said. "I have nothing to live for."

Then she wanted to know when I was going to make her a grandmother.

"We plan to start trying to have children as soon as I graduate from college. See? You have a lot to live for. You can look forward to being a grandmother."

We had Thanksgiving dinner. The next day Donna and I made the long drive from Alabama back to Lubbock, where I had enrolled to finish my last year of college at Texas Tech. I wanted to become an agriculture teacher like Guy Finstad, and Texas Tech was the only university in the Panhandle that offered a degree in agriculture education.

Donna and I had planned to spend Christmas in Lubbock, but on December 22, we got a call from Cecil. Honey had burned their house down. My brothers and I needed to come right away. She had gotten drunk, poured gasoline all over the garage floor and her car, and then lit a match. After the house was on fire, she crawled into bed to die. Their neighbor pulled her out through the bedroom window. The fire department arrived at the house, but everything was destroyed by fire, smoke, or water.

The four of us headed for Alabama at about 2:00 a.m. Bobby was following Donna, Karl, and me in his VW Beetle. Bobby fell asleep at the wheel, and I looked in the rearview mirror in time to see his car flipping and rolling off the road. I was so rattled. I could not bear to lose my brother. We turned around and headed back, and I saw Bobby standing, uninjured, beside his totaled VW. It was a miracle he was not hurt. We loaded his suitcase into our Ford Fairlane and had his car towed into Decatur, Texas. We then drove on to Foley, another seven hundred miles away.

When we arrived in Foley, we walked through the wreckage our mother had created, picking up a few photographs and other items that we thought could be salvaged. My heart broke when I saw the burned Christmas tree and what was left of the presents.

Cecil had arranged for my mother to be admitted to a state rehabilitation hospital in Searcy, Alabama. "Maybe they can help her," he said. Cecil and Honey had moved into a house he had just finished building. I held Honey's hand and told her about the plans for the rehab center.

She hung her head and would not look at me. She knew there were not a lot of options. "Are you sure they can help me?" she asked.

"I'm sure this is what you need," I said.

Honey raised her head and looked at me with very sad eyes and said, "I'm just so tired of living."

We talked a long time, and by the end, I was a little hopeful. The next day we all drove to Searcy to the state hospital. We turned into the entrance and drove down a long, treelined road. The main building was a two-story brick building with tall pillars. It looked like a southern plantation home. The man in the admissions office assured us that they could help Honey and slid some papers in front of me to sign. I noticed that Cecil had already signed the papers, and I thought that was odd. I signed and asked if I could take Honey to her room.

I walked with her and another man to a different building. It looked like an army barrack with two rows of six beds facing each other. Some patients sat on the beds. I could not look at any of them.

"This is your mother's bed," the man said.

Honey and I sat on the bed. She kept her head down and held my hand tight. "This is what you need to get well," I said, hoping it was true. "I love you so much, and I'm very proud of you."

I looked around at the other patients and realized that we were in a mental institution. Honey knew it too, and I felt her body stiffen.

I shook my head. "This isn't right. I'm getting you out of this place." I headed toward the door and then looked back at my mother. She was so lost and pitiful sitting on the edge of her bed. She held her hands in her lap, and her knees shook.

"I'm taking my mother home," I told the attendant in the admissions office. "I had no idea this was a mental institution."

"You and her husband both signed the papers committing her," he said. "You both have to agree to release her." I looked at Cecil.

"I'm not signing any release papers," he told me.

I realized that he wanted Honey out of the way. The administrator stepped in and said, "This is where we place alcoholics."

"My mother is not crazy!" I said furiously. I glared at Cecil. "My brothers and I have been waiting for the day for her to admit she needs help. Now that she finally does, she is put in a mental institution?" I turned to the door. "I am taking my mother out of here!"

A big man grabbed me. "It's time for you to leave," he said.

Another man ran over, and the two of them dragged me out of the building while I screamed at them. My brothers were as upset as I was.

"I'm getting an attorney! My mother is not staying here." I had no choice but to get into the car with Cecil and Donna. "Why wouldn't you sign the release forms?" I demanded.

"Because she burned my house down!" he shouted. "I'm filing for divorce."

"Fine," I said. "When we get back into town, I'm going straight to the courthouse."

"You're wasting your time," he said.

We drove in silence. When we got to his house, Donna and I loaded our car and left. That was the last time we saw Cecil. Donna and I drove to the courthouse. I found an attorney and explained everything. He shook his head slowly. "Cecil is her husband, and he signed the papers to commit her, along with the local judge. There's nothing you can do."

"What do you mean?" I asked, dumbfounded.

"Her husband signed the forms to commit her before you got here. She's going to be there for six months. You can't do anything about it. You can't even visit her without Cecil's permission."

I knew Cecil would never sign the release. We had no option but to go home. Bobby flew back to El Paso, where he was taking part in a mission trip. Donna and I drove Karl back to Amarillo and then went back to Lubbock. I cried for days and could not sleep. All I thought about was my mother sitting on the edge of her bed with her hands in her lap in that place. I had told her I was going to get her out. I prayed that she would be OK and did not think I had deserted her.

I vowed to change this broken system. I would find some way to get help for people with substance abuse problems. I knew I could do it. I had to.

In May, the school year finally ended, and I graduated from Texas Tech with a bachelor of science and a teacher's certificate. I hurt inside knowing that my mother was in a mental institution and could not be there with me to celebrate this special occasion. I knew she wanted to be there, but she still had another month at the mental institution before her release. Still, I wished my mother could have been at my graduation to share that special day with me. She had never given up on me and always gave me the encouragement I needed. Honey felt like she was a failure as a mother, but she was my motivation. I wanted her to be proud of me, and I so wanted to hold her hand and tell her how much she meant to me. I later learned that when Honey was in that institution, she worked with the other patients, teaching them crafts and art. She loved to help others, and she inspired me to do the same.

The Peggrams and the Finstads came to my graduation. I was so glad that Mr. Peggram was there; I remembered when he was the only one who thought I would even finish high school.

"I owe you and Boys Ranch so much," I told him. "I was so afraid of you, but now I know you cared a lot for me and my brothers."

I had always thought Mr. Peggram felt sorry for me the day Honey dragged me off the ranch bus and slapped me around in front of the other boys.

When the day finally arrived for Honey to be discharged, Donna and I drove to Foley. My mother looked great, and she gave me a plaster mold of praying hands that she had made for me during one or her art projects at the facilities. Honey was well liked. When she was sober, she was the most wonderful and caring person, but when she was drunk, she was unbearable. Donna and I drove her to Jackson to stay with her parents. Cecil had divorced her and left her with nothing. All she had was a few items of clothing in a suitcase.

It was wonderful to see my grandparents, but Granddad's health was deteriorating. His eyesight was failing, and he had a hard time getting around. We talked for hours sitting in his backyard. I hated seeing him struggle. Donna and I stayed in Jackson for a few days before I had to get back to Amarillo. I was looking forward to starting a new job: assistant director of admissions at Cal Farley's Boys Ranch.

Sherm gave me my new position, and it was the most difficult job I ever had. I had wanted to work as a vocational agriculture teacher, but they already had four people in that role. I enjoyed working in the Boys Ranch town office. My office was next to Sherm's, and we shared a secretary. I learned to use a dictation machine. I had never been a good speller and thought it was cool to speak into a microphone and have the secretary type the letter for me.

My job was to work with Sherm to select the boys from the thousands of applicants who would come to Boys Ranch. I gathered as much information as possible on each boy. After a file was completed and interviews were conducted, Sherm and I would review the material to make the final decision. We could accept only one in fifteen applicants.

Then I had to call the parents of those children who had not been accepted. They always cried, asking me what would happen to their son. Every night I went to bed agonizing over what would happen to the other fourteen boys.

While in this job, I learned how broken our childcare system was, and in my opinion, it still is today. Under Texas law, if the state has custody of a child, the first option for the child is adoption, the second option is foster care, and the last option is a permanent placement childcare facility, like Boys Ranch. I remember one case involving four brothers whose parents were on drugs. The parents were at a party, and the mother fell into a swimming pool and drowned. The father dove in to help her and hit his head on the side of the pool and was paralyzed from the neck down. Their grandmother agreed to take care of the youngest boy, who was two years old; Boys Ranch took in the other three boys. When the boys arrived at the ranch, they had never been to a dentist, and their health was very poor. They were all behind in school. Over a short period of time, their grades began to pick up, and they were doing great. Every time I went out to the ranch, they asked me when their little brother was going to join them, and I would tell them when he gets a little older and their grandmother believes the time was right. Months later the grandmother passed away, and the young boy became a ward of the state. The three brothers were excited and couldn't wait for their youngest brother to join them. The state put him up for adoption, and a couple agreed to adopt the child. I had to tell those three brothers about their younger brother. I will never be convinced that was the right decision, but those were the rules.

Most of the cases we received were teenage boys who were trying to get accepted into the ranch. But Boys Ranch did not discriminate—we accepted boys of all ages. A lot of the cases I worked on were kids who had been placed in many foster homes before the decision was made to send them to permanent placement homes like Boys Ranch. I remember a case of one boy who was seven years old and had lived in fifteen foster homes. There were people who adopted kids into foster care only to receive money from the state. In my opinion, permanent placement provides more stability for the kids instead of being moved around to multiple foster homes. Foster parents and homes are wonderful, and they help many kids in need, but oftentimes there are limited resources to ensure appropriate follow-up after a child has been placed. When the Texas legislature convened in 2017, the governor claimed that this issue would be at the top of the agenda. Unfortunately, when the legislative session ended, not much had changed. More funds, which were badly needed, were provided to the Texas Department of Family and Protective Services (DFPS), but nothing changed with respect to the way children are handled in the foster system. Throwing money at a problem is not always the answer.

We stuck to Cal Farley's philosophy by selecting the kids who were most in need and who would benefit most from Boys Ranch and our programs. Most applicants had similar profiles: the parents were either separated or divorced; the boy was behind in school and making bad grades; the parent(s) were out of work; the parent(s) had drug and/or alcohol problems; the boy was in trouble with the law or had been in a bad foster environment. Many kids had been abused and had never seen a doctor or a dentist. One boy had lived in fourteen different foster homes by the age of nine. We accepted him.

One time, I interviewed a ten-year-old boy, Pete, whose father had full custody. They lived in Littlefield, Texas, a small town between Amarillo and Lubbock. When I arrived at the gas station where the father worked, he said in front of his son, "Take this piece of shit and get him out of my life."

"Your son has not been accepted yet," I said. "This is only an interview. Could I talk to Pete alone?"

The father pointed at a small trailer behind the station. "Go in there."

Pete and I went inside. The trailer had one small bedroom, a tiny kitchen, and a couch. The place was filthy and smelled. We sat on the couch with the door open.

"It's important that I understand that you really want to come to Boys Ranch," I began, and I tried to explain what life would be like. Pete could not sit still. As I looked around the small trailer, I asked him, "Where do you sleep?"

"On the couch. If Pa brings a girlfriend home, he makes me sleep over there." He pointed out the door, toward the school across the street.

"Where do you sleep over there?"

"Under the stairs going into the school."

"What if it gets cold?"

"I crawl up under the school and find a place that's warm."

That did it. I made up my mind. I would do whatever it took to take this little boy to the ranch. I found a pay phone, called Sherm, and explained the situation.

"We have to go through the normal procedures to accept a boy in the ranch," he said.

"I'll never be able to sleep, thinking about this kid crawling under the school to keep warm," I said. "I have a custody agreement with me. If I can get the father to sign the papers, can I bring Pete to the ranch?"

Sherm Harriman had a big heart and always cared for the boys. He chuckled and said, "If you can get the father to sign it and then get the agreement notarized, I'll call the ranch and make all the arrangements."

I walked over to the father and made my offer.

"Give me the papers," he said without hesitation. "Get that piece of shit out of my life."

I told the father that we needed to go to the courthouse to have his signature notarized.

"I'll sign the papers, but I can't leave the station." He grumbled and spit some chew on the concrete.

I was exasperated. "I'll be right back," I said.

I drove to the courthouse and went to the clerk's office. "Do you have a notary?"

A woman stood and walked to the counter. "What do you need?"

"Would you ride with me to the gas station and notarize a father's signature to give custody of his son to Cal Farley's Boys Ranch?"

She looked at me in astonishment. I told her the whole story. "I'll get my coat," she said.

The father signed the papers. Pete watched with a big smile on his face. I went back to the pay phone and called Sherm. He chuckled again. "You remind me of myself when I started this job. I wanted to take care of every boy."

I told Pete to pack his things while I drove the woman back to the courthouse. Thanking her for her help, I handed her a ten-dollar bill. She gave it back to me. "Give it to Pete."

I drove back to the trailer, and Pete was waiting on the steps with a cardboard box next to him. He ran to the car, grinning from ear to ear. I put the box in the car, and he jumped into the front seat. "Can we go to my new home now?" he asked, still with the same big grin across his face.

"You should say good-bye to your father." He dropped his head and would not look at me. I knew his father abused him. I drove back to the gas station. The father walked to my window, looked in, and said to the boy, "I hope I never see you again, you little piece of worthless shit."

"We have a long ride," I told the father, and I gave him my card. "Call me if you ever want to know how your son is doing." That man took my card, tore it up into small pieces, and threw the pieces at Pete.

Pete bombarded me with questions about the ranch. We had been on the road for about thirty minutes when Pete looked at me and said, "Can I ask you one more question?"

"Sure."

"Do you mind if I call you Dad?"

My heart got caught in my throat. "I would be honored," I replied.

CHAPTER 12

Honey

When Donna became pregnant, both of us were elated. I loved putting my hand on her belly and feeling our baby move. Honey was ecstatic and could not wait to become a grandmother. The employees at the Boys Ranch town office threw a baby shower for us. Donna's obstetrician, Dr. Hands, told us that he planned to induce labor and asked us what day we wanted our child to be born. I suggested May 24 because it was my mother's birthday. He said that it would not be a good day for him, but he would deliver the baby on May 25. Karl was getting married on May 25 in Abilene, so unfortunately, Donna and I couldn't be there.

On the morning of May 24, 1973, Donna went into labor. I drove her to Northwest Texas Hospital. Dr. Hands arrived and said, "Well, I guess God wanted the twenty-fourth."

I called Honey to tell her that Donna was in labor. She was on her way to Karl's wedding in Abilene, so she stopped every thirty minutes along the way to call me from a pay phone for an update.

I stayed with Donna in her room and held her hand through the labor pains. She looked so beautiful, and I loved her so much. At 4:46 p.m., our son was born. It was the happiest day of my life. I was twenty-five years old. The first time I saw David was through my camera lens; I was taking pictures as the nurses rolled Donna out of the delivery room. I wanted to cherish that moment forever. I called Honey and told her that she was finally a grandmother; now she had a grandson, born on her birthday. She said she would come see us as soon as Karl's wedding

My son, David, was born on Honey's birthday. Courtesy of the Sarpalius family.

was over. I will never forget the look on Honey's face when she held her grandson for the first time. I put my hand on her shoulder and reminded her that she had a lot to live for.

Donna and I didn't have much, but we were very happy. We lived in a small rental house in Amarillo. I couldn't wait to get home from work every day to spend time with our son.

A year later, Honey married Louis Joyce in Fort Worth. Louis was much older than my mother. He was hard of hearing, and whenever Honey started drinking, he just turned off his hearing aid.

Donna, David, and I drove to Fort Worth on May 24 so my mother and my son could celebrate their birthdays together. Honey had baked a cake and wrote in icing, "Happy Birthday Honey & David" on the top. She was crazy about David and held him every chance she got.

On the evening of their birthday, Honey got drunk again. She was very depressed. When she and I were alone, she told me again, "I am tired of living."

"But now you have your grandson, plus you have Louis. You have so much more to live for."

"But I'm so unhappy. I don't want to live anymore." I knew she was suicidal again. We sat talking on the couch all night, and she finally fell asleep with her head in my lap.

The next morning, she made breakfast for all of us. I looked at Louis and prayed that he had the patience to help my mother. But Louis said he could not tolerate her drinking and didn't know what to do with her. I promised Louis I would try to find a place where we could get Honey some help. But I wasn't very hopeful. Texas still ranked last in the nation in treatment centers for substance abuse.

When it was time for us to leave, Honey gave me a big kiss and hug and told me she loved me. We were so close and had such a strong bond; I swore I knew what she was thinking at times.

"Hang in there," I whispered. "With God's help, you'll find happiness."

"I hope so," she said. "I have nothing to live for."

"Look at your grandson!" I told her.

Honey walked over to Donna, who was holding David. Donna handed David to Honey, and she held him close to her. She cried and slowly passed David back to Donna. We got in the car and drove off. When I looked in the rearview mirror, Honey was waving at us and crying. My heart was breaking once again.

Larry Johnson, an agriculture teacher at Boys Ranch, oversaw the dairy barn. His parents, Mr. and Mrs. Daylon Johnson, had been teachers at Boys Ranch for years, so Larry grew up there and graduated from Texas Tech a few years ahead of me. When he was a student at Boys Ranch, we talked about our dream of someday becoming agriculture teachers.

One day Larry was lifting a piece of metal irrigation pipe that was too close to a live electric line, and he was electrocuted. Regrettably, that tragic accident accelerated my teaching career at Boys Ranch. I wished it had been different. Now I was in charge of the dairy program, which meant beginning the day at 4:30 a.m.

Donna, David, and I moved into a home at Boys Ranch. Donna earned a salary cooking for five to ten guys who lived in the bunkhouse. I asked the school superintendent how I could make more money. He suggested I go back to school to get my master's degree, so when I signed the new contract, I also enrolled in the master's program at West Texas

State University. For the next two years, I drove 110 miles round trip every day to school and then back to the ranch, usually getting home around midnight. I later graduated in 1978 with a master's degree in agriculture. I was thirty years old, and my son, David, was five years old.

Being a vocational agriculture teacher was the most rewarding time of my life. My teachers had such an impact on me and helped me so much, and now I had that same opportunity to help students. At one time, I was helping three students prepare for a five-minute farm skill speech. This was part of the FFA program at Boys Ranch. I had been there, and I knew how difficult this was. The three boys were behind in school and lacked self-confidence, and one of the boys stuttered. I wrote a script on plant propagation and worked with the boys early every morning before breakfast. When it came time for them to compete against the other schools in the district, they won first place and then competed on the area level and again won first place. They advanced to the state level, competing against the top ten schools, and won second place. Once again, Boys Ranch had some more heroes. All three of those boys went on to finish college and became very successful. The boy who stuttered never stuttered again and became the quarterback of the football team. In my opinion, teachers have always been underpaid. Watching those boys succeed, though, was a payday for me.

～

We spent Christmas with Honey, but things continued to get worse. On March 1, 1975, she phoned long after Donna and I were in bed. I picked up and spoke to her; she was drunk again and told me that she was going to commit suicide. I got out of bed and took the phone into the living room and spent several hours speaking with her. She had been calling like this for months, but the calls seemed to be more frequent now. I told her that David's second birthday was right around the corner and that we would be there to see her. The conversation was going nowhere—which is what usually happened. She continued to cry, and before she hung up, she told me she loved me. I went back to bed and, once again, prayed for God to help her.

The next day, Donna and I went to teach Sunday school class and attend church. When we got home, the phone rang; it was Louis. He told me that Honey had overdosed on pills and died during the night. I fell to the floor. It was as if my world had stopped. I started crying uncontrollably. Donna took the phone and told Louis that we would drive there right away. I got up, walked outside, looked into the sky, and screamed, "Honey!" as loud as I could, over and over. That was the most painful moment of my life.

I was still in shock when I phoned Bobby and Karl. Karl had no money to buy a ticket to Fort Worth, so I bought his ticket. Then I had to call my grandparents in Jackson to tell them about Honey. That was one of the hardest phone calls I have ever had to make. Donna loaded up the car while I called Guy Finstad. He told me to stay in Fort Worth as long as necessary.

During the four-hour drive to Fort Worth, I thought of our last visit with Honey and had the picture of her in my head when we left that day—in the rearview mirror waving good-bye and crying. That was the last time I ever saw my mother alive. I could not comprehend that she was gone. Her only joy had been her sons and grandson. Her only relief had been the bottle and pills.

We pulled up to the house and walked to the front door. I glanced at Honey's plants on a rack by the door and envisioned her watering them. Louis opened the door, and we walked inside. Louis's two sons were there with their wives, and Bobby was standing in the kitchen. On the floor in the middle of the living room was a pile of photographs that had been taken out of their frames.

As I looked down at the pile, a heavyset woman, Louis's daughter-in-law, informed me, "Those pictures are the only things you will take out of this house."

The photographs were family pictures of my brothers and me. Honey had hung them throughout the house. I could not believe what I was seeing or hearing. Our mother had just died, and her husband and his children were treating us like we were thieves.

"Louis, can I go into Honey's room?"

"Go ahead." The heavyset woman followed me.

The room was dark. All the curtains were closed. I turned on the light and felt sick. I walked over to her record player, and there was an album by Tennessee Ernie Ford on top with a note in Honey's handwriting: *"These are my favorite songs, and I would like to have them sung at my funeral: 'The Old Rugged Cross,' 'How Great Thou Art,' and 'In the Garden.'"*

I stood there looking at that note and somehow felt responsible for her death, for not being able to talk her out of taking her life. Honey was only forty-eight years old.

I walked back into the living room. "Louis, can I talk to you alone?" I followed him into the garage.

"I don't like what is happening here. There are some things that belonged to Honey before you were married that mean a lot to my brothers and me. She always said she would put our names on the bottom of the things that she wanted us to have. We would like to take those things with us."

His sister-in-law stepped into the conversation and told me, "My family and I will go through her belongings first and then give you and your brothers any items with your names on them." Louis agreed. I could tell Louis cared a lot for Honey and was in a daze, but his sister-in-law had no compassion at all for Louis or my brothers.

I told Louis about the note I had found in Honey's room and the songs that she had requested to be sung at her funeral. Louis had no objections. He added that he and his first wife had bought four graveyard plots. "I'll let your mother be buried in one of them." He paused and then asked, "Who will pay for her funeral?" Clearly he did not intend to do so.

Donna and I checked into a nearby hotel. I didn't sleep all night. The next morning, we met Bobby and Karl at the funeral home, where we chose a coffin and a light-blue dress for Honey's burial. We reminisced about all the good times that we all had spent together growing up.

The funeral director reviewed Honey's funeral costs with me instead of Louis. We could not believe how much it would cost to bury Honey. Bobby and I shared the cost. I called the bank in Amarillo to get a loan.

The next day, we met at Louis's home, and a limousine from the funeral home picked us up. There were no more than ten people in attendance, including my brothers and our wives. The pastor and a church worker served as pallbearers. I thought I was holding up just fine until a woman from the church choir started to sing "In the Garden" by C. Austin Miles.

I come to the garden alone
While the dew is still on the roses
And the voice I hear, falling on my ear
The Son of God discloses.

And He walks with me,
and He talks with me,
And He tells me I am His own;
And the joy we share as we tarry there,
None other has ever known.

He speaks, and the sound of His voice
Is so sweet the birds hush their singing,
And the melody that He gave to me
Within my heart is ringing.

And He walks with me, and He talks with me,
And He tells me I am His own:
And the joy we share as we tarry there,
None other has ever known.

I'd stay in the garden with Him
Though the night around me be falling,
But He bids me go; through the voice of woe
His voice to me is calling.

And He walks with me, and He talks with me,
And He tells me I am His own:
And the joy we share as we tarry there,
None other has ever known.

Honey walked with Jesus, finally at peace.

Following the service, we all returned to Louis's house, where Bobby, Karl, and I took turns picking photographs from the pile on the floor. On a table were a few items with our names written on the bottom in Honey's handwriting. My mother had left me a bronze statue of a Japanese woman wearing a full kimono that she had bought when we lived in Japan.

As Donna and I walked out of the house, I glanced again at the plant rack and picked up a Christmas cactus in a small pot. I still have that Christmas cactus today. Over the years, I propagated the plant and gave it to my brothers and son. As Donna and I drove away, I looked in the rearview mirror, half expecting to see Honey waving good-bye.

Honey was a good mother, and we had a wonderful life until my father abandoned us. Honey did the best she could, but even her best was not good enough for her. My love for my mother is eternal.

～

After my third year of teaching at the ranch, I was becoming frustrated and did not see many opportunities to advance my career there. I was ready to leave. I had lived there for six and a half years as a boy and worked there for five years as a staff member and teacher. I was ready to teach in another school and head up my own vocational agriculture department.

I applied to several schools, but as the year ended, I had not received any offers for teaching positions. The ranch's school superintendent, Garland Rattan, gave me a contract to sign for the upcoming year. I brought it home and talked to Donna. I sensed she did not want to make a move. Our lives at the ranch offered our little family some stability. I did love teaching. We had four agriculture teachers, and the FFA chapter at the ranch was one of the most active and successful programs in Texas.

The Sunday after my mother died, there was a lot of excitement outside the Boys Ranch Chapel, and I thought that someone important must be expected at the services. When Donna and I walked into the church, I spotted a familiar face: state representative Bill Clayton, except now he was Speaker of the House Bill Clayton.

In Austin, the legislature hosted a Speaker's day honoring the Speaker of the House. At that time, it was customary for lobbyists and friends to give the Speaker gifts. Instead, Clayton had asked contributors to donate money instead of gifts, and then he would split the proceeds between Boys Ranch, located in the northern end of his district, and Girls Town, located in the southern end of his district. He received thousands of dollars in donations. That Sunday he had come to present the check to Boys Ranch.

After services, Donna and I left the chapel and headed toward the dining hall for lunch. I looked back at the chapel to see Speaker Clayton exit through the doors, surrounded by several directors of Boys Ranch. He spotted us and called out to me.

As I approached him, he turned to the directors and asked them to wait. He wanted to speak to me alone. Speaker Clayton and I stood a bit apart from others outside the chapel. Everyone was watching us.

"How are you, Bill?" he asked gruffly. He was a tough-talking but kindhearted man.

"Just fine, sir," I said innocently.

"You've made quite an impression on me, young man. Do you think you'd be interested in working for me? I'll pay your expenses if you fly to Austin so we can discuss what I have in mind."

Of course, I accepted his invitation.

When I caught up with Donna, I told her about my conversation with Speaker Clayton. I told her I was interested in finding out what he had in mind. I was thrilled. I was already intrigued with politics, and I wanted to learn more about how government worked—and I especially wanted to find a political solution to the lack of treatment centers for people with substance abuse problems.

PART III
State
Politics

CHAPTER 13

A New Road to Travel

I flew to Austin to meet Speaker Clayton at the state capitol. A tall man in his early thirties introduced himself as Rusty Kelly, Clayton's chief of staff. Rusty introduced another man, Jack Gullahorn, attorney for the Speaker's office. The two of them had similar lively personalities; both were smart, and both cared deeply about their service. Rusty explained that they wanted to hire a district director for the seven counties Bill Clayton represented. They described the responsibilities: travel to all seven counties that Clayton represented, maintain constituent contact, provide information regarding any problems or issues, and keep Clayton informed about important issues. Speaker Clayton joined us, and we went to lunch in an adjoining dining room, and the Speaker asked me if I would accept the position as his district director.

It paid less than what I was making as a teacher at Boys Ranch, but I was very interested. This was an opportunity for me to help people and get feet-on-the-ground experience of politics and government.

I knew that Donna would be concerned; it involved less money and a relocation. Boys Ranch did provide stability, especially for David. But I knew I would not be content teaching school for the rest of my life. Donna and I went through a difficult time.

"Remember when I had the opportunity to run for state representative but dropped out of the race?" I asked. "That was because you didn't like the idea, and because I love you, I gave it up. But I can't give up a second chance to improve our future."

She agreed to move to Hereford, Texas. Donna got a secretarial position at the Deaf Smith Electric Cooperatives. With our combined salaries, we could afford to buy a house. We found a nice two-bedroom redbrick house. Now we were first-time homeowners.

Speaker Clayton told me to find a preowned van to use as a mobile office as I traveled the seven counties that he represented. He did not like spending his money, so my budget for the van was a maximum of one thousand dollars.

I searched for a van for weeks and finally found a high-top van that an old man had stored in his barn. I paid him a visit. The van was bright orange with a white top high enough that I could stand up inside. It was perfect for a mobile office except for three small problems: it had no air conditioner, the heater was broken, and the engine was missing. The old man pointed at the engine on top of a bale of hay. "I'll have that van runnin' fer ya in two days," he promised.

I thought to myself, *There's no way.*

But a few days later, I showed up again, and to my surprise, the man had the old engine back in the van, and we took it for a test-drive. It ran just fine. I called Speaker Clayton, and he told me to buy it.

Bill Clayton's home in Springlake, Texas, had a private landing strip with a metal hangar beside it for his airplane. That day he was flying back from Austin, so I drove to Springlake to wait for him so I could show him his new mobile office. I hoped someday I could ride in his plane.

He taxied to a stop, cut the engine, climbed down, and met me with a big smile and a firm handshake.

"Your new mobile office is parked in the driveway," I told him, eager for his approval.

We walked around the airplane hangar, and when he saw the van, he said, "My God. It's orange and white!" He turned to me. "Those are the school colors for the University of Texas." I quickly learned that Speaker Clayton was a diehard Aggie from Texas A&M. The University of Texas and Texas A&M have always been huge rivals.

"I can't have you driving all over my district with those colors." He was momentarily annoyed. He looked at me and saw the disappointment on my face. I told him I hadn't known when I purchased the vehicle. Then after a few minutes of looking at that one thousand dollars bright-orange van, he grinned. "Well, maybe if we paint a big sign on it, no one will notice it." He chuckled.

So I had a big sign painted on the van that read, "Speaker Bill Clayton's Mobile Office," and scheduled visits to every town in his district. I always parked in front of a local bank, school, or courthouse and ran an extension cord so I could run a fan in the summer or a heater in the winter. I loved meeting and greeting all those people, listening to the constituent's issues, and helping develop solutions alongside the Speaker and his team.

On one of my many trips, I learned that the city of Littlefield, Texas, needed help with a water problem. They requested the Speaker's assistance, and Speaker Clayton filed a bill to put a water district in Littlefield, but the bill got held up in the Senate. I went to Austin and asked Clayton about the status of the legislation. He suggested that I talk to Senator Bob Price, who had sponsored the bill in the Senate. I had met Senator Price previously when I had my picture taken with him on my one and only trip to Washington, DC, back when he was a congressman.

When the state of Texas had been redistricted, Bob Price and Congressman Jack Hightower ran against each other. Hightower defeated Price, but then Price ran for Texas Senate when my friend Senator Max Sherman ran for attorney general. Now I needed to discuss the status of the water bill that Clayton had filed for Littlefield with Senator Price.

"He's too busy," his secretary informed me. "Come back next week."

I was floored. This issue meant water for people in Littlefield, a town in his district, and I could not believe he was too busy to address this.

I went to the Senate gallery and spotted Price, talking and laughing on the phone. I had no clue if his call was business or personal, but he certainly wasn't paying attention to the issues being debated. I sat there and watched him for his entire hour-long conversation, but I also watched the Senate members debate various issues. I was fascinated.

I started daydreaming about running for the Texas Senate someday and being down on that floor doing what they were doing. Then I thought to myself, *Who am I kidding? That will never happen.* I was just a kid from Boys Ranch and an agriculture teacher. Most of the Senate members were very successful, wealthy, professional attorneys. Even Senator Bob Price owned a large ranch with oil and gas wells. I could never compete on that level.

~

The two years working for Speaker Clayton went by fast. Before I knew it, David's first day of school arrived. He was so excited and nervous. Donna and I took pictures of him in his brown pants and red shirt. His hair had just been cut, and he was wearing his new cowboy boots. He looked so cute. I dropped him off in front of the school and watched him walk up the sidewalk to the schoolhouse. Then he turned back and waved at me. I will always cherish that moment.

I remained in close touch with my grandparents and called them every Sunday night. My grandmother updated me on her garden and her church activities, and Granddad would ask how I was doing. Their constant encouragement and love meant so much to me now that Honey was gone. I still missed my mother terribly. I could tell from my granddad's voice that he was growing weaker. I flew to Jackson to spend an entire week with them, helping with house repairs. I slept on the same foldout couch that my brothers, Honey, and I had slept on for years.

I got up with my granddad at 6:00 every morning, drank coffee with him, and listened to his stories about his years on the railroad. He had a green-and-white 1956 Buick that he used to drive Grandmother to the grocery store and to church. I loved that old car, and Granddad let me clean and wax it. Eventually, his eyesight got so bad that he couldn't drive anymore, so they had to sell the Buick.

One evening, we were watching the news on TV. Grandmother was in her tiny kitchen cooking dinner. She called to Granddad to get a bowl from a high shelf that she couldn't reach. I heard her cry out, "Oh, Clarence!" as he fell to the floor. I jumped up to try to help him. His eyes were unfocused, and his nose was bleeding. We helped him get to a chair.

"I'm all right," he kept repeating. "I just had a dizzy spell." We managed to get Granddad into my rental car and drove to the hospital. It turned out that he had two broken ribs.

When I left to head back home, I somehow knew that this was the last time I would see my grandfather. He hugged me good-bye and told me I was his favorite grandson. That meant more to me than anything.

A few months later, Granddad lapsed into a coma. Grandmother stayed by his side, and when she couldn't be there, my aunt Kat, Honey's older sister, stayed with him. He remained in a coma for several days, and I called every night to check on him. Aunt Kat was with him one night when I called and the phone woke him from the coma. He asked who was on the line, so Aunt Kat handed him the phone. We talked briefly. He said he loved me. I told him the same. Then he said, "I'm so tired," and handed the phone back to Aunt Kat.

Later I learned that Granddad fell back to sleep immediately after we talked, so I was the last person to talk to him. He passed away that night.

My grandfather, Clarence Maxwell, was such a significant influence on me. He never complained and never said a bad word about anybody. He loved life, nature, and his family. He had a big heart, and everyone else came first. He and Grandmother faithfully attended church every Sunday. He was a wonderful husband who loved my grandmother unconditionally and treated her with kindness and respect.

Donna and I drove to Jackson for the funeral. My granddad was the closest I ever had to a real father. Grandmother and I walked hand in hand around her backyard garden. I will never forget what she said that day.

"God answered my prayers," she said. "I prayed every day that your grandfather would keep his mind and that I would never have to put him in a nursing home."

My grandfather was nine years older than my grandmother, and to me they were a perfect couple. At his funeral, my grandmother opened my hand and gave me my grandfather's Masonic ring, the only jewelry he had worn. "He wanted you to have this."

With the encouragement of my granddad, I had become a Mason when I was a teacher at Boys Ranch. It meant a great deal to me because I knew how much it meant to my granddad. I slipped the ring on my finger, and Grandmother smiled. I wore that ring until it had worn down so badly that I was afraid I would lose it. Masonry is about brotherhood and a commitment to helping others. Later, when I was campaigning for office, my ring was often acknowledged and admired by other Masons. The ring was special to me; it was a reminder of what a positive influence my grandfather was to me.

His funeral service was beautiful, and the church was packed with all his family and his many friends. He was a role model to me and the most positive family influence in my life. Without him and Boys Ranch, I don't know what would have happened to me.

My granddad and Honey. Courtesy of the Sarpalius family.

~

Working for the Speaker was a great experience but a difficult job. I had to get up early every morning and drive to a different town and set up on the courthouse square or by the school. The weather was brutal, especially driving a van with no heat in the winter snow. When the weather was bad, I would just hang out in the courthouse, or I ran an extension cord to the van to power an electric heater. I met with the constituents and listened to their concerns. Then I would call Crockett Camp, who worked in the Speaker's office, and he would research the issues and get back to me. I had to call from a payphone on the corner of the courthouse square, and on those brutally cold days, I told Crockett to give me an answer ASAP, or I would freeze my ass off. Crockett and I became very close friends, and together we helped a lot of people. He is still a dear friend to this day. I eventually sought his advice about running for the Texas Senate. He told me that if I was elected to the Senate, I would have to find another job to generate enough money to pay our bills. The Texas legislature only met for five months in alternating years. Most members were already successful enough to accommodate this schedule, and the $7,200 annual salary for a Texas legislator was no problem for them. This annual salary, rooted in the Texas Constitution, could only be modified or increased by an amendment that required a vote of the citizens of Texas. Any pay raise was unlikely.

My expertise was agriculture, and finding a job in in this field that would allow me time to campaign for office and then attend the legislative sessions would not be easy. I knew teaching was not the solution, so I read in the jobs section of every newspaper, hoping to find something that would work.

There were twenty-seven counties in the Thirty-First Senate District of Texas; seven were in Speaker Clayton's district. I thought I might be able to find a job with one of the companies within the Speaker's district. I wrote every possible contact I could think of on an index card—I had hundreds of cards.

Donna wanted me to return to teaching while I was looking for another job, but I did not want to. I asked anyone I thought might be helpful about agricultural jobs that would be a fit for me. One Sunday I read a story in the only paper in Amarillo, the *Amarillo Globe*, about Center Plains Industries acquiring all the anhydrous ammonia from Phillips 66. Center Plains Industries sold anhydrous ammonia, a fertilizer that adds nitrogen to the soil to aid plant growth, which was used in nearly the entire Thirty-First District. I thought this might be a great opportunity and that they might be hiring, so the next day I jumped in my car and drove to Amarillo.

Their office was located between Amarillo and Canyon. I walked in and asked the receptionist if I could speak to the president of the company, Wesley Masters. I had read about him in the newspaper. She asked for my name and asked me to wait in the reception area.

Mr. Masters himself came to the lobby to greet me. I instantly liked him. He invited me into his office, and I immediately noticed the many awards and certificates from Texas Tech that were displayed.

"Are you a Tech graduate?" I asked.

"I sure am. BS in agriculture at Tech, and my master's from West Texas." I figured we were off to a good start. I told him that I had read the piece about Center Plains Industries in the paper and was interested in working for him.

"Are you interested in running for public office?" he asked.

I was taken aback. "I hope to someday soon."

"I heard you speak at the Plainview FFA banquet," he told me. "I was very impressed. I thought you would run for public office eventually."

I told him that I someday I would like to run against Bob Price for the Texas Senate, maybe in two years, when Bob Price was up for reelection. We talked about Bob Price and how it was time for him to go.

"I'd put you in sales and public relations," he said, nodding. "You'd travel to the co-ops and feed stores all over the Panhandle, giving you the chance to meet a lot of people. That would work out well for both of us. You would also speak to civic clubs as a representative of Center Plains Industries. This offers you great exposure and will be excellent for my company."

I stood up and shook his hand. "OK! Thank you so much for this opportunity!" This job was a godsend.

That was the beginning of a lifelong friendship. My workspace that Wesley assigned to me was in the attic of the building. It was tiny, only big enough for a desk, a chair, a file cabinet, and a bookcase, but I didn't care—it was better than the mobile van and I had my own phone in my office.

My first sales call was to the Farmland Industries co-op in Dalhart, Texas. I told the manager this was my first stop on my new job. He invited me into his office and told me he had been very impressed with my speech at an FFA banquet a year earlier. He greatly admired Wesley Masters and was pleased with his service from Center Plains. But he didn't increase the size of his order with Center Plains.

The next day Wesley called me to his office. I was afraid I had done something wrong and that he would be disappointed that I hadn't returned with a larger order. Instead he said the co-op manager phoned him to say he was impressed with me and that he would continue to buy his fertilizer from Center Plains. I was thrilled, so I continued to travel all over the Texas Panhandle daily, meeting customers of Center Plains Industries. I was pretty used to the travel by now.

～

That job seemed perfectly suited to my skills and ambitions. I began to dream again about my next steps and my political career. Whenever I got the chance, I discussed politics and tried to get a read about Bob Price from his constituents. I discovered that not a lot of voters thought he was doing a good job. In 1979, he was listed by *Texas Monthly* magazine as one of the ten worst legislators for the session.

On my long-distance drives throughout the Texas Panhandle, I began to plan my campaign for the Texas Senate for the next election year. I read every book I could find on managing a political campaign. The more I read, the more determined I became.

Everyone I talked to about running for public office said it would be a great experience, but not much support was offered, and they asked me how I planned to raise the money needed to finance a campaign. I was continually reminded that it was hard to win a race with no money and little name recognition.

My thoughts continued to return to Honey and her struggles. I kept thinking that if I could get elected to the Texas Senate, it would give me a chance to do something that would have helped my mother. I outlined my announcements, the issues I would address, and my plans for building a grassroots movement in each town. As I planned advertising and TV spots, I wondered where and how I would get the money.

I did question myself at times, wondering how I could possibly defeat Bob Price, a decorated fighter pilot, who had been popular and was a wealthy rancher, oilman, and landowner. And he had served in the US Congress and was now a Texas state senator. He was experienced in running campaigns, and he knew how to win. He had a large group of supporters. I studied everything I could find about Bob Price and his career.

Bob had a lot going in his favor. I could not measure up to him in any way. The one thing I did have going for me was that I was young, ambitious, and not afraid to work hard. As past president of the Texas FFA, I had become a good speaker and had developed a good reputation. Additionally, I had met hundreds of voters throughout the Texas Panhandle working for Speaker Clayton and now Center Plains Industries. And I was a graduate of Cal Farley's Boys Ranch, a distinct advantage in the Thirty-First District. I loved the idea of political service and what I might be able to accomplish for the people of Texas. This would also give me a chance to address the issues that my mother faced her entire life: alcohol and drug addiction with no rehabilitation available to people with no money other than mental institutions.

Speaker Bill Clayton. Courtesy of the Sarpalius family.

For the next two years, I continued to work for Wesley and Center Plains Industries. The filing deadline to announce my candidacy was rapidly approaching; I had to decide whether to throw my name in for the Thirty-First District's Senate seat.

In November, I called Speaker Clayton to ask if we could talk the next time he came home. We met at a drive-in restaurant in Dimmit, Texas. He pulled up in his pickup; I climbed in the cab. We ordered hamburgers, fries, and chocolate shakes.

"What's on your mind, Bill?"

"I'm thinking about running for Senate, and if I can win, it would give me a chance to do something about the problems of alcohol and drug abuse."

He smiled. "Others have already talked to me about running. Clint Formby, a radio station owner from Hereford, and state representative Foster Whaley, from Pampa."

My heart sank. Texas had an April primary, so I would only have four months to campaign and raise the needed funds.

"Go talk to Representative Foster Whaley and Clint Formby," the Speaker advised. "Tell them you are interested in running, and do your best to persuade them not to run." He told me they had a lot of money and didn't mind spending it.

"Would you endorse me?" I asked.

"I can't do that until after the primary."

"Can you give me some advice on raising money?"

"No one will contribute money until you announce your candidacy."

"This is like the chicken and the egg," I reckoned. "I won't know how much money I'll raise until I stick my neck out. But without money for TV, radio, and newspaper ads, I won't have a chance of winning."

He nodded sympathetically. "You'll need to raise at least four hundred thousand dollars to run a good race against Bob Price, a conservative Republican. If you have an opponent in the Democratic primary, you'll need another three hundred thousand dollars."

The next day, I wrote a letter to the Senate clerk's office requesting Bob Price's last campaign filing. Price had more than two hundred thousand dollars in his campaign account. My current salary was one thousand dollars a month, and I had little to no savings. I was in trouble.

Speaker Clayton advised me to talk to anyone that might support me if I decided to get in the race. I started making my list and began developing my shoestring campaign budget. I could not afford an advertising firm, so I designed all my own campaign material. The funds I would raise would go toward printing costs for brochures, signs, and bumper stickers—and for the gasoline needed to campaign all over the twenty-seven-counties in the Thirty-First District, which covered 28,929 square miles, more square miles than all but ten of the other states in the nation. I was convinced I could make a good run for it, and

I did all the work myself. I figured one hundred thousand dollars would be enough to pay for the print materials and maybe a few TV and radio spots late in the campaign. I went to meet with Pete Gilvin, a successful road contractor in Amarillo and a member of the Boys Ranch board. He was very gracious and told me the same thing Speaker Clayton had told me—that nobody would write a check until I got into the race. I asked if he would be willing to host a fundraiser for me if I got in the race. When he told me he would, I made my decision that day.

My plan was simple: I would do what Boys Ranch taught me—I would work hard. I would do the same thing that I had done during my FFA competitions: shake as many hands as possible and ask people to vote for me. I planned to campaign from sunup until sundown every day until the primary. But first I needed to approach my potential opponents and try to talk them out of running against me. I met with both Foster Whaley and Clint Formby and let them know that I planned to run and that I was going to give them a run for their money. I tried to appear confident; inside, I was shaking like a leaf. Clint Formby never filed to run. Foster Whaley decided to stay in his House seat.

I told Donna that we needed to have a serious discussion and that I needed her support. I told her that even if I didn't win, I at least had to try, and I needed her support and wanted her by my side when I announced my candidacy and on election night, win or lose. I told her that my goal was to help people with their issues, and more than anything else, I wanted to be able to establish treatment centers for people like Honey. Donna agreed to support me and said she would do everything to help me with my campaign—and to win. The next morning, I went to the bank and opened my campaign checking account. My initial deposit was twenty-five dollars. It was all I had to start my campaign.

I wrote my press release to announce my candidacy for the Texas Senate, and I prayed for strength. I mailed it to all the newspapers in the district. I recorded my announcement for my candidacy on a cassette tape and mailed it to all the radio stations. At nine in the morning, I held a press conference in the boardroom of a local law office. I grew nervous as I watched technicians from TV and radio stations setting up their equipment. There was no turning back now.

Donna and David stood with me on the podium with my supporters, including Gene Peggram, Sherm Harriman, Roy Turner (one of the first six boys at Boys Ranch), Wesley Masters, Boys Ranch board member Pete Gilvin, and my brothers Bobby and Karl. I was deeply moved by the support from my Boys Ranch family.

My initial speech was short, to the point, and focused mainly on how I could do a better job than Bob Price. I offered to answer any questions from the press. I did not really have much history, other than my time spent as the FFA state president, so the press had very few questions. Right after that, I jumped in my car and drove to the newspaper offices and radio stations in Pampa, Borger, Spearman, Dalhart, and finally Hereford. That was a very long day.

The three TV stations in Amarillo covered 90 percent of the entire district. So far, other than Bob Price, I was the only known candidate for the Senate. The next day my big announcement was buried on the third page, a blip in the newspaper. I was crushed. I had a long road ahead of me, but I was determined to succeed. I still could not believe I was running against Bob Price—I had my picture taken with him twelve years earlier, when I met him for the first time while serving as FFA president.

CHAPTER 14

The Primary

C rockett Camp called to let me know that Gerald McCathern had filed for the Democratic primary thirty minutes before the deadline. McCathern was a farmer who had gained national recognition as the founder of the American Agriculture Movement. He was from Hereford and lived only a few blocks from me.

In 1977, McCathern led the farmer's strike protesting the Farm Bill. The farmers, who were faced with increasing fixed costs and rising interest rates on their farm loans, also protested the FHA (Farmers Home Administration), who was trying to force land foreclosures for past-due loans. In a huge protest movement, McCathern led a "tractor-cade" of three thousand tractors driven by farmers across the nation to Washington, DC. It was a brilliant idea, and every night the national news featured the hundreds of tractors traveling across the highways of America, American flags flying above each. There was negative press though because the tractors blocked traffic for miles on the highways. The farmers had the public's sympathy until some of them started plowing up the ground around the Washington Monument.

The first time I saw Gerald McCathern was on ABC's *Good Morning America*. His interview focused on the problems of American farmers. During the interview, he declared his candidacy for the Texas Senate and emphasized his dedication to helping US farmers.

McCathern, an aviation engineer during World War II and a Texas Tech graduate, had a huge following. He was a hero to the farmers in the Thirty-First District of Texas and its twenty-seven agriculture-producing counties. The tractor he drove to Washington, DC, is on display in the Smithsonian Museum.

I knew I was in big trouble. I was an unknown running against a national hero.

When McCathern held his press conference for his formal announcement, the room was packed with supporters, farmers, and ranchers. He was on the front page of the Amarillo paper. I felt helpless and had no idea how I could possibly beat this well-known and popular farmer with national name recognition. I was still determined to give it my all.

Pete Gilvin hosted that promised fundraiser for me—a bird hunt at his ranch with business leaders from Amarillo. Some of the men I met at that event are still lifelong friends. I met Jerry Hodge, a young drug store owner who became a good friend and supported me throughout my career. Jerry started Maxor Drugs and became one of the most successful men in Texas. Maxor eventually became a national pharmacy, providing thousands of jobs. When the fundraiser was over, Pete handed over the checks totaling a little more than five thousand dollars. It was a fair start.

I called Speaker Clayton seeking advice and encouragement. He told me to not give up. I asked if I could buy his old mobile office. It was on its second engine and had more than 250,000 miles on it. He agreed to sell it to me for five hundred dollars. I picked it up and had my logo painted on both sides and on the back.

To cut costs, I designed my campaign brochures and included family pictures of Donna, David, and me, as well as pictures of me as the FFA president engaged in conversation with a farmer in a cornfield. I took my draft campaign brochure to a printer and told them I wanted five thousand brochures printed. My campaign colors were deep blue and gold. The colors of Boys Ranch and the Future Farmers of America.

I bought an eight-track tape of the soundtrack from the movie *Rocky*. That tape became my motivational music that I listened to while traveling the Thirty-First District in my mobile office. I glued a road map of the twenty-seven counties in my campaign district to a piece of cardboard and developed a campaign schedule where I would visit every town at least five times before the election. Election Day was only twelve weeks away. Sunday was my only day to spend at home with Donna and David.

I had spent almost all my campaign money and only had enough left to buy gas for the van. I had to hit the road and start talking to the voters. I called Farmland Industries Co-op in Dalhart to speak to the manager I met when I made my first sales call for Wesley. I asked him what the best time was for me to catch most of the farmers to speak to them. He told me that most of them showed up for coffee around five thirty in the morning.

"Would you mind if I stop by on Monday morning to shake a few hands?" I asked.

"Not at all," he said. "I'll make some calls on your behalf to make sure some of the farmers are here in the morning." Then he added, "I must warn you, the American Agriculture Movement is big in this town, and they all love Gerald McCathern. Some of them drove their tractors to Washington with him."

"I understand," I told him. "But I'm not going to avoid areas where McCathern has a big following."

On Monday, wearing my only suit and tie, I left our house at 3:30 a.m. and drove to Dalhart while listening to the *Rocky* tape. At 5:30 a.m., I pulled up in front of the co-op. There were already about twenty pickup trucks in the parking lot. About half of them had bumper stickers that read, "American Agriculture Movement." I knew that each one of those bumper stickers was a vote for McCathern.

I grabbed a handful of my blue-and-gold brochures, took a deep breath of cold air, and went inside. At each of the eight round tables sat three or four farmers in jeans or coveralls drinking coffee. When I walked in, they all stopped talking and stared at me. I felt totally awkward, overdressed, and out of place.

The co-op manager greeted me, walked to the coffeepot, introduced me to everyone, and asked me to say a few words. I gave a short talk explaining why I would be a good choice for state senator. I knew everyone there was a friend of my opponent—though I never mentioned McCathern's name. I had learned you should never mention your opponent's name because you want voters to remember your name. Then I told them about what I would accomplish for the people of the Thirty-First District if elected. I told them about growing up at Boys Ranch, thirty miles down the road, and that I had served as state president of the Future Farmers of America and earned my master's degree in agricultural sciences. I went on to tell them that I had been a vocational agriculture teacher at Boys Ranch and that I was currently working for Center Plains Industries selling anhydrous ammonia, an agriculture business product. My point was to emphasize that McCathern was not the only candidate who understood farmers and agriculture. In addition to promoting agricultural issues, I added that I wanted to create desperately needed alcohol and drug treatment centers, improve public education, and create new jobs in the Texas Panhandle.

I thought I did a good job and asked if anyone had any questions. The first came from a farmer wearing a cap with the American Agriculture Movement logo.

"Would you consider dropping out of the race to help defeat Bob Price? We all know you don't have a prayer of beating Gerald McCathern. If you drop out now, you'll save Gerald money for the race against Price. Then all the farmers will respect you and get behind you the next time you run for office."

That one caught me completely off guard.

"My mother and Boys Ranch didn't raise quitters," I answered, maintaining my confident demeanor. "I have a great deal of respect for the other candidate and the American Ag Movement, but this is not a race against him. This is an opportunity for each of us to demonstrate what we plan to accomplish for the people of the Thirty-First District."

More questions were asked, and I did my best to answer them. I told them Dalhart was like a second home since I grew up at Boys Ranch only thirty miles away. I had competed against Dalhart in football and several other sports. I told them that Dalhart had one of the best football teams in the state, and they kicked our asses. The farmers all laughed. The tension in the room seemed to let up.

When I left, I felt like the meeting went very well. I knew there were a lot of supporters for McCathern, but I thought I might've picked up a few votes—and in McCathern's backyard.

Roy Turner, a friend and former Boys Rancher, asked me to stop by his office, and he gave me several campaign checks. Roy was a successful brick contractor. As I was leaving his office, I turned and asked him if he would be willing to serve as my treasurer. He said he would be honored. That was the best and quickest decision of my campaign and the beginning of a long friendship.

Several Amarillo small businesses supported me. McCathern was viewed as a one-issue candidate, and many local businesses did not approve of his tactics. I was beginning to feel some momentum. I didn't know many of the people who were now contributing money to my campaign to help me win the Democratic primary in a Republican district.

One of my main obstacles was zero name recognition. Many people told me that voters would have a hard time remembering my name, but I hoped that because my name was different, voters would remember it. I decided to promote only my last name. I also chose nontraditional campaign colors: a dark-blue background with my name in bright yellow. To make my last name stand out, I designed the logo *SarpaliuS*, with a capital *S* at the end.

I didn't have enough money to pay for billboards, but I had enough money for advertisements to cover the sides of ten city buses that traveled around Amarillo. That decision was a home run. I had ten moving billboards for a fraction of the cost of one billboard.

I ordered the least expensive poster at the local print shop and had my logo and photograph printed. I planned to display these in store windows throughout the Panhandle. I also ordered some name-only vertically aligned signs, planning to staple them to utility poles and to use them for yard signs.

The printer promised to have my materials ready in one week. This did not leave me with a lot of time, but I did not have any other options—I was on a tight budget. This meant I would have to place my materials in the store windows and staple them to the poles myself.

I visited local restaurants, schools, businesses, banks, courthouses, hospitals, and anywhere else voters gathered. I hit the coffee shops at 5:00 a.m. and finished my day when the restaurants closed. If there was a local high school basketball game, I stood at the gym door handing brochures to every person who entered. I often worked two schools in one night. In some towns, I could rally a few volunteers, but for the most part, I was on my own. McCathern was strong in every rural town, and I was facing an uphill battle against him. I continued to listen to my *Rocky* tape, which kept me motivated. I campaigned late into the evenings, walking door to door asking for votes.

One day I knocked on the door of an old house and could hear movement inside, but nobody answered the door. I opened the screen door and knocked a little harder. Again I heard movement, so I waited. I was about to leave when a little old lady with white hair slowly opened the front door. She was stooped over and looked very angry. I opened the screen door, held out a brochure, and told her I was Bill Sarpalius and I was running for the state senate and would appreciate her vote.

She cocked her head and looked at me. "Young man," she said, "when you are eighty-six years old, you don't give a shit who your state senator is," and she slowly closed her door. Well, that was a surprise.

I kept going, working every town and hanging signs on poles and in store windows. The days were long, but the *Rocky* tape kept me going. I drove home when I was close to Hereford and then got up early the next morning to drive to another town.

Roy Turner and Wesley Masters were my greatest supporters. They raised enough money for me to buy some radio time. I wrote the radio spots myself because I couldn't afford a scriptwriter. The radio time was the best use of the little campaign money I had left. Election Day was only three weeks away, and I was anticipating a huge media bombardment from McCathern.

I spent the final three weeks making rounds to every town in the district, hitting every restaurant, coffee shop, business, and courthouse. I also attended every candidate forum to which I was invited. Most of the forums were held in small towns and allowed three minutes for each candidate to give his speech. At some of the forums, local charities held cake auctions. Anyone could bid on the cakes to raise money for charities. Of course, the candidates running for office should always place the highest bid. The local newspapers and radio stations covered these forums.

Donna worked just as hard as I did—typing letters to help me raise money, stuffing and licking envelopes, making phone calls, and whatever else she could do to help me. It became a real team effort, and I was so happy to have her support and have her by my side.

On my way to a campaign forum in Perryton, I was traveling on a farm-to-market road about twenty miles from town when I heard a loud *thump*, and my old van rolled to a stop. I looked in the rearview mirror and saw something in the middle of the road. The gas tank had fallen off! I dragged it back to the van but had no idea what to do. I noticed some baling wire wrapped around a barbwire fence and tried to grab enough of it to wrap around the gas tank. I crawled under the van wearing my only suit and got to work, and after about an hour, my gas tank was secured with the baling wire. I climbed back into my van, said a prayer, and pumped the gas pedal. The van started.

I drove very slowly to Perryton and arrived an hour and a half late. There were tons of pickup trucks in the parking lot with the American Agriculture Movement bumper stickers. Every eye was on me when I walked into the high school auditorium.

I was filthy. My suit was badly wrinkled and stained with oil. About twenty candidates who were running for local office sat behind long tables lined up on the stage. When I walked into the room, every head turned, and I know they were all wondering what on earth had happened to me. I sat down in the only empty chair, and the man at the microphone said, "Mr. Sarpalius, you got here just in time, because everyone else has spoken."

I got back up, took the microphone, and apologized for my appearance. I explained that my van was ancient and that its old gas tank was now held together by "a lick and a promise" and some baling wire. I assured them that as their state senator, I would represent them in much cleaner attire. As I finished, I could feel the support from the voters in that room.

That night I met McCathern for the first time. He was an older man. Every time he walked on a stage, he seemed to lack enthusiasm. He acted like he was the only spokesperson for the farmers and had already won the election. On the drive back to Amarillo, I tacked up more pole signs and began planning my television ad. At a gas station, I phoned Donna, who told me to return a call from Roy Turner as soon as possible.

"Good news, Bill, your radio ads are paying off," an excited Roy said.

I had paid to run the three radio ads I had recorded five times over the course of three days.

"Momentum is growing," he continued. "I've raised several thousand dollars more. You should have enough money now to pay for another week of radio, with maybe some left over for a TV ad."

When I got home, I dug through my scrapbook and found some old black-and-white photographs to use for a TV spot. I wrote the script and then took the pictures to a local television station. I paid for my only television spot and felt like my entire campaign was riding on this one thirty-second TV ad.

A local disk jockey with a good radio voice offered to read the script that I had written. A cameraman zoomed in very slowly on each of the black-and-white photographs. The first one was of Honey, my two brothers, and me. The voice-over narrated about the time when we were homeless in Houston. Next was a photo of Bobby and me in our FFA jackets next to an Angus steer. The script told our story of growing up at Boys Ranch. Then the voice-over touted my stint as state FFA president as the camera focused on a shot of me wearing my FFA jacket. Another showed me in my role as an agriculture teacher and emphasized my understanding of agricultural problems facing the farmers in Texas. The final photograph was of me handing my campaign brochures to senior citizens as the voice-over praised my hard work campaigning for the office of state senator for the Thirty-First District.

As I was leaving the TV station, one of the employees told me that McCathern had paid for a heavy TV blitz for the two weeks leading up to the election.

My television ad was a huge success. I could only afford to run it a few times, but the TV station began receiving phone calls from viewers asking when my spot would run again. The TV stations told me that was a first for them.

I now felt like my campaign was picking up speed. People began to volunteer to help. Some volunteers offered to put out yard signs, but I had none left. I asked for as many volunteers as possible to work the polling places on Election Day. Some college students volunteered to hold up homemade signs in support of me at the most heavily traveled intersections in Amarillo and at the entrances to shopping malls. On Election Day, I asked the volunteers to stand on the overpasses of the main highways and flash the signs at cars. No one had ever done that before, and I thought it was a good idea. I told the volunteers I would meet them at the donut shop at 5:00 a.m. on Election Day.

Meanwhile, McCathern's TV and radio campaign dominated the airways. All his TV and radio spots focused on his leadership of the American Agriculture Movement and his vision of helping the farmers and the future of agriculture. His main message was agriculture and how he would help farmers get a better price for their crops.

After hearing his ads, I quickly wrote and recorded another radio spot. I told voters I would not be a single-issue state senator. Not only would I work to help farmers; as a former teacher, I would also do my best to improve the Texas education system. As a businessman, I would work to help small businesses. I promised to do my best to help every citizen in the Thirty-First District.

I planned to run that spot the final week of the campaign. During that week, I received an invitation to a candidate forum in Wellington. I made the three-hour drive to Wellington, pulled up to the building, went inside, and started shaking hands. There were only two chairs on the stage. McCathern and his supporters were the only ones there. I had been set up.

The audience began asking very pointed questions. I did my best to answer, but it was a hostile atmosphere. It was obvious I was not going to win any votes there, and I got up to leave. As I walked to the door, one man pushed me up against a wall and started cussing at me and shoving me. Several men surrounded me. One was holding a camera, ready to snap a picture. I realized that this attack was planned. They wanted me to hit the guy who had attacked me so they could get pictures of me fighting with one of them—an effort to sabotage my campaign. I ran for the door. They tried to grab me, but I made it outside, jumped in my van, and took off. My heart was racing the whole way home.

For the live debate the Friday night before the Tuesday election, I had requested only one thing: that McCathern and I stand next to each other. It would show the contrasts between us. He was much older and shorter than me. McCathern also wore his suit coat open and applied way too much makeup.

For me, the debate was a huge success. While speaking, I looked straight into the camera, while McCathern looked at the person asking the question. Our debate lasted thirty minutes on prime-time TV on the most popular TV station in the Texas Panhandle.

When it was over, McCathern looked troubled. He apologized for what had happened in Wellington. For the first time, I admired what he had accomplished for the farmers.

"No matter who wins," he said, "we'll work together to beat Bob Price in the general election."

I agreed and shook his hand.

Over the weekend, student volunteers waved my signs at every major intersection in Amarillo. I shook hands and campaigned everywhere I could. On the day before the election, I drove to Pampa and visited every business on the square. Pampa was a key town because it was a

Republican stronghold, and there was always a big turnout on Election Day. It was also Bob Price's hometown.

I was physically and mentally drained. I could only sleep a few hours each night. During those months, I had lost twenty-five pounds. I had visited every town in the twenty-seven counties five times, in accordance with my plan. In addition, I had visited as many businesses as I could as many times as possible. I put everything I had into the race.

On my way home from Pampa, I played the *Rocky* soundtrack. As the sun was setting, the Texas sky was spectacular. I had five pole signs in the back of the van, so I decided to pull off the road and hang them.

After tacking up four signs, I held the final sign against the pole and used my heavy-duty staple gun to staple it, but I missed. I drove the staple all the way through the fingernail on my left index finger. I pulled my finger away from the pole, and my fingernail ripped off. There was blood everywhere. The staple had gone all the way through my finger. I pulled the rest of the staple out of my finger and searched for something in the van to stop the bleeding. I wrapped a rag around my finger, got back in the van, and drove home.

When I got home, Donna took me to the emergency room. The doctor bandaged my finger, gave me some pain pills, and told me to rest for a few days.

"I have an election to win," I remember telling the doctor matter-of-factly. I think he admired my stubbornness. This was not going to stop me.

The next day was Election Day. I met my student volunteers at the donut shop, thanked them for their help, and invited them to join me that evening at a local hotel to watch the election returns. Then they returned to their spots at key overpasses to hold up my signs. Then I went to all the polling places and shook hands with as many voters as possible and asked for their votes.

My brothers, Bobby and Karl, worked polls all day long for me. My brothers had been there for me throughout my entire campaign.

That afternoon Donna and I went to our voting place in Hereford. I thanked Donna for helping me and supporting me in the campaign. When I saw my name on the ballot in the voting booth, I couldn't help but wish Honey were alive to see it. I hoped I would not disappoint all my supporters at Boys Ranch. Whatever the outcome, God had brought me this far for a reason.

The odds were stacked against me. McCathern had outspent me four to one. His political ads saturated TV and radio, plus he had been running full-page newspaper ads. He also had support from the national farmers' movement.

That evening my campaign workers and friends met at the hotel ballroom. Roy Turner had arranged to have three televisions set up in three corners of the large room, one for each of the three Amarillo stations. We had a reception table with snacks for tired volunteers who had spent countless hours working the polls. The first arrivals were the student volunteers who had held up signs on every roadside. They were in good spirits.

Bobby and Karl kept a running total on a big blackboard. I was nervous. I did not want to let anyone down, most of all my family—including Boys Ranch.

The absentee ballot total, which represented only about 3 percent of the votes, finally came in. I had won a few more votes than McCathern.

As the evening wore on, about two hundred more supporters showed up to watch the returns. Everyone wished me luck.

The phones began to ring, with the results reported for the smallest counties in the district. Bobby and Karl grew more excited as they tabulated those results on the chalkboard. At that point, I was leading in every county. Amarillo comprised two counties, Potter and Randall. If I had a good showing in those two counties and added to my lead in the smaller precincts, I might win.

When the results were in, I had carried all twenty-seven counties. I had won! I think Donna and I were both in surprised. She was at my side while everyone celebrated. I could not have done this without her. We walked through the room and thanked everyone for their support.

As I stood in front of a TV camera talking to a reporter, I noticed David watching me, taking it all in. He was all dressed up in his suit, a tie, and cowboy boots. I motioned for him to come to me. I picked him up and hugged him so hard.

A reporter asked how I thought I would do against Bob Price, a giant and a legend in the Panhandle. I felt a knot in my stomach thinking about what I was up against—all his power and money. I responded to the reporter, "I am the underdog in this race, and I know he will outspend me, but he won't outwork me."

CHAPTER 15

The General Election

T he day after the election, I returned to my job. Wesley said he was proud of me and was happy that his sales had increased during my Senate primary. He continued his support and encouraged me.

I called everyone who had helped in the primary. They were all eager to help defeat Bob Price in November. With the primary over, the Democratic county chairmen could help. When I had visited the Democratic county chairs before, they had all promised their help if I won the primary. Now it was over.

Speaker Clayton called to congratulate me and offered to help me raise money from groups in Austin. Lieutenant Governor Bill Hobby called with the same offer. I told them I could win if I could raise enough funds for an aggressive advertising campaign.

A few checks arrived in the mail. I decided to spend them on the bus signs. They were my best buy for building name recognition.

At a meeting with my key supporters, I got commitments for several fundraisers. I was ready to hit the road again. I had seven long months of campaigning ahead of me, and I was up against a political powerhouse.

Driving to all twenty-seven counties, I thanked all those voters who had cast their ballots for me. I stopped at each small and large business and expressed my thanks to the owners and their employees. I also visited the Democratic chairmen in each county, promising that the money I raised in each county would be spent in that county. They loved that idea. All too often, the campaign money that they had helped raise was spent on Amarillo media and not in their local counties. I said that

Amarillo would be responsible for Amarillo. Obviously, Price could and would outspend me. I had to stretch every campaign dollar.

In the Thirty-First District, about 30 percent of voters would vote a straight Democratic ticket, and about 30 percent would vote straight Republican. I had to convince the uncommitted voters to support me.

I found a small vacant storefront across the street from the Amarillo National Bank that had been empty for several months, so the rent was cheap. I got some folding tables and chairs and made a big sign to hang in the window. Now I had my own campaign headquarters, complete with a telephone. There were no computers at that time.

I had some name recognition because I had won the primary, but Bob Price was a household name. One of the best things I did to raise awareness about me and my goals was to design football schedules with my logo on the front. On the inside left of the brochure was the local town's high school football schedule, and on the right side was a picture of David, Donna, and me along with my stated campaign goals. On the back was the Dallas Cowboys' football schedule. Football in Texas is a religion, so this was a really smart move. Gathering the high school football schedules for so many towns was extremely time-consuming, but it was time well spent. During my campaign visits to each town, I put the cards next to every cash register in every store I visited. They were a wild success.

Speaker Clayton organized a fundraiser for me in Austin, which was a great opportunity for me to meet lobbyists as well as elected officials. It was very successful. Speaker Clayton gave me a wonderful introduction, and my speech went over well. Many of the attendees were previous supporters of Bob Price, and they had to be careful not to offend Price or jeopardize their relationship with the Speaker, who backed me.

Each town had a parade and celebration in the summer, and many fell on the same weekend. So I focused on the most highly populated towns and on the towns where Price had a lot of support. I had been advised not to waste my time in those towns that Price always carried, but I decided to work those even harder.

My first parade was in Turkey, Texas, on Bob Wills Day. Bob Wills, a Turkey native, was a famous country singer and the father of western swing. For the parade, I joined about ten other elected officials inside a cotton trailer pulled by a John Deere tractor. The cotton trailer was about thirty feet long and enclosed by a metal cage made of chicken wire. We proceeded down Main Street on a hot April afternoon; hundreds of people lined the street. The county judge told me to try to stay in the middle of the trailer. I didn't understand why—I wanted to wave at the crowd and be seen. Most of the crowd was drunk when the parade started, and it was only about 3:00 p.m. The crowd started throwing beer bottles at us. I was in shock that they would throw bottles at their elected officials. I moved back to the middle of the trailer and silently thanked God for the chicken wire. That was the first and last time I attended Bob Wills Day.

When Texas joined the Union, the only thing of value the state had was its land, so Texas kept the rights to it. Texas wanted the largest state capitol in the Union, so in 1879, the Texas legislature gave three million acres of land to a construction company in Chicago, Illinois, in exchange for them to build a new Texas State Capitol in Austin. This is what started the well-known phrase "Everything's bigger in Texas." And the annual XIT Rodeo and Reunion in Dalhart lived up to that phrase, and it was one of my best campaign events.

More than ten thousand people attended the three-day event commemorating the famous XIT Ranch. The Saturday of that event was one of the world's largest free barbecues. The preparations for the barbecue began late Thursday and ran all day Friday. Workers dug several pits and filled them with mesquite wood, then lit the fires. Thousands of pounds of beef were hung over the coals, the pits were then covered with sheets of tin, and finally the tin was covered with dirt. For the next twenty-four hours, that beef smoked. To this day, it is still the best barbecue I have ever eaten.

Donna, David, and I spent all day shaking hands and passing out my brochures to thousands of people in line for the free barbecue. The day was long and hot, and we were very tired, but we were looking forward to the rodeo.

When the barbecue was over, my campaign helpers and the three of us found seats in the stands for the annual rodeo just in time to see the grand entry of the riding clubs from across the state. I was so proud when the Boys Ranch Riding Club entered the arena; I almost started crying. I had competed at this same event when I was at the ranch on three different occasions. I also rode bulls at this very event twice after leaving the ranch. This was a very special event for me.

Then the announcer came on the loudspeaker and told the crowd, "We have a special guest, our own state senator, Bob Price!"

I hoped I'd also be introduced, but that didn't happen. Bob Price rode into the arena on a white horse, swept off his white hat, and waved at the crowd. Suddenly, his horse stopped abruptly, and Senator Price went sailing over the horse's head. The crowd roared with laughter. I was silently laughing with them and figured Honey was looking down laughing as well. Price stood up and struggled to get back on the horse. Throughout his political career, he had tried to create an image of a rancher, cowboy, and oilman. Maybe he was good at being an oilman, but it was clear to me that he didn't know anything about riding horses.

By the end of the day, my hand was swollen, and I could not make a fist. I had shaken several thousand hands and was tired. Times like these, I wondered if all of this was worth it.

My daily campaign schedule was grueling, but I continued to listen to my *Rocky* tape, and it kept me going. Thankfully, the local papers and radio stations strongly promoted my events. They liked my advertising plan: any money I received from contributors in that town stayed in that town. I knew that my plan would result in less radio and TV for Amarillo, so I planned to use the same TV spots I had used in the primary—I focused on managing my budget. My radio spots focused only on what I would do if elected, no mention of my opponent.

Three Democratic county chairmen phoned and told me they had raised enough money to rent a billboard until Election Day. Those three billboards were the only ones I had.

Jerry Johnson, Danny Needham, and E. T. Manning agreed to host a fundraising event for me at their law firm. My friend Jerry Hodge was also in attendance. It went very well. On a hot August day, their office was packed with attorneys and their staffs. That event raised a lot of money. Danny Needham became a close friend. We were the same age, and we had a lot in common.

"Call me any time. I will help," he offered.

I call Danny one of my pallbearing friends—one who would carry me to my grave.

KGNC radio and Channel 7 planned to broadcast a live debate during the last week of the campaign. The radio debate would be held at noon on Wednesday that week, followed by the television debate on prime time that Friday night. Together the two stations would reach most of the viewing and radio audiences in the district, so the pressure was on. I needed to nail those two debates to win this election.

Every Friday night, I continued to work the high school football games with hundreds of people in attendance. This gave me the chance to work two towns at one game. At the beginning of the game, I stood at the home field gate to greet constituents; at halftime, I stood on the other side of the stadium to shake hands.

Price flooded the Panhandle with his billboard, radio, and newspaper ads. For the entire month prior to the election, his TV spots were broadcast nightly during prime time.

I met with my primary volunteers at Amarillo College, and as it turned out, the new student body president was David Rattan, whom I had taught at Boys Ranch. I was in luck. David helped me recruit more students to wave my signs at Amarillo's main intersections on the final three weekends prior to Election Day. Also, some of the members of the local labor unions in Amarillo agreed to display my yard signs during the last two weeks of the election.

We held a large fundraising event at the Big Texan Restaurant in Amarillo and invited all my county chairmen and supporters. Lieutenant Governor Hobby and Speaker Clayton both attended. The press covered the event. About three hundred people attended, and we raised a lot of money—enough to pay for some radio and TV advertising.

As planned, the TV spot I made for the primary began to run the week before the election, so I continued to gain more name and face recognition. People began pointing at me in public. This was good—my efforts appeared to be paying off.

Finally, it was time for my debate with Senator Price on KGNC radio. I was so nervous. I listened to my *Rocky* tape just before I went inside the radio station. I prayed for strength and thanked God for bringing me to this point.

The moderator asked us questions for the first thirty minutes of the debate, and then the phone lines were opened for questions for the final thirty minutes. It was common to arrange for supporters to call in to the radio station to promote candidates. The problem was trying to get the calls through. I had some of my volunteers call Price's headquarters to tie up his phone lines while the rest of my volunteers called in questions to the radio station. During the first thirty minutes, I did well. When the phone lines opened, most of the calls were from my supporters. Price seemed confused. There were not many calls coming through from his supporters. So for me, this debate was going very well.

The local newspapers began publishing their endorsements. The first was the *Canyon News* in Randall County, which was the strongest Republican county in Texas. When President Lyndon Johnson ran for reelection, he lost Randall County by the widest margin.

The day after the election, Johnson spitefully closed the Amarillo Air Force base, the largest employer in the city. No surprise then that Potter County leaned Democratic. The Randall-Potter county line divided the city of Amarillo. The *Canyon* paper endorsed Bob Price.

The only newspaper endorsements I received were from the cities of Hereford, Wellington, Dalhart, Friona, and Clarendon. All other local newspapers in the twenty-seven counties endorsed Price. They all cited his experience as a US congressman and as a Texas state senator.

Danny Needham told me that the newspaper endorsements were not good indicators of how the people would vote and encouraged me to push forward. The TV debate was next. The TV station had been promoting it for weeks. I called my grandmother for encouragement; she was my rock.

Bob Price was a pro. He had served eight years in the US Congress and three years in the state senate, had debated many times, and was so much more experienced. I knew I could not influence anything—I had to win the debate on my own, hands down.

The debate could not have gone better. I answered each question honestly and confidently. I was pleased with my closing remarks. I felt that I had done my best and was satisfied with the entire debate. Thankfully, my experience and training at Boys Ranch and as the FFA state president had prepared me better than I thought.

Donna, David, Roy Turner, and some of my campaign workers went out to dinner to celebrate.

In the final days of the campaign, I needed to buy more advertising but was almost out of campaign funds. Speaker Clayton warned me not to go into debt.

"I've seen a lot of candidates get personal loans to buy more advertisements in the final week of a campaign," he said. "Most of them lost the election and were stuck with debt. I know you can't afford to pay off a loan." He was right, and I respected his good advice.

I bought a one-inch ad in the *Amarillo Globe-News* with my remaining campaign funds and placed some ads in various rural newspapers from funds raised in those towns. My radio ads had been running for three weeks and my TV ads for one week. But Price was outspending me five to one. His ads were all over every radio and TV station.

I could not have worked any harder. I had started this race with only twenty-five dollars. Everyone had told me that the experience would be good for me, but I was running to win, not to gain experience. My campaign team and supporters had worked tirelessly. After winning the primary, I truly believed I could win the election. Now for the first time, I wondered if I had made the right decision.

At 4:00 a.m. on Election Day, my team started posting signs at the Amarillo polling places. My college student volunteers held signs on top of the overpass on I-40, where hundreds would see them on their way to work. I went from one polling place to another, from courthouses to schools, and stood outside shaking hands and asking for votes. In the afternoon, I drove to Pampa and worked all those voting places, then I drove to Hereford, then back to Amarillo.

When the polls closed, my team gathered at a local hotel ballroom. Bobby managed the chalkboard again, keeping track of the results from every county as the results were reported. The absentee votes came in quickly. Bobby wrote them on the board. Price was ahead. Danny Needham put his hand on my shoulder and said, "It's still early."

The hotel ballroom began to fill with supporters. TV stations were setting up their cameras, and reporters had their recorders ready. My son, David, stayed right by my side.

The results from the smaller counties began to roll in. I was carrying all of them. The key counties, however, were Potter and Randall. Most of the votes in the district were in those two counties. This election was far from over. The excitement and anxiety built as we waited for the results from Potter and Randall. At 10:00 p.m., I was live on all TV stations with David at my side.

Finally, Potter County reported. I had carried it! Now it all came down to Randall County. I knew my chances of winning Randall were slim, but I didn't have to carry it to win. I just needed enough overall votes to win the election.

Doug Dodson, one of my supporters, was at the Randall County Courthouse and called to say the ballot boxes were locked up inside a room on the top floor of the courthouse. Supposedly, the punch-card machine that counted the ballots wasn't working, and the votes would have to be counted in the morning by hand or whenever the machine was fixed.

Something wasn't right. I called Sheriff Travis McPherson, a good friend in Hereford, who offered to drive over to Canyon to find out what exactly was going on.

When Sheriff Travis got there, he phoned to report that the ballot boxes were, in fact, locked in one room. If we didn't do something about it quickly, he was afraid someone would tamper with the boxes. I asked Travis to please help me and make sure that there was no tampering with the ballot boxes. A few minutes later, he called me back to say he had met with the Randall County sheriff and recommended the ballot boxes be moved to Potter County so the ballots could be counted with their machines.

"Something's not quite right about any of this," he told me. "But we're not going to let them steal this race!" He said he would personally escort those boxes to Potter County.

Two hours later, Travis phoned again. "You have enough votes to win the county. You've won the election, Bill!"

I really was in shock! While the TV reporters announced my victory, the hotel ballroom went wild. Everyone cheered and clapped, people started blowing horns, and balloons were released. I was numb. Donna and David joined me on the stage as the TV cameras rolled and I thanked everyone for their help and support. I acknowledged Donna's support, and then I picked up David and told the crowd that my win was due to my "campaign manager," my son. David had watched me and traveled with me along the campaign trail, along with Donna, to the many parades, picnics, barbecues, cook-offs, football games, and other events. Besides me, I think he was the happiest person in that room.

Bobby came to tell me that Speaker Clayton was on the phone. The first thing he said was "Congratulations, Senator." It was the first time anyone called me "Senator." A few minutes later, I got a call from Lieutenant Governor Hobby, who said the same thing.

I called Grandmother to tell her I won. She started crying. We talked about how we wished Honey and Granddad were there to celebrate my victory.

"Thank you for all your prayers," I told her. "Can you be here when I'm sworn into office?" I knew she wouldn't miss it for the world.

I went back to the ballroom to shake hands with my supporters and volunteers and to thank each one of them personally. I will never forget the grin on Danny Needham's face when he shook my hand to congratulate me. "I will always be here for you," he said, and I knew he meant it. Roy Turner had worked so hard, carefully managing my limited campaign finances. He had believed in me from day one. I could never have made it without his expertise. I gave him a big hug and thanked him for everything.

Pete Gilvin, grinning from ear to ear, shook my hand and slapped me on the back. I reminded him, "You got me started with that first fundraiser you hosted at your ranch."

The only other person happier than my son and I was Wesley Masters. He hugged me and said, "You've come a long way since you walked into my office looking for a job!" I still cannot put into words how much Wesley meant to me. He had given me the opportunity to campaign and work at the same time, and I would never forget that.

Finally, everyone left, and Donna, David, and I went to our hotel room. David wrapped his little arms around my neck and told me he was happy for me. Donna also told me she was proud of me. I was exhausted, but when my head finally hit the pillow, my mind started racing again. I had won! I was only thirty-two years old. I once again prayed to God to give me the strength and wisdom to do this job.

Years later, after I had left political office, Lieutenant Governor Hobby told me that I had done many great things during my years of service as a legislator but that the best thing I had ever done for the great state of Texas was to defeat Bob Price.

~ CHAPTER 16 ~
Am I In Over My Head?

I was at home when the phone rang. A woman introduced herself as Betty King, the secretary of the Texas Senate. She said, "I look forward to meeting you, Senator." That title still seemed so strange to me. "I'm letting you know that freshmen orientation will be the week after Thanksgiving. The session will start on January 3."

Speaker Clayton called to let me know he was coming home for the weekend and asked if I would like to fly back to Austin with him. "It'll give us a chance to talk," he said. "You'll need to start assembling a staff as soon as possible. I'll provide any support I can. I suggest you meet with Lieutenant Governor Hobby to let him know what committees you'd like to serve on. Then you'll want to make some calls to lobbyists and associations to ask for financial support. After the session starts, it will be illegal to ask for any funds."

Asking for money was a side of politics I didn't care for, but it was necessary to stay in office and get ready for the next race. The more he talked, the more I realized how much I had to learn and do in a few short weeks. He told me not to waste any time.

I met with Lieutenant Governor Bill Hobby, who presided over the Senate. He invited me into his capitol office, shook my hand, and welcomed me, calling me "Senator." I asked him to call me Bill.

"I still feel uncomfortable when everybody calls me that," I said.

"You've earned that title. Respect the position and the title that comes with it. It's a title you can use for as long as you live, the same as a person who earns a doctorate degree. Respect those many people who earned the title before you, and do everything possible to bring honor to the title."

That explanation completely changed my perspective.

We discussed committee assignments, and I told him I would like to serve on State Affairs, one of the most influential committees in the Senate. "Everyone applies to serve on State Affairs," he said, "so giving one of those seats to a freshman will be difficult."

"I just won a Republican's seat," I said, hoping that might help my case.

"I'll take your wishes into consideration," he said. The committee assignments would be announced on the first day of the session.

Hobby asked me what specific legislation I intended to focus on. I told him about my desire to establish licensed addiction rehabilitation centers and added that I wanted to work on issues related to agriculture, education, and health care. I also wanted Texas to raise the drinking age from eighteen to nineteen. Hobby was familiar with my story and background. I left his office and was hopeful that I might get the committee assignments I wanted.

That afternoon, I began interviewing people to staff my team. I had never in my life interviewed or hired people. In 1981, of the thirty-one members of the Senate, eight were freshmen. Our class members became very close. To this day, I stay in touch with several of them. All eight of us drew a number for seniority. That number determined the order in which we'd pick our offices and desks on the Senate floor.

My desk was in the second row, next to Senator Ray Farabee from Wichita Falls. Ray was a very successful attorney and one of the most respected members of the Senate. He became my mentor and a close friend. My understanding of the law and its complexities was about the same as every other nonlawyer in Texas. Ray helped me with that a lot, and I learned so much from him. I had to work harder than the lawyers to understand the law and the issues that we were trying to address and change. On the flip side, not being a lawyer allowed me to look at issues from a different perspective.

That afternoon I went to my new Senate office, closed the door, and sat in the large leather chair with the Texas seal embossed on the back. I felt inadequate and thought I was in way over my head. I was not as well educated as other members of the Senate, and I was afraid I'd make a fool of myself and embarrass my district. I prayed for strength and wisdom.

I recalled how terrified I was when I first went to Boys Ranch, uncertain what would become of my brothers and me, and I remembered my fear of failure at Clarendon College. Now sitting in my new Senate office, I had that same feeling. I wasn't even sure what legislation I should work on other than the establishment of alcohol and drug treatment centers. But I had assured my supporters that I would not be a one-issue senator.

The first member of my team that I hired was Joel Brandenberger, my press secretary, who had worked for the Amarillo newspaper. His job was to keep my constituents informed and keep me updated on various legislative issues. Joel wrote quarterly newsletters that were mailed to voters and also weekly columns for each newspaper in the Thirty-First District about the issues of local interest before the legislature.

The night before the session began, the wives of current and former members of the Senate hosted a black-tie dinner. I had never worn a tuxedo, so I rented one and bought a new pair of black cowboy boots. I thought they looked good with the tux.

During the reception before the dinner, Senator Walter Mengden, an attorney from Houston, introduced himself and asked me what legislation I was going to work on. I answered that I wanted alcohol and drug rehabilitation centers to be established across Texas. He was holding a drink.

"That will be a great issue for you to generate some press," he said, "but it'll never pass. The Texas alcohol and beer lobby is too strong."

"I'm not doing it for the publicity," I replied. "Texas ranks last in the entire nation in treatment centers, and something has to be done."

He smirked and said, "Well, we will see." And he walked off.

When it was time to sit at our table, I was honored to find my name card next to my friend, former senator Max Sherman. Max was so proud of me and was grinning from ear to ear. Max and I talked about when he had hired me to be his campaign manager during his run for the Texas Senate—and how that was my first experience in managing a campaign. Max also gave me some great advice about what to expect from my colleagues.

Each member of the freshman class and the current and former governors of Texas gave a short speech and then presented a yellow rose to their wives. I was sizing up my colleagues, and I know they were doing the same.

Sarpalius family: my family and my brothers' wives and kids. Courtesy of the Texas Senate.

The big day arrived to be sworn into office. I hosted a reception in my office for my guests and family before the ceremony in the Senate chamber. Both my grandmother and my aunt Kat had come to share this day with me. I wished Honey could be there. Grandmother held my hand with her small, wrinkled hand, looked at me with her sparkling blue eyes, and said, "Bill, Honey is here for you."

The Texas Constitution required the legislative session to commence at noon on the first Tuesday in January every other year. At 11:30 a.m., we entered the Senate chamber and went to our desks. Behind my Senate chair were four wooden chairs with the Texas seal embossed in gold on the back. Donna, David, Grandmother, and Aunt Kat sat in those chairs. On my desk was a large flower arrangement sent from the staff of Boys Ranch.

Lieutenant Governor Hobby entered the Senate chamber and approached his desk, which was on a large, raised platform. A painting of Stephen F. Austin, the father of Texas, hung on the wall directly

Roy Turner, former Boys Rancher and my campaign treasurer. Courtesy of the Texas Senate.

behind him. The chamber was large, with several hundred chairs in the gallery. Beautiful chandeliers hung from the ceilings, and each chandelier had a star in the center with a letter on each point of the star that spelled *Texas*.

I looked to the gallery for my other guests, which included Wesley Masters, Danny Needham, Roy Turner, Sherm and Genie Harriman, and most importantly, my brothers, Bobby and Karl.

Lieutenant Governor Hobby kept an eye on the old clock just above the door as it ticked closer to noon. There were two paintings on either side of the back door; one detailed the battle of the Alamo and the other the battle of San Jacinto. I still love those paintings.

Television cameras circled the chamber just outside the brass rail. Only members of the Senate were permitted inside the rail, except during the swearing-in ceremony, when family members could join for the opening session.

Genie and Sherm Harriman—Cal Farley's only daughter and son-in-law. Courtesy of the Texas Senate.

Lieutenant Governor Hobby rapped his gavel three times. "The sixty-eighth Texas legislature will come to order." He made brief welcoming remarks and then asked the new members to approach the front of the chamber to be sworn into office. I stood with the other members, raised my right hand, and took the oath of office.

Lieutenant Governor Hobby congratulated the new members and then handed Secretary Betty King a piece of paper that contained the committee assignments. She then read the names of the members appointed to each committee. My appointments were to the Economic Development, Human Resources, and Natural Resources Committees, as well as several subcommittees within those three main committees.

I was surprised to hear that I had been appointed to chair the Agriculture Subcommittee. I was the only freshman member who had been appointed chairman of a subcommittee. Our committee would hear

Lieutenant Governor Hobby presenting me my gavel as chairman of the Agriculture Subcommittee. Courtesy of the Texas Senate.

every bill related to agriculture in the state of Texas. As chair, I would have to hire three additional staff to assist the committee and the committee hearings.

Dr. Norman E. Wright from Amarillo also attended my swearing-in ceremony. During my campaign, Dr. Wright helped raise funds for me from the medical community and the Texas Medical Association.

He pulled me to the side and said, "I'm very glad you've been appointed to the Subcommittee on Public Health." He was very serious. "The next time you're in Amarillo, I'd like you to call me. I have something to show you."

"I know little to nothing about health care," I told him. "I'll need your expertise and advice."

"Consider it done," he said, and then he smiled.

Carl King, with the Texas Corn Growers Association, had driven down from Dimmit. He was a steadfast Democrat. After the primary, he influenced the state's corn producers to support me. Carl was also an early promoter of ethanol fuel production.

"I couldn't be more pleased that you're the subcommittee chairman of agriculture," he said, grasping my hand. "I have a bill I'd like you to carry for the corn producers."

"Let's discuss it as soon as you have it ready," I replied.

And, of course, Guy and Geneva Finstad were there for my big day. They had been there for me through so much. I was already thinking about who I could hire to help me on the Agriculture Committee. Guy was an expert in every aspect of agriculture. He didn't know much about the legislative process, but neither did I! And Geneva would make a perfect secretary. I trusted them both implicitly.

My mind was racing—how could I possibly ask Guy if he wanted a job working for me? He was my teacher when I was a student, and then he had been my boss when I was a teacher. This might be really awkward.

I asked Guy if we could talk over the weekend back in Amarillo. He invited Donna, David, and me to dinner with his family. We all gathered in the kitchen before dinner. I asked Guy if I could talk with him privately, so we moved to the living room.

"What's on your mind, Bill?"

I sat on the edge of the couch and thought it would be best to just get to the point: "Would you be interested in helping me run the state's Agriculture Committee?" Guy sat back in his chair.

I told him about the opportunities to improve agriculture in Texas and added, "I think I can pay you a decent salary. I also want to hire Geneva as secretary and bookkeeper." Then I waited.

Guy finally responded, "When Bob Wilson retired, I applied for his job as superintendent of Boys Ranch. The board gave the job to Lamont Waldrip." I never knew about this, and I was in shock and disappointed in Boys Ranch.

Guy had almost single-handedly built the agriculture program at Boys Ranch's from nothing into a major farm, producing almost 80 percent of the meat, vegetables, and milk for five hundred boys and staffers. Guy had also expanded the FFA program at Boys Ranch from a one-teacher department to a four-teacher department.

I could sense his disappointment that he had been passed over. He asked me a lot of questions about my offer, but I didn't have any answers.

"This is all new to me too," I said. "The only thing I know for sure is that you'll have the job for the next two years."

"Dinner's ready," Geneva called. The discussion ended for the time being.

The Finstads' three sons—Barry, Terry, and Gary—joined us for dinner. Their daughter, Sherry, was away at college.

We said grace and started dinner. About halfway through, Guy told Geneva about my offer. Then he asked her, "What would you think about moving to Austin?"

Geneva was surprised, and I suggested that they look around Austin before making a decision. I told Geneva I could use her help running the office as my administrative assistant and asked if she would be interested.

Donna, David, and I spent that night with the Finstads. I tossed and turned all night thinking that Guy was going to turn down my offer—and that leaving Boys Ranch would be very difficult for him and Geneva. He had promised to let me know something soon.

Guy called a few days later to tell me that he and Geneva were excited about making a change and that they would be honored to work for me. I was so excited. I needed Guy's expertise.

I also hired Rick Smith as a legislative assistant. Rick was one of my best friends growing up at Boys Ranch. Rick was a Vietnam veteran, and his primary focus was to assist with veterans' issues. He was so good at his job—very compassionate and caring. Rick is a dear friend of mine to this day.

~

Meanwhile, I scheduled an appointment with Dr. Wright in his Amarillo office. I was curious to learn about what he had to show me.

"I'm working on a difficult situation you may be able to help us with," he said. "Texas has a terrible ambulance problem. Currently, anyone can legally run an ambulance company out of the back of a pickup truck. There are absolutely no standards or licensing requirements. The only qualification is a Red Cross certification." Dr. Wright stood from behind his desk. "Come on. I want to show you something."

Guy and Geneva Finstad. Guy has been my teacher, my boss, my employee, and my friend. Courtesy of the Sarpalius family.

We walked outside and climbed into his Jeep Wrangler. He drove to a small brick building a few blocks away. A sign on the building read, "Amarillo Rehabilitation Center." It was not far from the Amarillo hospital. Dr. Wright showed me a room with about thirty hospital beds. Every single patient in that room was paralyzed from the neck down.

"Eighty percent of these patients were pulled from car wrecks by ambulance attendants who lacked proper training," Dr. Wright explained. Those patients made me heartsick.

"Besides these folks here, there are many other paraplegics who live at home," he continued. "Unfortunately, this is a major problem in Texas; thousands of people have been paralyzed because we have failed to enact the appropriate regulations for ambulance equipment and personnel."

"Since I know absolutely nothing about the standards needed for ambulance services," I said, "I'll need your expertise helping me find solutions for this problem."

When I returned to Austin, I called my small staff together. "We have a major problem that offers us a unique chance to help a lot of people. Find out everything you can about the existing ambulance services in Texas."

My team was beginning to take shape. We all had one thing in common: none of us had ever worked for the Texas Senate—or for any legislature, for that matter. The session began each morning when Lieutenant Governor Hobby rapped his gavel on a block of wood made by prisoners in Huntsville, Texas. Betty King called the roll in alphabetical order, then a guest chaplain offered a prayer. Lieutenant Governor Hobby then gave Secretary King a list of all bills that had been filed and named the committee to which the bill had been referred. After the list had been read, special guests were introduced. Then members could make their remarks on any subject.

The next item of business was the intent calendar. After a bill was referred to a committee and public hearings had been held, committee members voted on the bill. If the bill passed, it was eligible for the intent calendar. Every morning each member received a list of all the bills eligible for debate and a vote on that day. No member was allowed more than five bills on the intent calendar at one time.

If a member thought he had the votes to carry a bill, then he would call it for debate and a vote. Senate rules required a two-thirds majority for debate and a vote; eleven members could kill a bill. But we all needed each other, so even if a member did not support a bill, he typically would not vote to kill it, but would allow the debate to proceed.

I worked hard to understand and learn the procedures. Senator Farabee was so patient and spent a lot of time coaching me.

I was also surrounded by many veteran senators, all experts on the subjects and issues related to their professions. They were trial lawyers, defense attorneys, prosecutors, insurance salesmen, ranchers, oil and gas producers, and owners of large business enterprises. Seated to my left on the floor was Senator Bill Meier, a Republican lawyer from Euless. Bill held the record for the longest filibuster: forty-three hours to kill a bill. Under Senate rules, if a member stood to filibuster, he could not sit or leave his desk, and he could speak only about the bill under discussion.

Learning the Texas Senate. Courtesy of the Texas Senate.

At the end of my first week in office, I filed my first bill, Senate Bill 306, to raise the drinking age in Texas from eighteen to nineteen. Alcohol-related incidents, primarily involving drunk driving, were at the top of the list as causes of death for teenagers.

The alcohol and beer distributors in Texas were very powerful and spent millions of dollars each year lobbying the legislature in an effort to protect their business interests. Additionally, as I had already experienced, there were no alcohol and drug rehabilitation services for people with no money. My long-term goal was to make this a big enough issue to convince the legislature to spend the money to build those rehabilitation centers. In order to do that, I had to build public awareness so that the voters would support the issue. I knew what I needed to do, but I was still learning the ropes.

Shortly thereafter, I also filed Senate Bill 874 to set up stringent licensing standards for ambulance services, thanks to Dr. Wright. My proposed SB 874 would require licensed paramedics and trained emergency medical technicians on every ambulance in the state of Texas.

Immediate opposition came from funeral homes and many cities and counties that were running their own ambulance services. They said it would cost too much money to operationalize. With the help of Senator Farabee and other members, SB 874 eventually became law.

Donna and David had moved with me to Austin and into our small apartment for that first five-month session. David was seven years old and in the second grade, and we enrolled him in school. This was our first experience with traveling between Austin and my home district, Amarillo. Donna did not work during that initial session, but I was fortunate to still be receiving a salary from Center Plains Industries thanks to Wesley Masters. My only other income was the six hundred dollars a month that I was now receiving from the Texas legislature.

CHAPTER 17

My First Session

B ack in the Thirty-First District, I had the same van overhauled that I had been driving since I was the district director for Speaker Clayton. I had the signs repainted on my mobile office and hired a driver to travel throughout my very large district. My job was to serve the people.

In Austin, I was continually amazed at the depth of the discussions and debates and the intelligence of my colleagues. Many of the issues were repeatedly debated in each session, including education, finance, parks and wildlife, highways, health care, and agriculture. I worked hard, studied, and researched so that I could appear equally versed and intelligent. For the most part, I was debating against my lawyer colleagues. My staff and I started very early each day, and they did a great job of bringing me up to speed on the issues for that day.

Senate Bill 306 was gaining momentum. The press was interested, and every story noted that Senator Mengden had previously filed the same bill. Senator Mengden's nickname was "Mad Dog." He was large, loud, and had a short fuse, especially when he was opposed. His previously filed bill and my proposed bill were identical—we both were proposing to increase the legal drinking age from eighteen to nineteen. Mengden had filed his bill the previous session but was unable to get enough votes to pass it.

Senator Mengden approached me on the Senate floor and told me I needed to drop my bill and cosponsor his. I didn't like his suggestion or his attitude, so I proposed that he drop his bill and cosponsor mine. He pointed out I was a freshman and that I didn't even know how to

A mobile office: a way to bring government to the people. Courtesy of the Sarpalius family.

present a bill. He was right. "But," I replied, "each member has to have a first time and a first bill."

On the day of the committee hearing, when the two of us were to present our bills to the Committee on State Affairs, representatives from TV stations across Texas were present.

Senator Farabee, who chaired the committee, sat at the head of the long table for committee members in the Senate chamber. Staffers flanked him on both sides. The presenting senator, introducing his bill, sat at the other end of the table. Both Senator Mengden and I were to introduce our respective bills, which were the same. Any member for or against the bill would then state support or opposition.

I was asked to present first in the allotted thirty minutes. I was as nervous as a turkey in November. SB 306 was my very first bill, and I did not want to see it canned just because I was a freshman with no experience. "Drunk driving is the number one killer of kids between eighteen and nineteen years old," I said. I had two sets of parents there to testify. Each had lost a child in a drunk-driving accident. In each case the driver was eighteen years old and drunk. Their testimony was powerful. My goal was to make this an emotional issue so the members would have difficulty voting against it. I made my closing remarks, feeling that I had accomplished that goal.

Senator Farabee then called Senator Mengden to present his bill. Mengden told the committee that he did not have to explain his bill because he had explained it before. He then said he had been working on this issue for years, and since I had refused to cosponsor his bill, he expected the committee to pass *his* bill instead of a freshman member's bill. Both of our bills were passed out of committee. Mengden was furious.

The next day, my bill and Senator Mengden's bill were both on the intent calendar. Each member could request up to five bills that a member intended to bring up for a vote to be put on the intent calendar. The issue at hand was which of us Lieutenant Governor Hobby would recognize on the floor to carry the bill. This was highly irregular. The responsibility typically fell to the committee to make these decisions. I was pretty sure I had Senator Farabee's support, since he knew how much this issue meant to me. But Mengden had been in the Senate a long time, and Farabee would not want to offend him.

At one point, "Mad Dog" Mengden was speaking to Lieutenant Governor Hobby on the governor's platform. Mengden pointed in my direction. Hobby saw me watching and motioned for me to join them. I got up from my desk and approached them. Governor Hobby asked another senator to sit in the governor's chair and preside over the Senate. Hobby began walking toward his office, located just off the Senate floor, and motioned for Mengden and me to follow. He closed the door behind him, sat behind his desk, and asked us to sit.

Senator Mengden raised his voice at the lieutenant governor and told him that he would not allow a freshman member to steal his legislation that he had been working on for several years. He went on to say that he had received a lot of press coverage from the bill and that he wanted to keep it going.

I stared at him and held the courage of my convictions. "Hundreds of kids are out there getting killed by other kids who don't know how to drink responsibly. You want to keep this bill afloat so you can get good press? You had your chance. You couldn't get it passed, so step aside and let a freshman do it for you."

He got up from his chair. I was sure he was going to punch me. The lieutenant governor stepped between us and told us that we needed to settle this like grown men. Mengden grumbled.

Governor Hobby pointed at Senator Mengden, cleared his throat, and said, "Look, this has been your issue for a long time. We all know you have worked hard on it, but at the same time"—he pointed to me— "Bill has worked hard on it too, and it means a lot to him personally. The committee left it up to me to decide." Hobby looked at both of us. "To be fair, I'm going to flip a coin. The winner is the one I'll recognize when we go back onto the Senate floor."

We stood in the middle of his large office as he reached into his pocket and pulled out a quarter. He looked at Senator Mengden. "Call it."

"Heads."

Hobby looked at both of us. "If heads, I will recognize Senator Mengden. If tails, I will recognize Senator Sarpalius."

He flipped the coin over his shoulder, and it landed in the corner of his office, behind his leather chair. Neither of us could see it. We stared at each other.

"You two stay where you are," Hobby said, and he reached around the chair and pulled out the coin. "It's tails."

Mengden and I never saw the coin.

"Flip it again," Mengden demanded. "We couldn't see the coin."

"That wouldn't be fair to Senator Sarpalius," the lieutenant governor said. "You'll just have to trust me. Now let's go back into the chamber, and I am going to recognize Bill."

Mad Dog Mengden was *mad*.

All eyes were on the three of us as we entered the Senate chamber. I went to my desk. Mengden went to his. Lieutenant Governor Hobby pounded his gavel. Silence.

Lieutenant Governor Hobby always recognized a member by the county he or she lived in. Mengden was from Harris County in Houston. I was from Deaf Smith County in Hereford. Lieutenant Governor Hobby looked around the room and said, "The senator from Deaf Smith County will be recognized."

I stood, picked up my microphone, and said, "I would like for the Senate to consider Senate Bill 306 for consideration and action."

"Is there any objection?" Hobby asked. There were usually no objections to the consideration of a bill, but Senator Mengden stood and said, "I object, because you all know this has been my issue, and Lieutenant Governor Hobby gave it to this freshman."

Hobby asked for a roll-call vote. It was thirty to one. He called on me to explain the bill.

Cameras from TV channels across Texas were rolling when I explained my bill as I had previously described it to the committee. We voted, and my first bill passed.

Senator Mengden stood and publicly chastised me. Several members advised me not to take his comments personally. I still had to pass the bill in the House, but I had a good friend on my side: the Speaker.

I developed tremendous respect for Lieutenant Governor Hobby that day and an even deeper admiration for him over the years. He was fair, soft-spoken, and extremely intelligent, and he had the political pedigree and knew politics inside and out. Both of his grandfathers were in the Texas legislature, and his father was also the lieutenant governor and governor of Texas. He always said that his political career began in his mother's womb! I think he understood my struggles in trying to learn politics and the rules of the Senate. He knew my story—when we were homeless in Houston with Honey, the only income we had came from his family's newspaper, which I delivered as a paper boy.

That night I called Grandmother to tell her I had passed my first bill. She was so proud of me. "God is using you to help people, Bill. Never forget that you are working for Him."

With Speaker Clayton's help, the bill passed the Texas House. I was thrilled to attend the ceremony in the governor's office, when he signed my first bill into law. Then he gave me the pen he used to sign the bill.

～

Senator Ike Harris of Dallas filed the "Redfish Bill." Ike, a respected and well-liked attorney from Dallas, served as the chairman of the Economic Development Committee. He was a Republican, but at that time in the Texas Senate, there was very little emphasis on partisan politics.

In all my years in politics, my time that I served in the Texas Senate was the best experience of Democrats and Republicans working together to do what was best for the people of Texas. Lieutenant Governor Hobby had appointed several Republicans to serve as chairman of committees, even though the Democrats held the majority.

The Redfish Bill was supported by the Texas Parks and Wildlife Department. They wanted to designate redfish and speckled trout as game fish and prohibit the sale of these fish by commercial fishermen for two years, at which time the ban would be revisited. Commercial fisherman had been using dragging nets for fishing and were allegedly overfishing the waters and depleting redfish and speckled trout in the Gulf. The proposed bill, however, jeopardized thousands of jobs and would create serious economic consequences for the commercial fishermen along the coast. The sports fisherman strongly supported the bill. The bill was deferred to the Natural Resources Committee, which dealt with all bills associated with hunting, fishing, oil and gas, parks, agriculture, and water. The Natural Resources Committee was chaired by Senator Tati Santiesteban.

Tati Santiesteban was one of the Senate's most colorful and well-liked members. Tati was from El Paso and had worked in strip clubs and bars as a bouncer to put himself through law school. He had built a very successful law practice in El Paso.

A group of sports fisherman from Houston founded the Gulf Coast Conservation Association (GCCA) and raised money to hire two of the best lobbyists in Texas: Dick Ingram and Jack Gullahorn.

I hadn't paid much attention to this bill. There were no commercial fishermen in my district, and very few sports fishermen made the six-hundred-mile drive to the Gulf to fish.

The Natural Resources Committee, headed by Tati, was ready to hear the bill at the long committee table in the Senate chamber. The room was packed with people and TV cameras.

Senator Carl Parker, a resident of Port Arthur on the coast, spoke against the bill. Carl represented the towns along the Gulf of Mexico from Baytown, Texas, to the Louisiana border. Carl had made a lot of money as a trial lawyer. Carl had a short temper, but he was very shrewd and prepared. Carl explained that this bill would impact the livelihood of hundreds of families who had been in the commercial fishing business for generations; this was all they knew. He presented a very compelling case.

Ike Harris then presented the opposing side of the bill, stating that based on the research of the Texas Parks and Wildlife experts, within a few years, there would be no redfish left for the sports fishermen because the waters were being overfished by the commercial fishermen.

This was a tough issue.

Testimonies from commercial fishermen were heard, where they explained that they would be out of jobs and unable to feed their families if this bill passed. Then there were experts who questioned the accuracy of the Texas Parks and Wildlife studies. Then the Texas Parks and Wildlife experts testified, defending their studies—they had been monitoring the depletion of redfish for years.

After three days of testimony, I was still struggling with this issue and how to vote. Jack Gullahorn, the lobbyist representing the GCCA, had also become a good friend, and he wanted me to support the bill.

That night the phone rang in our apartment. I answered it.

"If you vote in favor of the redfish bill," an unknown voice said, "you may never see your wife and son alive again." Then the line went dead. I started shaking as I hung up the phone. Donna knew something was wrong. I didn't think it was a good idea to tell her about the threat, so I did not say anything.

I couldn't sleep that night. I figured the best solution, in order to protect my family, was to vote against the bill.

The next day I went to the office early and called the Department of Public Safety to tell them about the phone call I had received the night before. They contacted the Texas Rangers, who assured me they would assign someone to my wife and son.

The committee was scheduled to meet that morning to hear closing remarks on the bill and then vote. I was still deliberating and torn but also scared to death. A crowd of commercial fisherman gathered outside my office and barricaded me in. I called Lieutenant Governor Hobby and told him what was going on. Officers from the Department of Public Safety armed with shotguns arrived shortly and escorted me to the Senate chamber. The crowd was shouting. I had made my decision—I would vote to support the bill.

The bill was defeated in committee by one vote.

Ike Harris thanked me for my vote. He knew this was a tough issue, and he had done his homework. He knew every senator's stance on the bill, and he was certain that if he could get the bill out of committee and onto the Senate floor for debate, it would pass. Ike's strategy was to have the bill referred to another committee. He would need a two-thirds majority of those present in the chamber in order to do this. Ike kept a running list and was always counting and recounting for his two-thirds majority presence when members left and reentered the chamber. We all knew what Ike was trying to accomplish.

Carl Parker was determined to make sure Ike wouldn't get his majority vote.

Several weeks later, during an afternoon session, Carl Parker went to the men's room. Another member saw Carl enter a bathroom stall and raced back to the Senate chamber to tell Ike that Parker was in the men's room. Ike hurriedly counted the votes of the remaining members in the chamber and made his motion. Lieutenant Governor Hobby called the roll, and the bill was referred to Ike's committee.

As Hobby announced the results, Carl stormed back into the chamber. He was furious. Hobby told him the motion had been made and that it was unfortunate that Carl and his supporters had not been in the chamber at that time. Carl screamed about fairness and insisted that loudspeakers be placed in the restrooms so that this could never happen again.

I was a member of Ike's committee, Economic Development. He held his hearing, which was very similar to the Natural Resources Committee. The bill passed out of Ike's committee and then passed out of the Senate. It later passed the House and became law.

The Redfish Bill eventually turned into the "Redfish War," which continued for years along the Gulf Coast. Ike received multiple death threats and had to hire a bodyguard. Bob Brister, a sports columnist who wrote articles on hunting and fishing and supported the Redfish Bill, awoke to a bonfire in his front yard. Another supporter had a bag of rattlesnakes thrown onto his lawn. The GCCA president, David Cummings, and his wife and family were continuously threatened. His home in Port O'Connor was vandalized, and his boats were sunk. Another GCCA volunteer had property that was burned.

Willie Nelson. Courtesy of the Sarpalius family.

GCCA later became the Coastal Conservation Association (CCA), which now has seventeen chapters throughout the nation in coastal states. Members of CCA are still very active in their advocacy efforts in support of sports fisherman.

I learned quickly that I would be involved in many debates over bills that did not directly impact my constituents, but regardless, I remained true to my heart and committed to what I thought was the right thing to do.

I filed a bill to increase the license fees to sell alcohol in Texas. The license fees had not been increased in more than fifty years. All other license fees (for driver's licenses, hunting licenses, etc.) had continually increased, so I thought this was really a nonissue. The additional revenue generated by the bill, in accordance with my plan, would be used to develop alcohol treatment centers in Texas. I thought it made perfect sense. The alcohol lobby in Texas was so powerful, I never even got a hearing on my bill. So I continued to struggle to find a way to approach this issue. I had made that promise to myself and to Honey. There had to be a solution and a way around the lobbyists.

Wesley Masters and my son. Courtesy of the Sarpalius family.

One day, during my first session in the Senate, Willie Nelson paid me a visit. Willie knew that I chaired the Agriculture Subcommittee. Willie had an idea about farms and homeless people. I listened. Willie explained that there were a lot of vacant, run-down farmhouses throughout Texas. Willie thought it would be a good idea if the legislature could get involved and move the homeless people out of the cities to these farms and supply them with a few chickens and some milk cows—everyone would be better off. I explained to Willie that the legislature would have to appropriate funds for this and it would likely cost a lot of money. I also suggested that the homeless people probably wouldn't want to move to farms out in the country. Regardless, I respected his idea and his willingness to make an effort. This was the beginning of a good friendship, and over the years, he and I worked on several projects to help people, like his initial Farm Aid concert, which raised money for farm families. Willie is a good person and has done a lot to help others.

I learned a great deal during that first session. I had developed tremendous respect for the other members and for the rules of the Texas Senate. The hours were long, the pay wasn't even worth mentioning, and it was hard on me and my family, but I was making a difference, and I really enjoyed it.

David seemed to be adjusting well; however, I knew that Donna was concerned about our finances and the fact that I was only being paid six hundred dollars a month for this job. I still had my job with Wesley, which provided additional income, but it was not much. Wesley was thrilled to have a state senator on the payroll of Center Plains—his fertilizer sales had increased significantly. Regardless, we were barely getting by. I was not even making as much money as I had been when I was teaching school, which Donna constantly reminded me about.

After the session, David, Donna, and I returned to our home in Hereford, where David was enrolled in school, and I returned to my job in Amarillo at Center Plains with Wesley—until it was time for the next session. This would be our life while I served in the Texas legislature—live in Austin while in session and then return to the Panhandle when we were not in session. Even when we were not in session, my work as a legislator never stopped.

I continued to call my grandmother every Sunday. She was in her early eighties now, but she continued to be my strength and encouragement.

⌒ CHAPTER 18 ⌒

Fighting Mad

I received a lot of press after SB 306 was passed. People from across Texas began calling my office to report their stories about loved ones who they had lost in drunk-driving accidents. Their stories were compelling. My staff and I listened.

The program *60 Minutes* aired a story about the drunk-driving problem and a new organization in California called Mothers against Drunk Driving (MADD) that was lobbying the California legislature to crack down on drunk drivers. The segment focused on people who had been repeatedly arrested for drunk driving and were released. But each time they went back to court, they were considered first-time offenders! Some of these repeat offenders had killed others while driving drunk. MADD wanted the California legislature to stop those repeat offenders.

The next day I asked my staff to call the Department of Public Safety to determine if we had the same repeat-offender problem in Texas. This information might provide the angle that I needed to get a bill passed to establish treatment centers for substance abusers.

My staff and I read every article we could find about the drunk-driving problem. I knew firsthand the pain and suffering inflicted on a family due to drinking problems and alcoholism. I was committed to becoming an expert on the drunk-driving issue. This would become the number one issue facing the Texas legislature in the next session.

MADD began gaining popularity, and chapters began to form across Texas. I spoke at many of their meetings, giving me the opportunity to learn more about the problem and hear more painful stories. One woman told me a drunk driver killed her husband and three sons.

That driver had previously been arrested twenty-three times for drunk driving. Every time he went to court, he was given deferred adjudication, his offense was cleared, and the next time he was arrested for driving drunk, he was a first-time offender. When he had finally killed four people for driving drunk, he was sentenced to six months in jail!

At that time, judges and law officers were lenient on drunk drivers. MADD began to target the courts and the judges. Members of MADD sat in courtrooms to hear drunk-driving cases and were vocal about insisting on harsh punishments. MADD also began publishing DWI conviction records in local newspapers. They were instrumental in escalating the issue.

Judges often had no choice but to release the repeat offenders because prosecutors failed to produce adequate evidence proving how much alcohol had been consumed. At that time, breathalyzers were not reliable, and the only accurate way to test the alcohol percentage level was to draw blood. Very few drunk drivers agreed to the blood test, so it was usually the officer's word against the accused.

I began outlining my plans to draft a bill and spent a lot of time consulting with Danny Needham and Corky Roberts, my two attorney friends in Amarillo, about this issue. They were very helpful in outlining the legal challenges involved in getting a bill passed on this issue. One night we met at Danny's home, and I tossed out the idea of using video cameras to gather evidence. Video cameras were pretty new at that time. I told Danny and Corky that a video of a drunk driver could provide substantial evidence in obtaining a conviction.

Danny and Corky liked the idea, but they said that defense lawyers would fight it hard, and they had one of the strongest lobby groups in Austin. I still thought that if I incorporated the use of video cameras into a bill, those lawyers would have a hard time explaining why it was not a good idea.

We also discussed imposing mandatory penalties for repeat offenders. Under the law at that time, the judge or jury determined the penalty, and they were extremely lenient. One man who had been arrested thirteen times for drunk driving finally killed a man and his wife. He served just sixty days in jail. Any time a jury heard a case, the prosecutor could not bring up previous convictions, so the juries were in the dark.

Danny and Corky also told me that the judges and attorneys would strongly oppose the concept of mandatory penalties, so I proposed a discretionary range of punishment for each offense, except for a third offense, which would bear a mandatory penalty requiring treatment at an alcohol rehab center. Since Texas had no such facilities that would force the state to spend the money to build the centers; this was my path toward what I wanted to accomplish for Honey.

MADD was my biggest supporter in drafting the legislation. I encouraged them to publicly promote my bill, knowing that many watered-down versions would be filed. Once my bill, Senate Bill 1, was drafted, I began traveling the state to meet with local newspapers, the press, and anyone who would listen.

While I was speaking to a group in Dallas, a man stood and asked me if I had ever been in an accident involving a drunk driver. "Oh, yes," I said, and I told my story about the time my mother slammed into that tree, sending all of us to the hospital. I explained that we all had been very fortunate to not sustain permanent injuries. I told that story to other groups as well, and it gave validity to my motivation in trying to get this bill passed, even though my story was not nearly as tragic as others I had heard.

~

I had already started planning my next campaign. After the federal census results were tallied, the legislature divided the total population numbers in the state by the thirty-one districts to determine the number of people that each legislator would represent. This is known as redistricting. Every member of the Senate then had to run in these new districts. The newly elected senators would draw for a two- or four-year term; half the Senate would run for reelection in two years, and the other half in four years.

I drew a two-year term but had no problem getting reelected.

I called Grandmother and told her about the election results, Senate Bill 1, and my goal to get the state to build treatment centers. We talked about how we wished there had been a center available for Honey.

Not long after I had been reelected and was back in Austin, I began to tackle other important constituent issues. One day, a man and his sister visited my office. They had both been adopted and wanted to find their biological parents and potential siblings. At that time, the law required that records remained sealed after an adoption, and only a judge could decide to unseal the records to reveal the identity of the biological parents, and only for health-related issues. My staff researched the issue and learned that there were thousands of parents and adopted kids who wanted to reunite. I filed SB 777, and Representative Stan Schlueter from Killeen filed a companion bill in the Texas House.

This bill would allow an exchange of contact information only after the parties had reached legal age and if all parties agreed. The bill became law, and thousands of biological parents and adults who had once been adopted were reunited.

Another issue that I championed was to end dogfighting. Dogfighting was rampant across Texas, and it was horrible. The more I learned about the issue, the more disgusted I became. I was a dog lover; it made me sick to my stomach.

I filed Senate Bill 557 to make dogfighting a felony in Texas. Any person who participated in a dogfight would have his or her dogs confiscated in addition to any possessions used to promote or participate in the dogfight, including any vehicles used to transport the dogs. Tough penalties needed to be enforced to stop this awful practice. The dogfights primarily involve pit bulls, so many people who owned and loved pit bulls strongly supported the bill.

The dogfighting bill was getting as much if not more publicity than the DWI bill. Public hearings were held in the Senate chamber, and the gallery was packed with some pretty rough-looking folks. The people who provided testimony in opposition to the bill refused to admit that they had attended dogfights.

After three days of testimony, closing remarks began. The final testimony in opposition to the bill was from a woman who bred pit bulls. She spoke for a very long time about how wonderful pit bulls are and that there was no need for such severe penalties for those who chose to fight their dogs.

I had learned to smoke cigars by then, and at that time, members could smoke while in session in the Senate chamber. I straightened out a paper clip and stuck it down the middle of my cigar, which prevented the ashes of the cigar from falling. I lit the cigar and smoked it while the woman railed against my bill. Eventually, I had smoked two-thirds of my cigar, and the ashes remained intact, which began to attract attention. Everyone was watching my cigar, and nobody was paying attention to the woman testifying.

When she finally finished, I put my cigar down and asked her if she had ever been to a dogfight. She said no, that she bred pit bills because they were a superior breed. I asked her if she knew anyone who had attended a dogfight. She denied any knowledge of dogfights.

When it was time for my closing remarks, I told the group that before the vote was called, I wanted them to see a dogfight. I had a TV connected to a VCR player at the end of the long table. The chamber was packed. People sat in the gallery and stood on the Senate floor. Everyone was focused on the TV.

"The video you are about to see is a dogfight that was filmed by an undercover agent with the Department of Public Safety," I said. "This dogfight was held on the second floor of the Shamrock Hilton in Houston in their largest ballroom." The Shamrock Hotel was one of the oldest and most prestigious hotels in Houston at that time.

I pushed the play button. The woman who had just testified was the first face we saw on the screen. She stood in the middle of the ring and held a pit bull between her legs while the crowd yelled. She released her dog, and it charged after another dog. The dogfight was brutal, and the video was graphic. I pushed the stop button. The chamber went silent.

I broke the silence and spoke to the chamber: "If you vote for this bill, this outrageous cruelty will finally stop, and Texas will have the toughest dogfighting law in the United States."

Every member voted for the bill, and the committee adjourned.

The woman who had testified, the star of the video, began screaming and cursing at me. The crowd of dogfighters also began yelling at me. The police began to clear the room as quickly as possible. I was advised to return to my office immediately.

The next day, when I entered the Senate chamber, Betty King, the secretary of the Senate, told me that Lieutenant Governor Hobby wanted to speak to me. I found Hobby, and he asked me if I knew what was going on. I told him no. "Someone called a popular radio station," he began, "and threatened on the air to shoot you from the gallery at this morning's session. I'm not going to allow the public into the chamber today."

That day I received threating phone calls at my office and at home. A police officer was assigned to watch my family. For the next several weeks, undercover agents sat in the gallery of the Senate chamber.

The dogfighting madness finally settled down, and I continued my fight for my DWI bill. As expected, several drunk-driving bills had been filed. My bill, Senate Bill 1, which had been endorsed by MADD, had captured the media's interest. The biggest challenge would be to keep the language in the bill permitting the use of video cameras and imposing mandatory penalties for third offenses. Cameras could certainly help in providing evidence of the degree of drunkenness. No judge wanted to be told what sentence he or she was to impose. This was pretty radical legislation at that time.

Senate Bill 1 and all other similar bills on this issue were to be heard before the State Affairs Committee. The public was then invited to testify. Most of the testimony supported Senate Bill 1. Not surprisingly, most legal associations testified in opposition to the use of video cameras, and the judges opposed any mandatory penalties.

The testimonies continued for three days, and most of it was very emotional. A man from Houston testified that his parents, wife, and two young children had driven to a grocery store only a few blocks from home while he stayed behind to watch a football game. Not long after they had left home, he heard sirens. When they had not returned after a while, he began to worry, jumped in his car, and drove to the grocery store. Only four blocks from his home, he arrived at the scene of the accident. He cried as he described holding his dead son in his arms. Everyone in the chamber cried with him. The drunk driver, who had killed every member of this man's family, spent six months in jail.

I found it interesting that nobody attempted to amend my bill. It passed out of committee; every member had voted for it.

Senate Bill 1 generated a huge amount of press across the state—and that press, along with the help of MADD, made this the only issue of that session. I began polling the members of the Senate to understand how they would vote if I brought the bill to the floor. I knew I would not get most of the trial lawyers' support unless I was willing to amend my bill to eliminate the use of video cameras and the mandatory penalties. But I was determined.

I invited the members of MADD and told them that other senators were trying to weaken the bill. I asked the MADD members to meet with each member of the Senate to urge them to vote for Senate Bill 1 in its current form and to vote against any proposed amendments. I asked

Senate Bill 1, the DWI bill. Courtesy of the Texas Senate.

that they keep me informed about their meetings with other Senate members, specifically those who opposed SB 1.

A few days later, we had made great progress, and as I suspected, there were many efforts under way to weaken the bill. I asked the members of MADD to begin advocating in their districts and suggested that they set up tables in local shopping malls and urge people to sign individual postcards to be mailed to Senate offices.

The strategy worked. A few days later, thousands of postcards flooded members' offices pressuring them to vote for Senate Bill 1—with no changes.

After working on it for more than a year, I decided to bring the bill to a vote on the Senate floor. TV cameras from all over the state were there to cover the bill. The pressure was on—this would be all over the news that night.

I addressed the Senate and told them that thousands of letters had been sent by voters across Texas in support of Senate Bill 1—and specifically requesting no amendments to the proposed bill. I explained that SB 1 would create the toughest laws in the nation against drunk drivers by incorporating mandatory penalties and permitting the use of video cameras. Just these two changes would prevent thousands of drunk drivers from becoming repeat offenders. I asked the members to please remember those families who had lost wives, children, mothers, and fathers to drunk driving when they were casting their votes.

The bill passed overwhelmingly and was sent to the House of Representatives.

I finally had found an opening, through the mandatory penalty provision, to possibly create alcohol treatment and rehabilitation centers. I wasn't there yet though.

I was thrilled but thought this had been way too easy. I wondered why the Senate members who were defense lawyers had not tried to change or amend my bill. I soon discovered they had another plan.

∿

Every other Saturday, I flew back to Amarillo to spend time with Wesley. One Sunday evening, on a Southwest Airlines flight back to Austin, I sat in an aisle seat near the back of the plane. At that time, Southwest Airlines had a row of seats at the back of the plane that faced each other. A cowboy wearing a white straw hat walked down the aisle of the airplane, opened the storage bin above my seat, placed his hat inside, and sat down across from me.

He looked at me and said, "Aren't you Bill Sarpalius? I voted for you for state president of the Future Farmers of America." He explained that his band competed in the talent contest.

"What are you doing now?" I asked.

"My band's still together. We just released a song, and I think it will do well. It's called 'Amarillo by Morning.'" His name was George Strait. He would become a legend in country music.

For the entire trip, we talked about what an influence the FFA had made in our lives.

∿

After passing the Senate, Senate Bill 1 went to the chairman of the House committee that would hear the bill. He held a press conference and announced that Senate Bill 1 was very poorly drafted and that the committee would pass its own version.

I knew that my opponents' strategy was to weaken the bill that I had worked on for so long, and I knew they were trying hard to undermine all my hard work.

The House committee passed its version of a DWI bill. There were no mandatory penalties in the bill, and the use of video cameras was nowhere in the bill. I was determined not to let this happen.

Bill Clayton had retired as Speaker, and the House elected Gib Lewis from Fort Worth. Gib was handsome and engaging and a solid Democrat. He had also been very close to Speaker Clayton. He had already been very helpful to me, and I badly needed his help now. I went to his office and asked for his support in keeping Senate Bill 1 intact.

Speaker Lewis was in a bad spot. The chairman of the Committee on Criminal Jurisprudence had helped Gib with his campaign for Speaker. Gib told me it would be difficult for him to oppose the decision of the committee, but he would do what he could to help. As I was leaving his office, he told me he believed in my cause and advised me to remain strong and not give up. Speaker Lewis was a good man.

The Texas House passed the committee's version of the bill and sent it to the Senate. Lieutenant Governor Hobby asked me if I would accept the House bill. I refused.

The next step was to refer both Senate Bill 1 and the House version to a conference committee. Hobby would appoint five senators to serve on the committee, and Speaker Lewis would appoint five House members. The conference committee was tasked with working out the differences between the two bills.

Governor Hobby was kind enough to let me select the four senators who would join me on the conference committee. I met with all four of them, and they agreed to do whatever they could to help me. I asked them to stick with me and told them I was willing to play hardball. The House conferees were willing to play equally as hard.

Everyone in the legislature knew we had to pass a bill to address drunk driving. I was determined it was going to be Senate Bill 1. Since this bill originated in the Senate, the chairman would come from the Senate side of the conference committee, and as the bill's chief sponsor, I was chairman of the conference committee. I scheduled a meeting. The room was packed again with journalists and TV cameras from all over the state. The five House members sat on one side of the table, and the members of the Senate on the other side.

I was nervous. I had never chaired a conference committee. I began the meeting by asking every member to express his issues over the differences in the two bills. Much concern was voiced about the proposed use of video cameras. I also knew many on the committee were concerned about the mandatory penalties. And my proposed penalty for the third offense required mandatory treatment in rehab facilities that didn't yet exist. I knew this would force the state to establish treatment and rehab centers across Texas. I told the conference committee that if the state of Texas was truly serious about solving the drunk-driving problem in Texas, then Senate Bill 1 needed to remain intact. I moved that the conference committee approve the Senate version with no changes. The vote was called. It was tied, with the senators supporting me.

"I call this meeting adjourned," I said to everyone's surprise. "We will reconvene when the House has accepted the wisdom of the Senate."

As I stood, reporters approached me and asked what I was going to do. "I'm going to stand firm," I replied. "The people of Texas want to get repeat offenders off our highways. They don't want a watered-down version."

For the next several days, I was criticized in the press by the five House members on the committee. I fought back. I met with the members of MADD and the director of the Department of Public Safety and asked them to furnish daily reports of accidents caused by drunk drivers.

At the beginning of the session every day, I provided a report on the deaths or injuries resulting from drunk driving within the previous twenty-four hours. I read the victims' names, and I reiterated that we needed to pass Senate Bill 1. I focused on the deaths that occurred in the districts of the five House members on the conference committee. I used the TV cameras to my advantage every chance I got, saying, "If the people of Texas want Senate Bill 1 to pass, then phone these five opposing House members on the conference committee. I will provide their names." Several Senate members asked me to back off and to not provide the names of House members. I told them that I would continue to apply pressure and that I had no intention of backing off. This was too important.

In the last week of the session, the members of the Senate asked me to compromise on the DWI bill. Countless letters and phone calls from constituents had been sent to members of the legislature demanding action on the drunk-driving issue.

Every day, I continued to read the names of people who had been injured or killed by drunk drivers. It was a gamble, and I knew it. If we did not pass a bill, I would be blamed. If I gave in, I would lose everything I had worked for and believed in. Reporters contacted me constantly to ask when the conference committee would meet. My response was consistent: "Call the five House members, and ask them if they are ready to vote for the Senate bill." Then I gave their names and contact information to the journalists.

On the last day of the session, I was certain that I had lost on the issue. The pressure from the other senators was unbelievable. Governor White, Lieutenant Governor Hobby, and Speaker Lewis approached me on the Senate floor and requested that I meet with the House members on the committee and pass a bill. They told me that even if we passed a bill that was not as strong as I would like, we could work on improving it in the next session.

"This is the number one issue in Texas," I answered. "It has gathered tremendous momentum. How would you explain to the voters why we decided to pass a weaker version of the law? I am not the problem. Speak to those five House members causing the roadblock. Talk to them."

They respected my perspective, but I knew they thought I was not playing for the team.

Time was running out. The session would adjourn at midnight. At around 6:00 p.m. on the last day of the session, one of the House members on the conference committee asked me what I planned to do. I said I was ready to meet when the House members agreed to the Senate version of the bill.

"If we don't meet," I told him, "I believe the House members of the conference committee will be blamed, and they will have to explain to their constituents why they did not support a strong DWI bill."

"Do you have any room for compromise?" he asked.

"I cannot compromise on the lives of people affected by a drunk driver," I responded.

He exhaled slowly. "Let me talk to the other House members."

Two hours were left in the session. The five House members entered the Senate chamber, walked to my desk, and told me they were ready to meet.

"Are you willing to accept the Senate bill?" I asked. They said they would.

The conference committee met a few minutes later in a small committee room off the floor of the Senate chamber for the last time. We were surrounded by media. I called the meeting to order, and we briefly discussed the bill. Within a few minutes I called for a vote to accept the Senate bill unmodified. All members voted to pass Senate Bill 1 and send it to the Senate and House for final approval. I had to stay calm, but I could not believe what I had accomplished.

When the bill passed out of the conference committee, I had less than two hours to pass the conference committee report through both the House and the Senate and send the bill to the governor signature. Many bills passed the legislature during the final few hours of a session. Senate Bill 1 passed both houses and went to the governor for his approval with fifteen minutes to spare.

The session adjourned. This was a very stressful time for me, but it was also one of the most rewarding. It was also one of my most successful accomplishments as a state senator. Senate Bill 1 became a model that many other states across the nation similarly adopted and over years has been credited with saving thousands of lives.

A few days later, Governor Mark White had a signing ceremony in the governor's office. The room was packed, and many people who had worked to make this a reality were present. I was so proud of the members of MADD. Without their help, I don't think we would have accomplished what we did. After the governor signed the bill, he stood and gave me the pen, and everyone applauded. I was so thankful, but all I could think about was the next step—to get those alcohol and treatment centers established.

I phoned Grandmother and told her my good news. I explained that in the next session, I had a good chance of passing a bill to allocate funds for treatment and rehabilitation centers across Texas. The mandatory penalty for a third offense had provided that opportunity for me. My plan was working.

PART IV
The Painful Road
to National Politics

CHAPTER 19

Finding My Father and Saving the FFA

Rusty Kelly and I had dinner one night at a popular restaurant in Houston. Rusty and I had become close friends when he worked for Speaker Clayton, and he had been incredibly helpful during my election campaign for the Senate. Rusty was a very well-respected, self-employed lobbyist in Austin. He was a straight shooter and very candid about how I might be impacted politically by the issues he was lobbying. I appreciated him very much.

At that dinner, I thought a gentleman seated at another table looked very familiar, but I could not place him immediately. Finally, I recognized him as Mr. Crochet, a former neighbor in Houston, before my father had abandoned us. I approached his table to introduce myself and say hello.

Mr. Crochet stood as I neared his table. He greeted me and excused himself from the table, and we walked to the front of the restaurant together. We made small talk, but I really had only one question for Mr. Crochet: "Do you know if my father is still alive?" I explained that my brothers and I had not heard from our father for twenty-five years.

"The last time I heard from your father was several years ago," he said. "At that time, he was living in San Francisco, California."

I was stunned. The thought had not really crossed my mind that my father might actually still be alive. Mr. Crochet and I returned to our tables, and all I could think about was my father and what a son of a bitch he was.

The National Democratic Convention that year was in San Francisco. I was elected by my party to be a convention delegate. I wanted to attend for two reasons: I wanted to broaden my base of contacts in case I decided to run for Congress one day, and more important, I wanted to find my father. Donna went with me. When we checked into the hotel room, I grabbed the telephone book and searched for my father's name, Bob Sarpalius. There were no names with that spelling, but I did notice a different name, Bob Sarpolis. I dialed the number and then hung up. I didn't know what I would possibly say to him after all these years.

The convention was exciting, but I was totally consumed with Bob Sarpolis. Several days later, I sat on the edge of the bed in my hotel room, took a deep breath, and called the same number again, but this time I did not hang up.

A man answered.

"Is this Bob Sarpalius?" I asked.

After a long pause, he responded, "Yes."

I asked him, "Did you have three sons named Bill, Bobby, and Karl?"

After another long pause, he replied, "Yes."

I said, "Well, this is Bill."

It had been more than twenty-five years since I had heard my father's voice. I didn't know if I should feel disgusted or excited. We talked for a few moments and then agreed to meet for dinner that night.

Donna and I took a taxi to a local Italian restaurant. We got there early. I wanted to see my father walk through the door. I wanted to hug him, but I also wanted to hit him—and hard. I didn't even know what I should call him, except a "bastard" and a lot of other really bad names. I wanted to know as much as possible about him and where he had been for the last twenty-five years. I wanted him to apologize for abandoning us. I didn't even know if I wanted to be there. I was so conflicted.

He was late, and I figured he probably would not even show up. Finally, a tall, thin man with gray hair and piercing blue eyes walked through the door. There was no question it was my father. For a moment, I could not breathe.

A short, platinum-blonde woman followed him. She had on a very low-cut, white dress. A Hispanic boy who looked to be about thirteen was also with them. They looked around the restaurant. I stood slowly, and they spotted me. As they approached our table, Donna and I stood to greet them. I shook his hand.

"This is my wife, Lolita," he said, "and our son, Jonathan."

Lolita was my age, and she was a stripper in a local nightclub. Jonathan was very quiet. The conversation between my father and I was very strained. The only question in my head that I wanted to ask was why he had abandoned his family. But the only thing he talked about was himself.

He said he married another woman after he left us. All I could think about was that he had yet to apologize and how he had been so cruel to leave Honey with three little kids and no support. He then said he was proud of me, and I was taken aback. I certainly had never had any help, encouragement, or support from him.

Dinner was finally over, and I was nauseated. The waiter brought the check to the table, and I waited for him to reach for it. He made no effort and kept talking about himself. I paid the check, and we went outside to catch a cab back to the hotel. I shook his hand again. He had never mentioned one word about abandoning us. I watched as my father and his third family climbed into a bright-pink minivan and drove off.

We saw each other only a few times after that. Once, my father and his family showed up unexpectedly at our house when Lolita was touring strip joints across Texas. When they got ready to leave, my father handed me a fistful of one-dollar bills that customers had given to Lolita when she danced on the stage. Another time, his family showed up in the pink minivan unannounced at the Texas State Capitol and asked for a tour.

The last time I saw him, I asked him how he felt about abandoning his family.

"I never abandoned you," he said. "I'm the one who got you and your brothers into Boys Ranch. I sent money to the ranch and wrote you many letters. Didn't you get them?"

Not long after that when I was in Amarillo, I stopped by the Boys Ranch town office and told Sherm Harriman about what my father had said about the letters and the money. He left his office for a moment and returned with my file. "Here's your file," he said. "Go ahead and read it. That's everything the ranch has about you."

I had never seen my file before. It was about five inches thick. I took it into an empty office and read everything in it. There were many letters from Honey and my grandparents, addressed to Cal Farley, inquiring about my progress. There were copies of letters that Cal Farley had written to Honey and my grandparents about Bobby, Karl, and me. There were detailed statements of the contributions that my grandparents had made to Boys Ranch over the years. Each donation was for twenty-five dollars; that was a lot of money for them. I almost cried when I read my monthly progress reports that had been written by Mr. Peggram. I realized then how deeply he had cared and how badly he wanted me to succeed. There was not one piece of correspondence in my file from my father.

I knew he had lied to me. He left us and never looked back. I always felt like I had been cheated. I never had a father to watch me play sports, ask me about what I wanted to be when I grew up, help me with my homework, or give me a hug. My father never sent cards or letters or placed a phone call. The men at Boys Ranch were like fathers to me—Cal Farley, Mr. Peggram, Guy Finstad, and others. I was disgusted with my father.

About five years after I found my father, he died of a heart attack. He was still living in California. He had donated his body to science. I didn't care that I was not able to take one last look at him—dead or alive.

My half brother, Jonathan, later got into trouble with the law and committed suicide before he was thirty years old.

～

In January, I filed for reelection and had no opposition in the primary. I ran the same campaign that had worked for me previously.

Meanwhile, back in Austin, Governor Mark White appointed a commission to study the Texas public education system and make recommendations to him and the legislature for reform. He named Ross Perot to serve as chairman of the committee. Perot, one of the richest men in the state, had formed Electronic Data Systems (EDS), which sold data processing services to other companies. He eventually took EDS public and became a billionaire. In 1992, he also threw his hat in the ring as a candidate for president of the United States.

I was the only Senate member who had taught in a public-school classroom. I felt that I was a voice for the teachers of Texas and that they would be counting on me to represent them on the Education Committee.

During the summer, the committee announced its recommendations for consideration in the upcoming session. When I first read the recommendations, I thought none of the recommendations would ever make it through the legislature. The first recommendation was that every teacher in the state would be required to take a competency test. Teachers in Texas were already required to be certified and licensed by the Texas Education Agency and to have graduated with a college degree.

The next recommendation was called "No Pass No Play." This would require students to pass all their academic classes before they could participate in any competitive sports. High school football is a way of life in Texas. Even the smallest schools without enough players to fill a roster played eight-man football. On Friday nights, most members of the community could be found at the local high school's football stadium, supporting their home teams. No Pass No Play would prevent many star athletes from playing because of mediocre grades. It might also encourage teachers to be more lenient in grading so the best athletes could participate in sports.

The third recommendation was for the members of the Texas Board of Education to be appointed by the governor instead of being elected by the people. This would eliminate the people's right to choose who should serve on the board of education. The governor might be inclined to appoint his biggest supporters to sit on the board.

The final recommendation eliminated all state vocational funding in public schools. This would eliminate programs such as the Future Farmers of America and Future Homemakers of America. Nearly every high school in Texas had these programs, and they were strongly supported by the local communities.

I was in the right place at the right time. I was a product of vocational education, a teacher of vocational agriculture, and a past state president of the FFA. I owed my success to the FFA, the Houston Livestock Show and Rodeo, and Boys Ranch, who had the strongest vocational program in the state with more than fifteen different programs. I had to save this program.

A few weeks after the recommendations were published, Perot invited me to lunch in Amarillo. I picked him up at the airport, and we went to a new hotel on the east side of town that he recommended.

As we pulled into the parking lot, he asked if some of his friends could join us for lunch, and I told him that would be fine.

We entered the lobby, and there were two men waiting for us. Perot made introductions, and we headed toward the restaurant. When we got close to the restaurant, Perot instead turned and walked into a ballroom, where approximately three hundred Amarillo businessmen and women were seated for lunch. The press was everywhere. I was floored. Many of the people in attendance were supporters of mine. I later asked a few of them why they had not told me about the luncheon, and they said they assumed that I knew about it.

Everyone stood and applauded when we entered. We shook hands and sat at the head table on the raised platform. After lunch, Perot took the podium and thanked everyone for attending his luncheon. Perot gave a moving and inspiring speech outlining each of the recommendations for changes to the Texas educational system. He told the crowd that high school graduates in Japan were better educated than our college graduates, adding that there was a teacher in Texas who could not spell the word *Texas*. He explained that was why we needed competency tests. Then he criticized vocational education programs and told a story about a boy who had missed several weeks of school because he was showing a chicken at stock shows across Texas. He went on to outline the other recommendations and closed by saying that the people in Texas should have their children educated by the very best teachers.

Everyone stood and clapped, and then Perot turned to me.

He said, "Now let's hear from your state senator about these recommendations." He reminded the crowd that I served on the Senate Education Committee.

His strategy was brilliant, and he was one of the best salesmen I had ever seen, but there was no way he was going to get me to endorse any of his recommendations in front of my constituents and supporters.

I took the podium and told the audience that Ross Perot had spent countless hours researching our state's educational system; that Texas was fortunate to have a concerned, informed leader like Perot; and that he was one of the most generous people in the state.

I explained that education reform was a top priority for the legislature and that as a former teacher, I was committed to ensuring the best possible education system for our children. I told the crowd that I had not yet received Mr. Perot's committee report and, therefore, had not had a chance to read it and certainly was not prepared to speak about any of the committee's recommendations.

When I got back to my office, I called other members of the Education Committee and asked if they had received an invitation from Perot for lunch. They all had. I told them what had happened and advised them to be prepared.

The legislature convened in a special session on June 4, and education reform was at the top of the list. Perot had gained a lot of support. I opposed every provision. I was strongly opposed to the teacher competency test. I did not think a competency test would be fair to a teacher who had been teaching history for twenty-five years but never taught algebra—he or she would be at a disadvantage unless the competency test was evenly balanced. I tried to convince members to vote down the recommendation. I lost on that issue.

But of all the recommendations, I held the strongest opposition to the elimination of funding for the vocational education programs. I represented what those programs were about. I was very vocal on the Senate floor about this and explained that some kids might never finish high school, but if we provided the opportunity and education for them to learn a skill or trade, they might still become productive citizens and find jobs.

I became the swing vote on Perot's recommendation to have an appointed state board of education in fifteen single-member districts across the state. Governor White, Lieutenant Governor Hobby, Speaker Lewis, and Ross Perot all approached on me on the Senate floor and pressured me to support this recommendation. I knew they needed my vote.

I looked at all of them and said, "Let's make a deal."

I told them I planned to filibuster the recommendation to eliminate the funding for vocational education. I would do whatever it took to kill it. They were very aware of my commitment to this issue. I said that in exchange for my vote in support of the appointment of the state board of education, they would do away with their recommendation to eliminate vocational funding.

They had no choice but to agree, so four of the five educational reforms passed.

I have no doubt that if I had not been in the Senate at that time, all vocational education and training programs would have been eliminated in Texas and the FFA programs would have had to depend on local funding to keep their programs running, if even possible.

I took the new teacher competency test myself in order to maintain my teacher certification. The only other member who took the test was Lieutenant Governor Hobby. The local TV station filmed me while I was taking the test. I couldn't help but think how embarrassing it would be if I failed! A few weeks later, I, along with many other teachers, received a letter notifying me that I had passed.

CHAPTER 20

A Walking Miracle

E ach year, the Texas legislature attends the Southern Legislative Conference, providing it the opportunity to meet members of other southern state legislatures and learn from each other as to how the states addressed important issues. I became very active in the conference, and I was elected chairman of the Southern Legislative Committee for Children, Youth, and Families. As chairman, I got to choose the location for the conference the following year. I chose San Antonio, Texas, and began working to line up good speakers for the conference.

Many states were struggling to develop strong rehabilitation programs for juvenile delinquents. Very few of these programs existed, so most of the juvenile delinquents were sent to the adult prison system, costing taxpayers millions. Research and studies found that many of these juvenile delinquents could not read. When you can't read, it is hard to find a job. And when you can't find a job, many turn to crime. This could have been me, if not for Boys Ranch.

I asked my staff to research the most successful state rehabilitation programs for juvenile delinquents. They told me it was in Arkansas.

Each inmate was assigned a teacher who would work with that inmate one-on-one. If an inmate could not read, the teacher taught him or her how to read. The teachers worked to identify the inmate's skills and develop them. It was a very costly rehabilitation program, but it was also the most effective in the nation. Bill Clinton, the governor of Arkansas, was the brains behind this program. So I invited him to the conference to be one of our keynote speakers.

Another hot issue was whether to label the packaging of music that contained adult content and/or bad language. Tipper Gore, the wife of Senator Al Gore, was the leading spokesperson on this issue. I also invited Mrs. Gore to speak at the conference. The first day of the conference, Governor Bill Clinton; his wife, Hillary; Tipper Gore; her husband; and I went to a great Mexican restaurant on the River Walk in San Antonio for dinner. I thought both Clinton and Gore were brilliant and that both would make great presidential candidates.

The rest of the story is history. Years later I attended the inauguration of President Bill Clinton and Vice President Al Gore. At another event after Clinton had been elected president, he whispered to me, "Don't tell anyone about all those margaritas we drank in San Antonio." Clinton has an amazing memory.

My next reelection campaign for the Senate was no different than the others. I traveled to all the small towns in my district at least five times, walking the streets and visiting all the small businesses, schools, coffee shops, and courthouses. I won another term in the Senate.

The Sunday after the election in 1986, I was invited to attend my first professional football game—the Dallas Cowboys versus the Seattle Seahawks. I had been invited as a guest of Tom White, the local Miller beer distributor. He was a very good friend and supporter of Chet Edwards. Chet Edwards was a senator from Waco, Texas, who came in after me. He and I had become very good friends.

Tom told me he was going to be out of town on Thanksgiving Day and that I was welcome to his luxury private suite and that I could invite friends to the game. I asked him if it would be all right if I invited some boys from Boys Ranch. Tom White loved that idea and told me he would make all the arrangements for a Thanksgiving lunch. I agreed to organize everything with Boys Ranch and told him that this would be an unforgettable experience for the boys. I agreed to stay in touch with him.

I called Lamont Waldrip, the superintendent at Boys Ranch, and told him about the game and the plans and that we could host forty boys and staff in the suite. Lamont said he had some concerns about Boys Ranch accepting this from a beer distributor. I told him the boys would love it. He told me he would think about it and call me back.

A few days later, Lamont called me and told me he didn't think it was a good idea because it would be too hard to select which boys would get to go, and he still had concerns about the association with a beer distributor. I asked him, "Why don't you just let the varsity football team go?" I assured him no press would be there. I also decided to go over Lamont's head and called some of the board members of Boys Ranch, and finally a decision was made to allow the boys to go.

I called Tom White, and together we came up with a great plan for the boys. When the Boys Ranch bus arrived at Texas Stadium, I was waiting at the gate with David. The boys and staff were escorted to the private box. We had Cowboys caps and T-shirts for each of them. Those boys were so excited, and I was so glad that I had the opportunity to do this for them.

As the game neared the end, caterers arrived with several smoked turkeys, hams, and all the trimmings for a perfect Thanksgiving dinner.

The Cowboys lost the game but the boys did not care. The highlight of the day was when the Cowboys' coach, Tom Landry, walked in, and soon after, Drew Pearson, Tony Dorsett, Randy White, Herschel Walker, Robert Newhouse, and other players joined the boys for dinner.

David was as excited as the other boys. They all got autographs from the players. It was truly an unforgettable day.

～

Unfortunately, around this time, Donna and I began having marital problems. We began to grow apart, and I was spending less time at home and more time at work. I regret that now as a father and as a husband.

Years earlier, we had purchased a house on twenty acres just south of Amarillo and closer to my office at Center Plains. When I was home, I spent as much time as I could with my son. I bought myself a four-wheeler and David a dirt bike. David loved to ride and got really good at it. We rode all over our twenty acres, and occasionally, we loaded up the four-wheeler and the bike and headed to Boys Ranch, where we rode in the old dry riverbed. David loved it. We packed sandwiches, and after riding for a few hours, we would picnic under the large cottonwood trees.

For Christmas 1986, Donna and I gave David the best helmet we could find. He could not wait to ride and try it out. The next day David begged me to take him to the riverbed near Boys Ranch. We loaded up and drove to the back side of the ranch. David was thirteen. We rode for a couple of hours, refilled our gas tanks, ate our sandwiches, and took off again.

My four-wheeler was poorly designed—the front two wheels were much smaller than the back two wheels; it was the only year that model would be sold to the public.

We rode for about an hour beside each other. Suddenly, I hit a spot of soft sand. My four-wheeler flipped end over end four times. It happened so quickly, all I remember was praying to God to help me. The four-wheeler and I finally came to a stop. I landed in sand, and the four-wheeler landed on top of me. I could not move.

David ran to me and pulled the four-wheeler off me like it was a toy. He ripped off his helmet and threw it. He yelled, "I'm so sorry! It's all my fault!" He was in shock. I think I was too.

I was not in pain, but I was sure my back was broken. I tried to turn on my right side and get up but then thought it was better if I remained still. I could move my left leg so I knew I was not paralyzed. David was still crying and screaming. I told him that I needed him to put his helmet back on and ride his bike to the pickup, then drive to Boys Ranch and get some help.

David jumped on his bike and took off toward the pickup truck. As I lay there, I had plenty of time to think about how lucky I was to be alive.

I pulled my white helmet off, and it was covered with tire tracks. That helmet saved my life. My gray goose down coat was covered with tire tracks. I still have that coat today. I prayed to God. I was afraid to even try to move. That hour that I spent lying in the sand was the longest hour of my life.

I thought about how the day after Christmas seemed to hold so many bad memories for me. My brothers and I were taken to Boys Ranch the day after Christmas. Honey had been taken to the hospital one year the day after Christmas, following a car wreck when she was drunk. And now this accident. Then I told myself to quit feeling sorry for myself and to be thankful that I was alive.

After lying in the sand for an hour, I finally saw the ambulance approaching, followed by my pickup truck. The paramedics got out of the ambulance with the wooden stretcher. They examined me, put a collar around my neck, and slowly rolled me onto the board. Pain ripped through my body. They strapped me on the board so I could not move. I could not believe the pain. The paramedics put me in the back of the ambulance but would not let David ride with me. One of the staff from Boys Ranch drove David to the hospital in my pickup.

They called Donna and told her what happened and to meet us at Northwest Texas Hospital. That two-hour ride to the hospital was the most excruciating two hours of my life. When we finally got to the hospital, Donna tried to talk to me in the emergency room, but I was in so much pain, I couldn't speak. All I cared about was that I still had feeling in my legs. They rolled me in for scans.

Two doctors in the emergency room told me my back was broken and that a vertebrae in my lower back had exploded.

"Your spinal cord is exposed," one of the doctors explained. "It's a miracle it wasn't severed. We're taking you down to surgery; we need to put steel rods in your back."

As the doctor was talking, David came into the emergency room. He was still crying and looked so pitiful. He thought this was his fault. He kept apologizing to me, and I told him not to blame himself.

"You had nothing to do with me getting hurt," I said. "I will be just fine. You were heroic getting help for me so fast."

David looked at me. "I am so sorry I asked you to take me out today." Tears streamed down his cheeks. The last thing I heard him say as they wheeled me to surgery was "I love you, Daddy." That was all I needed to hear.

I woke up with a tube stuck down my throat. I could hardly breathe, my mouth was dry, and I could not talk. I wanted to pull the tube from my throat, but my hands and body were strapped to the bed.

A nurse gave me some ice chips. I was in the intensive care unit and drifted in and out of consciousness. Every time I came to, I struggled to ask them to remove the tube.

The doctor finally came in and said they could remove the tube. "We're not out of the woods yet," he said, "but it's a miracle you're not paralyzed. You must lie flat on your back. You must not move or get out of bed."

Friends from all over Texas sent flowers. My staff visited every day. Bobby and Karl drove to Amarillo to see me. I talked to Grandmother every chance I got. Donna brought her parents, sisters, and David to see me. Staff from Boys Ranch visited me, and I was particularly glad to see Mr. and Mrs. Peggram.

I watched the opening of the Texas legislative session on TV from my bed and wished I were there. I had already filed many of my bills, and I feared that by the time I got back to Austin, it would be too late to get them passed.

Following the passage of Senate Bill 1, I had spent years developing a plan to create a new state agency called the Texas Commission on Alcohol and Drug Abuse (TCADA) to provide rehabilitation services—my dream. Since the bill had gone into effect, there were thousands who needed treatment, but Texas had no facilities.

My plan was to consolidate all money that was being appropriated to different state agencies for drug and alcohol abuse and redirect those funds to my program. The governor's office, the Department of Health and Human Services, and several other state agencies received monies to help with alcohol and drug abuse programs, but there was not a sole state agency with oversight. My proposed bill combined all state money earmarked for alcohol and drug abuse into one state agency, which would establish guidelines and licensing for treatment centers. This had been my plan since before I stepped foot in Austin. I was so close to finally passing this bill, but now I couldn't be there to push it through. Instead I was lying in a hospital bed in Amarillo, Texas, while my dream of helping thousands of people sat on the desk of the Senate clerks.

I had paid to share an apartment in Austin for the session with Senators Ted Lyon and Chet Edwards before my accident. Ted and Chet called me on the first day of the session to tell me that the Senate had passed a resolution wishing me a speedy recovery. They also told me they would help me with my legislative agenda. I was a little comforted, but I wanted to be there to advance my own legislative agenda and pass the legislation I had worked on for years. I didn't want a "pity" vote.

Chet and Ted reminded me of the bills I had passed that saved my life in my recent accident. Ted Lyon had cosponsored the bill requiring the use of helmets when riding motorcycles and trail bikes. Had it not been for my own helmet, I likely would not have survived.

I also recalled the legislation that I had passed establishing standards for ambulances based on Dr. Wright's suggestions. Without the care of those trained paramedics that day, my spinal cord may have been severed. I might have ended up permanently paralyzed in one of those rehab centers that I had visited years earlier. I had personally benefited from the legislation that I had helped pass.

Two weeks after my surgery, I was still not allowed out of bed. I was getting very frustrated and wanted to see some improvement. I had lost a lot of weight, and I was very weak. The doctors showed Donna and me the X-rays of my lower vertebrae: there were two steel rods that had been screwed into my back.

"You really have only one option," one doctor said. "Another surgical procedure. We will take your intestines out of your body during the surgery and place them on your chest. Then we'll cut the tops of both your hips and use the bone to fuse your lower back."

My mind reeled. "You're going to fuse my back?" I asked. I'd never heard of that before.

"It's a relatively new procedure," one of the doctors admitted. "We'll operate from the front and side of your body."

"It's a high-risk surgery," another doctor said. "The odds are not great, but without it, you have a greater risk of becoming paralyzed from the waist down." He paused, looked at Donna and then at me, and continued, "If that happens, you'll have to wear a diaper and be confined to a wheelchair for the rest of your life."

"If you decide not to do the surgery," the third physician said grimly, "it will only be a matter of time. Just one fall is all it would take, and you'd be paralyzed."

"You two discuss it," the first doctor said. "We'll wait in the hall for your answer."

Donna paced the room. "What are we going to do? How can we live?"

I was still working for Wesley and still getting paid a salary from the Texas legislature, but this was not at the top of mind at the moment. I was on a lot of pain medication and felt like I was in a nightmare.

The doctors came back into the room. I looked at them and said, "Let's do it."

The next morning they came to get me for surgery. The second surgery was hard on me. I had no strength. When I awoke in the intensive care unit, the doctor pulled back the blanket, touched the soles of my feet, and asked, "Can you feel this?"

I started crying when I responded, "Yes."

After almost a month, the doctors finally got me out of bed. When I sat on the edge of the bed, I became light headed and weak. My body cast stretched from my armpits to my hips, but they put me in a wheelchair, and off I went to begin my rehabilitation. I had to learn to walk again. The therapy was painful. All I could think about was returning to Austin. I still had the steel rods in my back so I could not bend, and I had no flexibility. Every step on a staircase was excruciatingly painful. The rehabilitation seemed like an eternity.

During my recovery, I developed so much respect for the physical therapists, nurses, and doctors who cared for me day in and day out. At times the pain was unbearable. I prayed to God for strength and continued to talk to my grandmother every Sunday. I focused on the physical rehab—and it became my obsession. I had to get back to Austin.

CHAPTER 21

Agony Even in Victory

It was only a matter of time before Donna and I went our separate ways. After being married for sixteen years, we finalized our divorce agreement. I gave her everything, except my son. We had joint custody of David, but he lived with me, and I accepted the responsibility to raise him. I was equally to blame for the divorce. All my efforts had been focused on my work, with little time dedicated to my family. Serving in a public office is a sacrifice and is very stressful on the family. I put my job before my family.

Donna and I just grew apart. We did remain friends. I had given Donna the house, so I had no place to live in Amarillo. Fortunately, Rick Smith agreed to share an apartment and help me with David for a while until I was in a position, both physically and financially, to care for him on my own. David knew Rick very well, as Rick had been working for me for years in the Senate. Rick was also single, and his two kids were a little younger than David at the time. David and I later moved into our own apartment.

I was still very weak and could not walk without a cane, but I was ready to return to work. On my first day in Austin, when the session started, the members rose to acknowledge me. My heart was in my throat. I leaned on my cane and stood to talk. I thanked the members for helping me and the people of the Thirty-First District of the state of Texas during my absence.

I thanked my staff, who had remained committed during that time of my absence. I could not have asked for a more loyal and dedicated group

Speaking to the Senate with a broken back. Courtesy of the Texas Senate.

of people. I also thanked Senator Ted Lyon and Senator Chet Edwards for helping me with my legislative agenda.

On March 25, the Committee on Health and Human Services met to discuss my bill to create the Texas Commission on Alcohol and Drug Abuse (TCADA). It had taken me seven years to finally get a hearing, but my strategy to mandate treatment on a third offense for drunk driving had created a demand for rehab centers in Texas.

My Senate staff: Kevin Knapp, Paul Jardem, Wil Galloway, Laurie Dickerson, Geneva Finstad, Matt Powell, Joel Brandenberger, Bethany Boyd, Jan Gipson, and Guy Finstad. Courtesy of the Texas Senate.

While recovering in the hospital, I had mentally prepared for this hearing, replaying it in my head. I would not be denied the opportunity to be heard on this issue. I wanted the people that testified to leave a lasting impression in support of this legislation. It took a lot of courage, but I contacted two state officials who I knew were alcoholics to testify in support of the bill. It took even more courage for them to testify, but they both agreed to do so. The Senate chamber was packed the day of the committee hearing. I sat at the end of the long table and set my cane on the floor. I took a deep breath and told the committee my life story, all of it. I described the struggles we encountered trying to find help for my mother.

"Maybe all of you have been blessed with solid, stable families and have not experienced the pain that alcoholism can bring to a family," I told the committee. "Alcoholism is a disease, and we need professionals to help cure that disease. This is one of the primary reasons I ran for the Texas Senate. I have been a member for seven years and have waited for the day that I would stand before this group to hear me on this issue. Texas ranks last in the nation for treatment facilities for alcohol and drug abuse. This state has avoided this enormous problem for too long."

Bob Bullock, state comptroller, testifying in support of establishing rehab centers. Courtesy of the Texas Senate.

I further explained to the committee that most people are embarrassed or ashamed of family members who struggle with alcohol or drug problems. I had been there. I kept going, explaining that the State of Texas at the time did nothing to assist with this; people with substance abuse problems often lost their jobs, families, and marriages simply because they had no place to go for help. Those with substance abuse problems often ended up homeless—just like Honey, me, and my brothers. I wrapped up my talk and told the committee members that I wanted them to hear from two state officials who had agreed to testify because they both suffered from this disease. The chamber was silent.

Then I called the Texas state comptroller, Bob Bullock, to testify. Bullock sat at the end of the committee table and told everyone that he was an alcoholic. He said that alcoholism had destroyed his marriage and made his life miserable. He called on the Texas Senate to step forward and help people who were struggling with substance abuse. Bob Bullock went on to become the lieutenant governor of Texas, and the state of Texas even named the state museum in his honor.

I then called the state treasurer, Ann Richards. She sat at the end of the table and told her story. Ann spoke openly about her struggles

Ann Richards, Texas state treasurer, testifying in support of establishing rehab centers. Courtesy of the Texas Senate.

with alcohol and stressed the need for rehabilitation centers, stating that Texas had turned its back on people with substance abuse problems. Ann explained that addicts were not weak or lazy; they simply couldn't overcome their addictions alone, and professional help was needed. This testimony was difficult for Ann—it would have been difficult for anyone. But Ann Richards was one of the wittiest and most determined people I have ever met. She later became one of the most well-respected governors in the history of Texas. I always admired the courage of those two very respected elected officials to come forward and publicly tell their stories.

The bill passed out of the committee with unanimous support. The next day, Lieutenant Governor Hobby called me to present my bill to the entire Senate. I held my cane in one hand and the microphone in the other. I told my Senate colleagues the same story that I had told the day before. Other members spoke in support of my bill, and when the vote was called, it passed unanimously. I stood and thanked the members. I was numb.

When I came to the Texas Senate seven years earlier, I couldn't even get a hearing on an issue. This legislation was the most important and meaningful thing I had ever wanted to accomplish during my time in the Texas Senate, and I had the support of every member.

I silently dedicated my victory to Honey. Then I thought about Cal Farley and the day he died, when I had prayed to God and asked him to use me in some way to help people. I was pretty sure that God had heard me.

~

After only one week back in session, I grew very weak. I thought maybe I had pushed too hard. The following weekend, all the members of the legislature boarded buses to Galveston, Texas, at the invitation of the cities of Houston and Galveston.

We arrived on Friday afternoon, and I was exhausted. I checked into my hotel room and lay down on the bed for a nap. I lost consciousness. The hotel staff found me on Sunday afternoon, after former state senator Babe Schwartz's wife, Marilyn, began asking about my whereabouts and why I had not attended any of the events. I was rushed to the hospital.

I woke up in the hospital with my arms strapped to the bed. I itched everywhere, and it was getting worse. My whole body felt like it was on fire. My skin and eyes turned yellow, and the doctors kept me heavily sedated.

The diagnosis was hepatitis C, a virus that can destroy the liver. I had received several blood transfusions during my back surgeries, and apparently one of the blood donors had been infected. The doctors kept me strapped to the bed for several days. My entire body itched beyond belief. This would haunt me for decades.

I was transported back to Austin and hospitalized for another two weeks. I lost more weight, and the cast on my upper body became too large and had to be replaced. The virus compromised my immune system, so I got sick very easily.

Although I missed most of the session, I had a very productive year in the Senate, mostly due the efforts of Senators Chet Edwards, John Montford, and Ted Lyon—most of the bills I had filed became law. Chet and Ted were so good to me. They became such close friends during this time. We lived in an apartment together, and they helped me dress each day and drove me to the capitol. I am still great friends with them today.

Senator John Montford and me. Courtesy of the Texas Senate.

Senator John Montford's district covered Lubbock, just south of mine. He was also a very successful attorney. He was always very kind to me, and we became good friends. John had broken his knee and was on crutches, so the two of us hobbled from one committee hearing to another. John became the chancellor of Texas Tech University and president of Southwestern Bell.

Chet Edwards became a very well-known and respected member of the US Congress. He represented Waco and central Texas for fourteen

Me, Chet Edwards, and Ted Lyon. Courtesy of the Texas Senate.

years. Ted Lyon, from Tyler in East Texas, became one of the most successful trial lawyers in the nation. He received a lot of media coverage, including spots on *Good Morning America*, *60 Minutes*, and *Dateline NBC*. He gained national recognition when he won a case against the Koch brothers involving a gas leak that exploded and killed a young man and lady. Ted and his wife, Donna, are still dear friends.

Senator John Sharp is another dear friend. John is very personable. He and I served together on the Sunset Commission. The Sunset Commission was established to evaluate the effectiveness of state agencies and recommend proposed changes to the legislature to make the agencies more effective. Agencies were abolished if a bill was not passed to continue support.

One of the agencies up for overview was the Railroad Commission. John became interested in the Railroad Commission and made the decision to run for one of the three statewide elected commissioner seats. This commission regulates oil and gas industry, utilities, pipelines—all big business interests in the state of Texas. John was elected, and the

John Sharp and me at a Sunset hearing. Courtesy of the Texas Senate.

people of Texas loved him. He later was elected as the state comptroller and saved the state millions. John is now the chancellor of Texas A&M.

After the session ended, I rented an apartment in Amarillo and got a loan to buy furniture and a new TV from Sears. Then my apartment flooded. Amarillo never floods, but my apartment was located next to a deep-water reservoir, and water from Interstate 40 and other highways drained into the reservoir. After a really bad rain, the reservoir overflowed—and into my apartment.

I lost everything. I had no insurance, and now I had outstanding loans for the new furniture, TV, and clothes that I had just bought. I had been at the bottom before and had learned how to claw my way out, so I rented another apartment and started over again. I was still working for Center Plains, Wesley's company, but I was pretty much broke.

I added several key people to my staff who worked for me for years. David Escamilla was a smart, young attorney who loved politics. I hired him as a staffer. Years later, he became a Travis County attorney and a leader in Austin and the state of Texas.

I hired Kevin Knapp as my district director. Kevin was very nice looking and well known in Amarillo from his recent performance in the

My son, David, in the Texas Senate close to my desk. Courtesy of the Texas Senate.

popular outdoor musical titled *Texas*. Kevin had excellent communication and people skills.

I also hired Debbie Miller as my legislative director. She and her husband had served as missionaries in the Philippines. They moved to Amarillo with their two children to work at a local church. Debbie was incredible at her job.

My office and team had earned a great reputation among the constituents. We tried to help everyone—citizens seeking government assistance, senior citizens who had lost their social security checks, or mothers who had no money to take their children to doctors. I always reminded my team that we had been elected to serve the voters.

David and I spent as much time together as possible. He hung out around the state capitol when we were in session for those five months, but after Donna and I divorced, he remained in school in the Panhandle and stayed with Rick when I was in Austin. David never complained about the adjustment and tried hard. It was tough trying to raise a child and hold public office even though I did share custody with Donna.

In 1988, Beau Boulter, a sitting member of Congress of the Thirteenth District of Texas, announced his candidacy against US senator Lloyd Bentsen for the US Senate. This opened Boulter's seat in the Thirteenth Congressional District of Texas. Many of my supporters and friends encouraged me to run, and I started to think about it. One thing was certain: it paid more money than my combined salary from Center Plains and the Texas state legislature.

I called Congressman Jim Wright, who at that time was Speaker of the House in Washington. I asked if he remembered me from years earlier, when I spoke at a Fourth of July rally in Fort Worth. He didn't skip a beat and asked me if I was ready to run for Congress. He was very encouraging and offered to call some of his supporters in the Thirteenth District on my behalf. But he said he could not endorse me until after the primary—I knew what that was all about. Ed Lehman, then a successful farmer from Vernon, and Ernie Houdashell, then a radio disc jockey from Amarillo, had already announced their intentions to run in the primary.

I talked to Wesley, and as always, he was encouraging and promised to help me in any way possible.

I announced my intention to run for the US Congress in December 1987. The primary was in early March. I began campaigning hard, traveling to every town in the Thirteenth District and attending as many political events as possible.

January 10, 1988, was my fortieth birthday, so my staff planned a birthday party. We met at my apartment for birthday cake, and then we went to the Caravan, a local country and western dance hall. I seldom went to bars, especially during a campaign, and I had never been to the Caravan. There were a lot of people at the bar, and the music was good. There was a large dance floor in the center.

The waitress took our order. I ordered water—I was campaigning, and I seldom drank alcohol anyway. The others ordered beer. I danced for a few songs and returned to the table. When I took a sip of my water, it didn't taste right. Some of my staff tasted it and agreed. Rick said it tasted like Everclear (190-proof grain alcohol). I shoved it aside.

A couple of hours later, as I was walking off the dance floor, someone hit me so hard that I fell on the ground. Then I was kicked in the jaw. I saw stars, and my head exploded in pain. My attacker ran out the side door. I never saw his face, and no one else got a look at him. I held my jaw as people helped me to my feet. My jaw felt loose, and I knew it was broken. Not one employee from the Caravan offered to help. Rick Smith drove me to the hospital. I held my jaw in my hand and could not speak.

When we got to the emergency room, I asked the doctors to test my blood alcohol content. I was sure this had been a professional hit and wanted to prove I had not been drinking. I held my jaw with the palm of my hand. My mind was spinning as I tried to figure out who was behind this. I was pretty sure that someone wanted me out of the congressional race.

I was wheeled into the operating room and put to sleep, and when I woke up, my mouth was wired shut. My jaw had been broken in two places—close to the jawline and at the center of the jaw. I had just announced my candidacy for a US congressional office and now I could not even speak.

The next morning, Kevin Knapp walked into my hospital room with the local newspaper. The front-page story was about my broken jaw and an alleged barroom brawl. There had been no fight, but this would not be good for my campaign. Kevin provided my blood test results to the press to prove I had not been drinking.

The local radio station accused my doctors of lying about the blood test results to cover for me. Kevin, Rick, and Doug Dodson, my campaign manager, strategized in my hospital room about how to save the campaign. They asked me questions, and I wrote the answers on paper since I could not talk. They all offered to substitute for me at candidate debates and other speaking engagements. They then suggested that I might want to consider dropping out of the race. In response, I wrote, "I was set up, and I'm not going to quit." The primary election was only eight weeks away. I was determined not to let this set me back. I learned at Boys Ranch to never quit.

The local TV stations filmed me as I left the hospital in a wheelchair. The story was on the news that night. Everyone was speculating whether I would drop out of the race. Reporters interviewed Kevin, and he told them, "Bill Sarpalius has never quit before, and he is certainly not going to quit now."

I was furious and focused on finding out who had done this to me and why.

Since I was an elected state official, the Texas Rangers paid me a visit and told me they were working to find my attacker. They asked if I thought one of my opponents was behind the attack.

I wrote, "I don't think so. They have been running very positive campaigns and have never said a negative thing about me."

The Rangers promised to keep me informed.

The weekend after I got out of the hospital, there was an annual pancake breakfast in Wichita Falls, one of the biggest events of the year. Hundreds of people attended the event. Kevin and Doug told me they were going to work the event to campaign on my behalf. I decided to join them and work the crowd even though I could not speak. I had to get back on the campaign trail, and I asked Kevin and Doug to stand beside me and speak for me. Wichita Falls was the second-largest city in the Thirteenth District, and it was new to us—it had not been in my previous Senate district. I needed to make a good showing.

On that cold Saturday morning, we arrived in Wichita Falls and met with Jim Maddox, a young man who was very active in the Wichita Falls Democratic Party and had volunteered to help with my campaign. I began walking the lines and shaking hands. Kevin walked on one side of me and Jim on the other. They asked the townspeople to vote for me in the March primary. I was the only candidate there.

I campaigned hard in Wichita Falls for several weeks and stayed in a hotel. I hit every business I could, shook hands, and left my brochures at the cash registers. I visited all the surrounding towns.

A few weeks later, I could speak through my teeth, so I could finally get a few words out. I had to speak very slowly. I had lost a lot of weight, since I could only drink liquids through a straw.

About two weeks after the attack at the Caravan, I got home to my apartment and found everything David and I owned piled in the middle of the living room. Our apartment had been ransacked. I called the Texas Rangers. As far as I could tell, nothing was missing. The Ranger who came to our apartment said that whoever did this was trying to scare me.

A week after that incident, I received another threatening phone call on my red "brick" cell phone while Kevin and I were on our way back from campaigning. The gruff male voice on the other end of the line told me I was lucky that only my jaw had been broken and that if I did not tell the Rangers and district attorney to drop the investigation, David would be next. Then the line went dead.

Kevin heard the call, and he turned the van around and headed back to Amarillo. "You have to inform the Texas Rangers," he told me. "You and David need protection."

Kevin and I met with a Texas Ranger in District Attorney Danny Hill's office. Danny and I had become friends when he served in the Texas House of Representatives. He had supported me in every election.

I told Danny and the Ranger about the phone call. Danny asked me if I had considered asking the Texas Rangers to drop the case. The Ranger, Kevin, and I just stared at him in disbelief. Danny then said he would do whatever he could to help.

I picked David up after school and told him about the phone call and told him that we had to be very careful. We got to the apartment and opened the door—the place had been ransacked again.

I called Kevin, who phoned the Texas Ranger. He came right away.

When he came in, he looked stunned. "This is worse than I expected," the Ranger said. "Do either of you know how to use a pistol? It would be wise for you to carry a gun."

Kevin walked in and overheard the conversation with the Ranger. Kevin knew that I had very little experience with firearms. I told Kevin I did not want to carry a gun, but if he wanted to carry one, that was fine. We agreed to keep a pistol in the glove compartment of the van.

The threatening phone calls continued, and my apartment was repeatedly ransacked. We kept all this very quiet on purpose. A Texas Ranger was in attendance with us at all the events. David was by my side at all times, whenever possible. We moved to four different apartments in three months.

The campaign was the worst ever. I could not talk. I was weak and worried about our safety. I had no idea who was behind all of this or his or her motive. The election was rapidly approaching, and it was a close race, so I had to stay focused on my campaign.

I attended as many candidate forums as possible as Election Day approached. I held the microphone close to my mouth and talked through my teeth: "I am the only candidate running for Congress who will keep his mouth shut."

The crowd roared with laughter.

The week before the primary election, two live TV debates were scheduled, one in Wichita Falls and one in Amarillo. This was very risky. Kevin, Rick, Doug, and I discussed whether I should attend the debates or have Kevin stand in for me. I wanted to do the debates to show the voters I was not a quitter.

It was embarrassing to try to debate my opponents with my mouth wired shut. The press had agreed in advance not to ask questions about how my jaw had been broken; the reporters were to focus only on the campaign issues.

On Election Day, I worked the polls from sunup until sundown. I was optimistic and thought we had run a strong campaign, despite my significant challenges.

My staff, my supporters, Bobby, David, and I gathered at a local hotel. Bobby and David tallied the votes on the chalkboard as the results were reported. Key cities were Wichita Falls and Vernon.

The final vote count was Randy Hollums, 10,906 votes; Ed Lehman, Jr., 19,629 votes; and Bill Sarpalius, 37,745 votes.

I had won the primary, but now it was time for a face-off with Republican candidate Larry Milner, the president of the Amarillo Chamber of Commerce, who had never held a public office but had strong name recognition and a lot of money.

CHAPTER 22

From Slot Machines to Congress

T he threatening phone calls continued, and I was really worried about David. We moved back to Rick Smith's apartment so he could help me take care of David while I was on the road campaigning. I was also still working for Wesley's Center Plains Industries.

District Attorney Danny Hill called and asked to see me. I thought he might have a lead in my case. When I got to his office, he closed the door and told me I needed to drop the investigation and pull the Texas Rangers off the case. I was in shock.

"Danny," I pointed out, "someone attacked me and threatened to harm my son. I want to know who did this, and more important, I want to know why."

Danny leaned over his desk. "You don't know who you're messing with," he said. "You could just as easily have been shot dead in the parking lot. You got off easy."

At that moment, I had a feeling that Danny knew who had attacked me. I walked out of his office. Suddenly the threats stopped, and I was able to refocus on my campaign.

My opponent, Larry Milner, was an aggressive campaigner and raised a lot of money. The Republican Party desperately wanted to hold on to the party seat and was pouring money into Milner's campaign.

This campaign was as hard as any I'd ever run before. I put the old *Rocky* eight-track tape in the player in my van and went to work. I needed a young, energetic person to help me with my campaign—somebody who was willing to travel and put in the long hours.

I called Aaron Alejandro, who was working for the state agriculture commissioner. Aaron had graduated from Boys Ranch and had been elected FFA state president. He had proven himself a very capable leader and an effective public speaker. I offered Aaron the job, and he accepted. Aaron was probably one of the most loyal, hardworking employees that I had ever hired. He is one of my best friends to this day.

In July 1988, Wesley Masters sold Center Plains and most of the employees were laid off, including me. I had no idea what I would do for a living. My salary as a state senator, still just six hundred dollars per month, was not enough to pay the bills and care for David.

I called everyone I knew and asked for a job, but nobody would hire me because I was in the middle of a congressional campaign. If I was elected to office, I would have to quit any job within six months and would need time off to continue campaigning. If someone hired me, then it would become a campaign issue.

I tried to get a loan to help pay the bills, but no one would lend me money because I had no job and I was in the middle of a campaign. I had no money in savings; my divorce from Donna had cost me everything. David and I ate most of our meals at campaign events. We were still sharing an apartment with Rick.

I was able to meet a lot of people while on the campaign trail, and I knew they all thought I was successful with plenty of money available to carry me through my race. I felt like such a loser. I was broke and practically homeless, again. I thought if they knew the truth, they would never vote for me. I had to find a job to take care of my son, so I was trying to figure out how to drop out of the race. I had reached a point where I just couldn't handle any more setbacks. But I had worked so hard and had never quit at anything in my life—if I quit now, it would be such an embarrassment to me, to my supporters, and to Boys Ranch.

Lobby work had always intrigued me ever since I had been elected to the state senate. Lobbyists were a great source of information. I thought that was something I would enjoy if I were no longer in public service. I even thought about which company I'd like to represent as a lobbyist.

Texas had no income tax, so every session we dealt with an increase in the sales tax for additional revenue for the state. I noticed that Walmart never testified or showed interest in the issue. Walmart, an Arkansas-based company, was just beginning to take off, and it was doing very well. There were several Walmart stores in my district, so I figured I was the perfect candidate to lobby for them. I could not believe they had no lobbyists.

David and I drove to Bentonville, Arkansas. I was going to see Sam Walton, the founder of Walmart. I walked into Walmart's corporate headquarters, expecting to find large, fancy corporate offices. Instead, the headquarters were in a plain white, old building. When I asked the receptionist to see Sam Walton, she showed me to the waiting room of the management division, which had several metal folding chairs and a few other pieces of furniture. I sat on a folding chair, and David sat next to me.

After a few minutes, a middle-aged man introduced himself as the corporate vice president. I followed him into his small office and told him why I was there—that I want to become a lobbyist for Walmart. He told me that he had encouraged Mr. Walton to develop a government-relations division, but Sam was a pretty simple guy.

He told me to sit tight, and then he left the office. He returned a few minutes later with a tall, thin, gray-haired man, who extended his hand to me, smiled, and said, "I'm Sam Walton. Welcome to Walmart."

He invited me to sit and shook David's hand and asked us both a lot of questions. Sam was down to earth and didn't waste time getting to the point. He seemed genuinely interested in my background. After a while, he asked if we had dinner plans. When I said no, he invited us to his house for dinner.

We arrived at Sam's modest house, and he introduced us to his wife, Helen, who was just as friendly. Their house was on a lake. As we drank iced tea, David looked out a large window at a ski boat that was tied to the end of a pier. Sam asked David if he had ever been on a boat ride.

"No, sir," David said, and his face lit up.

Sam asked Helen to find us some swimsuits. We put them on and walked down to the pier, and Sam helped us into his boat. David pointed at a pair of water skis and asked Mr. Walton what they were.

"Have you ever water-skied?" he asked David, who shook his head. Sam turned to me.

"Do you know how to drive a boat?" I told him I did. "Then let's teach your son how to water-ski."

We drove to the center of the lake, and Sam jumped in the water with David. After several tries, David managed to stay upright for a while. Sam Walton had taught my son how to water-ski!

We got back to his house and had a wonderful dinner. Sam told me that he was not interested in hiring a lobbyist to represent Walmart's interests. I told him that I was surprised, especially considering that the Texas legislature was considering raising the state's sales tax. "We heard every single major store chain testify against it," I said. "Except Walmart. Why?"

Sam explained, "I was a poor boy who grew up on a farm milking cows by hand. Now I'm one of the wealthiest men in the United States. This country has given me so much, so I don't mind giving some back. Paying more taxes is an investment in our country's future."

I thanked Sam and his wife for a wonderful dinner in addition to his time, but most especially for teaching my son how to water-ski. As David and I left that evening, Sam wished me luck in my election and said that if for some reason I did not win, I should come back to visit him.

I didn't want anyone on my campaign team to know I was broke. We were campaigning every day, so we at least had something to eat; I could use campaign funds to pay for our meals. But I felt like such a phony; I was the Democratic nominee for the United States Congress, and I didn't even make enough money to provide for my son and me. I prayed to God to help me find a way to survive. I needed about $4,000 to make it through the next five months. That was assuming I would win the election.

Before I was elected to the state senate, I had earned money as a public speaker and had been paid up to $5,000 for one speech. As a state senator, by law, I could not accept more than $250 per speech. I thought if I could get a few speaking engagements, then I might make enough money to get by.

I began calling every organization I could think of, asking if they needed a speaker for their conference. I got an invitation to speak at a conference in Las Vegas in August. My expenses would be paid, and I would receive a $250 honorarium. I was thrilled. I couldn't afford a ticket for David, so Rick took care of him till I got back. I flew to Las Vegas and checked into my room. I only planned to stay for one night because I had to get back to the campaign trail. I gave my speech and received my $250 honorarium. Feeling lucky, I decided to try the slot machines, so I got $50 in quarters from the cashier.

On my way to the slot machines, a tall man wearing a white straw cowboy hat, cowboy boots, and jeans approached me. "Aren't you Bill Sarpalius? I'm from Guymon, Oklahoma, and I've seen your TV spots." Guymon was within the Amarillo TV market.

He told me he was a professional gambler. He glanced down at my bucket of quarters. "Let me show you how to win on the slots," he offered. "Cash in those quarters for dollar coins."

I did, and then I followed him to a one-dollar slot machine.

"Play this machine, and after you win some money, go to that machine." He pointed at a five-dollar machine against the wall. "After you hit on that machine, move to the ten-dollar machine." He showed me which machines to play.

I had no idea what I was doing, but I followed his advice.

"Always load up the machine," he said. "That means three dollars a pull on the one-dollar slot."

I did the math. At three dollars, a pop, I would be out of money quick. I pulled the handle anyway. I was almost out of coins when it hit. I won $300.

I returned to my hotel room at 2:00 a.m. with $7,000, all of it won on that same slot machine! I threw the cash on the bed and rolled around in it. I was in disbelief and so happy! I said to myself, "I am saved, I am saved." I thought about going back to the casino to play some more but decided to quit while I was ahead.

My plane left at noon, which meant I had to leave the hotel by 10:00 a.m. I decided to return to the casino at 8:00 a.m. and play the slots—there was no way could I lose all my money in two hours.

I found my lucky machine; nobody was on it. I went to the machine and loaded it. About thirty minutes later, the cowboy approached me and put his hand on my shoulder.

"Well," he said, "how did you do?"

I smiled. "Great!" I said. "I won seven thousand dollars."

He looked puzzled. "Is that all?" Then he asked, "You been playing this same machine?"

I nodded. He told me I was supposed to go to the five-dollar machine and then the ten-dollar machine. So I cashed out and headed to the second machine. He followed me. "Did you give the casino workers a big tip?" he asked.

"What do you mean?"

"The casino employees are assigned to work certain machines. You should always tip them big." He winked. "They always know what machines are cycling in."

We talked for a while, and then he said, "Good luck, Bill," and left. I had often wondered if that cowboy was an angel sent to me to help me in my time of need. I never saw or heard from him again.

I hit another jackpot and won another $7,000. A crowd gathered around. My heart was racing. I could not believe this was happening. I looked at my watch to check the time.

"Are you getting ready to leave?" a man next to me asked.

"I don't know. I have a plane to catch, but this machine is really paying."

"I'll give you five hundred dollars in cash right now if you will give me that machine," he said.

I shook his hand, took the $500 and my winnings, tipped the casino workers, and left to catch my plane. Now I had enough money to get me through the election!

CHAPTER 23

What Does He Have Planned for Me?

L arry Milner and I had two televised debates. One would be taped and aired the night before the election in Wichita Falls and the other would be televised live from Amarillo the night before the election. On the day of the taping, I was scheduled to speak at a luncheon in Amarillo, so my plan was to fly myself to Wichita Falls in a rented plane; I had earned an airline pilot's license several years earlier. I got in the plane after the luncheon and took off to Wichita Falls. The wind picked up as I flew over US Route 287. I was flying straight into the wind; when I looked out the window, I saw cars moving faster than I was—something was wrong. The winds in the Texas Panhandle are very strong.

When I landed, I called the TV manager and told him I was running late. He said it was not a problem; they would film the debate when I got there. I arrived an hour later. When I entered the studio, Larry Milner, wearing a three-piece suit, was standing behind his podium. He looked at me. "I have been waiting for over an hour."

I apologized. A newspaper reporter nearby was taking notes.

Larry was very short and had a complex about it. In planning the debate, both campaigns work together to agree on how the stage is set up, who enters the room first, and who gets the first question. I had requested that our podiums be placed right next to each other. At over six feet tall, I knew I would tower over Larry.

I looked at Larry. He was standing on a wooden Coca-Cola crate box behind his podium. The station director asked if there was anything else we needed before we got started.

"Yes, sir," I said. "I would like to have a Coca-Cola box just like the one Larry is standing on."

Everyone looked confused, but they brought me a crate and I stood on it.

Larry glared at me. "You are going to look very tall and stupid."

"Oh, no, Larry," I responded. "You will look very short."

The station manager advised that this did not look good.

"I've got an idea," I said. "Why don't we both stand on the floor like normal people so the voters can see us for who we really are?"

The station employees removed the boxes, and the debate started.

Larry was angry. He had red hair, and when he lost his temper, his face turned the same color. His face stayed red throughout the debate.

The debate went well for me, but even better, the next day the local newspaper ran a story about the Coke boxes. On Sunday, the same paper endorsed me.

It was Election Day. The first name on the ballot was George H. W. Bush, the Republican candidate for president of the United States, who was from Texas, and underneath his name was the choice for the US Congress. I knew almost everyone in the Thirteenth District would vote for Bush, so I was hoping that voters would cross over to the Democratic side of the ballot to vote for me.

My son, brothers, friends, supporters, and staff were all with me at a local hotel on Election Day, just as they had been when I began my political career more than eight years earlier. Once again, Bobby worked the election board and posted the results on the chalkboard. The results were reported: Larry Milner—88,981 votes; Bill Sarpalius—98,401. I had won!

I called my grandmother. She told me she was proud of me, adding, "Let's see what God has planned for you next!"

A few weeks after the election, the Texas Rangers caught the man who had broken my jaw. As we suspected, he was a professional hit man, and he had been hired by the Caravan's owners, who were suspected drug dealers. I had worked on a bill to increase the penalties for dealing drugs to minors and to raise the drinking age, and they wanted to get even with me. When I entered their club, they called their hit man. When the hit man was caught, they put a wire on him, and the police got enough evidence on tape. The Rangers arrested the owners.

For some reason, District Attorney Danny Hill went easy on the prosecution, so they got off with a light sentence. They were placed on parole for six months. I suspected that Danny was involved with all of this somehow and that he might have been buying drugs from the owners of the Caravan. Danny had problems with alcohol, depression, and substance abuse. A few months later, Danny Hill committed suicide. He was forty-seven years old. Danny Hill was a good friend; we served in the legislature together. He was in the House while I was in the Senate. I attended his funeral along with many others who respected Danny. Nine years later, his daughter, Hallie, took her life at the age of fourteen.

I had only a little over a month to find an apartment in DC, attend freshman orientation for a week, and hire staff to help me with my offices in Washington and my district. I also needed to get to know the members who would select the committee assignments. I had a lot to do in a short amount of time.

~

I quickly found myself with a new set of friends. Congressman Charlie Wilson from Texas's Second District called me on election night to congratulate me and offered to host a fundraiser for me to retire my campaign debt when I arrived in Washington. Charlie was a tall man with thick, dark hair, a great sense of humor, and a deep, distinct voice. He taught me how to get things done in Congress, and our friendship grew. Charlie also served in the Texas Senate, and we had a lot of the same friends. He served on the Appropriations Committee and the subcommittee that funded all military programs. Charlie was a highly respected and well-liked member of Congress.

Over the next several months, I used some of the gambling money to take care of my son until it was time to move to Washington, DC, and be sworn in as a congressman. Charlie hosted his promised fundraiser for me at his condo on the top floor of a high-rise building overlooking the US Capitol, the Washington Monument, the Thomas Jefferson Memorial, and the Lincoln Memorial. The view from his living room window was one of the most spectacular and beautiful views I had ever seen. Charlie had invited about fifty guests, including defense contractors and lobbyists. It was a huge success. Because of Charlie's fundraising party, I was able to retire my campaign debt. I asked Charlie how he found this place. He introduced me to the realtor who had helped him find his condo.

Charlie's realtor found me a condo with a gorgeous view of Washington—right next door to Charlie. The view was so incredible—I used to rent square footage on my balcony to photographers for Fourth of July fireworks. My life had changed so very much in just four short months.

Over the next few years, Charlie and I became close friends, and I learned how Charlie got the nickname "Good-Time Charlie." We were both single, but neither of us had time to date. Charlie enjoyed life and he always made everyone laugh. He was always surrounded by beautiful women, and I was glad to tag along with him.

Charlie also taught me how to raise campaign money from lobbyists. In DC, there were thousands of them, and they all had checkbooks. Fundraising was necessary in order to keep your job. Unless you were rich, you had to spend at least half of your time trying to raise money.

Charlie also introduced me to Tricia Wilson, to whom he had once been engaged, and told me I should interview her to be my executive secretary. Tricia had previously worked for two other members of Congress who had run for state governorships. She was experienced in running an efficient federal office and knew her way around Washington, so she would be a good teacher for my staff from the Texas office. I interviewed her and hired her the next day. She was one of my most valuable employees. Guy and Geneva Finstad, Joel Brandenberger, and Debbie Miller moved to DC from Austin to be a part of my staff.

One time, Charlie and I wanted to do something special for young kids in school. Our staff worked with the teachers in DC to plan an Amtrak train trip to Philadelphia to see Independence Hall. We had lunch prepared for the children, and Charlie and I spent the afternoon on the train talking to the kids. It was a great experience.

Charlie became a legend in Texas. In 2007, Tom Hanks and Julia Roberts starred in the movie *Charlie Wilson's War.* It was the true story

Charlie Wilson and me with kids we took on a train ride. Courtesy of the Sarpalius family.

of Charlie's secret back-door efforts to help arm the Afghani Mujahideen freedom fighters against the Soviet invaders. Charlie funded the covert war in Afghanistan with private and government funds. He just happened to be on the right committees at the right time to pull it off.

~

Greg Laughlin, another Democrat from Texas, had also been elected the same time I was. Greg was from West Columbia, Texas, where he had served as the assistant district attorney. Our wins reflected well on Speaker Jim Wright. The Republicans had spent millions of dollars to hang on to the seats we had taken. Since Greg and I had defeated Republicans and Speaker Jim Wright was from Texas, we thought we stood a good chance of getting the committee appointments we wanted.

We met with Speaker Wright. Greg expressed interest in serving on the Energy and Commerce Committee, and I requested Appropriations. The Speaker explained that he had to balance the committee assignment requests from all other states. He also explained that freshman members could not be appointed to major committees.

Each member of the freshman class was provided a temporary office in a cubicle located in the foyer of the Rayburn House Office Building.

Our freshman class met to elect our officers and draw numbers for seniority rank, which determined the order in which we selected our offices. I drew a number in the middle. Tricia knew which office to choose: a second-floor office in the back of the Longworth building. It was small but close to everything.

There were thirty-two members in our freshman class, and we had to elect a class president. Every freshman member wanted that role. I decided to run for class president. Greg Laughlin and John Tanner from Tennessee both worked hard on my behalf. The race was between Mike Parker from Mississippi and me.

I called my grandmother that night and told her I was in another race already. Mike Parker was her congressman, and she said she liked Mike and that she had voted for him. The vote was by secret ballot, and I was elected. Now I was the spokesperson for our class. It sounded impressive on a press release, but our class was very small, and it didn't mean that much.

The US House of Representatives hosted a beautiful dinner for the freshman class in the National Statuary Hall in the Capitol. The host was House Speaker Wright of Texas.

The tables were all set with fine china and candles, and there was live music and wonderful speeches from senior members, who welcomed us to the US House of Representatives. I had never seen anything so elaborate, and I could not believe I was there. Speaker Wright was proud of me when he introduced me as class president.

Tricia had my small congressional office repainted and furnished. It had two rooms, one for my staff and one for me. I walked into my office and sat down in the chair behind my empty desk. I prayed for guidance to help me do the best job I could representing the people who put me there.

On the first day of the session, I walked from my new office to the US Capitol with Bobby, David, Danny Needham, and Wesley Masters. Each member had been given two gallery-seat tickets for the opening day of the session. Texas Congressman J. J. "Jake" Pickle, who served

David and me on the steps of the US Capitol. Courtesy of the Sarpalius family.

from 1965 to 1995, had been kind enough to give me his tickets, so I had four. David and I entered the House chamber and took our seats in the brown leather chairs where members had sat since the Civil War. I received a small box that contained a member's most prized possession: a congressional lapel pin and a voting card. The blue-and-gold lapel pin had an eagle in the middle and number *101* under it, representing the 101st Congress. The voting card had my picture on it with puncture holes all over the card. The card identified the member when slid into voting boxes throughout the house chamber. The clerk of the House called us to order and asked us to record our presence. That was the first time I used my voting card. He asked us to stand and take the oath of office. With David at my side, I raised my right hand and took the oath. Once again, I silently thanked God, Honey, Cal Farley, and Granddad.

To make my committee request, I had to appear before the House Democratic Steering and Policy Committee, which was charged with making all committee assignments. They appointed me to the Agriculture and Small Business Committees. I attended my first committee hearing on the Agriculture Committee. We sat in order of seniority, and there was a nameplate in front of every seat. My seat was in the center of the bottom row, right below the chairman of the committee, Kika de la Garza from South Texas.

Next to me sat Ben Nighthorse Campbell from Colorado, who would eventually get elected to the Senate. On my other side was Mike Espy from Mississippi. Several years later, Mike was appointed by President Clinton to the secretary of agriculture. I met Robin Tallon, who represented South Carolina and had a deep southern drawl. We hit it off instantly and became long-lasting friends and are still great friends today. We spent hours talking about politics. Robin encouraged me to write this book. Robin and I became active members of the Congressional Prayer Breakfast, composed of Democrats and Republicans, who gathered every Thursday morning for prayer. The group still meets every Thursday, and Robin and I have been going together for more than twenty-five years.

Charlie Stenholm was from Texas, and his congressional district was just south of mine—our political issues in our districts were very similar. He was known as a moderate, and he and I had the same voting patterns. Charlie and other members from Louisiana, including Billy Tauzin and Jimmy Hayes, wanted to form a conservative Democratic caucus. Pete Geren (TX), Billy Tauzin (LA), Jimmy Hayes (LA), Greg Laughlin (TX), Gary Condit (CA), Collin Peterson (MN), John Tanner (TN), Mike Parker (MS), myself, and others all met often to discuss the formation of this coalition. We all agreed the Democratic Party was moving too far to the left and the Republican Party was moving too far to the right. There was no place for the moderates. So we named our coalition the "Blue Dog Coalition"—after the blue dog paintings that hung in Tauzin's and Hayes's offices; the Cajun artist was George Rodrigue. We agreed to do our best to vote as a block. The Blue Dog Coalition grew over the years and played a major role in bringing issues to the center.

I quickly learned that the Agriculture Committee was the key committee in negotiating all the trade agreements with other countries. It gave me an opportunity to help with the North American Free Trade

Texas delegation. Courtesy of the Sarpalius family.

Agreement (NAFTA) and General Agreement on Tariffs and Trade (GATT).

The Texas delegation was very strong. We had the Speaker of the House and five committee chairmen in our delegation. We met every Wednesday for lunch in the Speaker's dining room to discuss what we could do together to help Texas. I was so impressed and felt so blessed to be among such great Texas giants.

During my third week in office, I attended the inauguration of George H. W. Bush, the forty-first president of the United States. Current members of the House and Senate met on the House floor and were escorted down the hall and through the old house chamber, known as the National Statuary Hall. The House of Representatives met in Statuary Hall for nearly fifty years (1807–57). It is now the main exhibition space and an art gallery. Six future presidents served in that room as members of the House of Representatives, including Abraham Lincoln. One former president served in that chamber as a member of the House: John Quincy Adams, who died of a stroke in that room. We went downstairs in single file onto a large platform at the rear of the Capitol. The outgoing president and vice president, the new president and vice president, and their immediate families sat in the front row of bleachers on the platform. Current members of the US Senate and US House of Representatives sat behind them.

We began filling up the bleachers. I had an aisle seat in the fourth row on that platform, looking at thousands of people on the mall staring back at the Capitol. The band played "Hail to the Chief." President Ronald Reagan and President-Elect George H. W. Bush walked down the aisle to their large leather chairs, only inches from me.

President Bush was sworn in as the forty-first president and gave his speech. At the end of the ceremony, as Nancy and Ronald Reagan exited down the center aisle, President Reagan made eye contact with me and smiled. As he got closer, I stepped in the aisle and shook his hand. He was much taller than I had expected. I will never forget that moment. I was the first person to shake his hand as he left the office of president of the United States. After I shook his hand and stepped back to my seat, I realized that many other members were staring at me. Apparently, I was not supposed to step into the aisle.

After that ceremony, I got a letter from President Reagan, and we communicated a few times over the next several years. When he died, I was asked by the family to be one of a handful of Democrats to accept his body into the rotunda of the US Capitol. It was a great honor.

The Texas State Society of DC hosted the biggest inauguration party of all, the Texas Black Tie and Boots Ball. Tickets sold for a premium. Everyone wanted to attend because Texas was President Bush's home state. I rented a black tuxedo, polished my black cowboy boots, and put on my black cowboy hat. The only thing I didn't have was a date.

That was the largest party I had ever attended. It spanned several ballrooms in one of Washington's largest hotels. Country and western bands played in every ballroom. The highlight of the evening was the introduction of all the Texas members of Congress along with Senator Lloyd Bentsen and Senator Phil Gramm. President Bush; his wife, Barbara; Vice President Dan Quayle; and his wife, Marilyn, were all on the stage with us. I was so proud to be a Texan.

My new job in the US Congress was very demanding. I usually started the day by attending two or three breakfasts held by constituents or associations, or I went to a fundraiser for one of my congressional colleagues. When I got to the office each day, the staff briefed me on the day's topics, the committee hearings, and the votes to be cast on the House floor. Many of the issues were new to me. I was fortunate to have a very patient and diligent staff. At the end of each day, Guy Finstad handed me a folder of briefing papers to prepare me for the issues the following day.

I attended several committee hearings every day, and often the hearings overlapped, so I had to jump between hearings and try to not miss any votes and keep up with the issues.

Every member had a pager. When there was a vote on the floor, our pagers went off. Someone from the Democratic cloakroom advised us as to what vote was being called. When a vote was called, we had fifteen minutes to get to the floor, place our card in the voting box, and cast our vote. There was a running tally of how each member had voted—and we could all see how our colleagues had voted. A lot of the time you got to know the experts of several issues (agriculture, air and space, health care, or foreign affairs) and followed their vote. There were so many issues to deal with and vote on—it was very difficult to keep up with all of them, especially for a freshman member learning the ropes. Votes on many issues often lasted late into the night. You had to be present to vote.

Tricia did an outstanding job managing my calendar and scheduling meetings with staff, lobbyists, and constituents. I usually had lunch with a constituent in the members' dining room in the Capitol and then attended two or three receptions or fundraisers in the evening. I got home late at night and then read all the information provided by my staff to prepare for the next day.

David had made the move to Washington with me. He was a teenager trying to adjust to this new life as well. He came to my office after school each day, and I tried to make him feel a part of our team. But the busy lifestyle took its toll on us. David had always been very excited about my campaigns, but as he got older, he began to lose interest. The move to DC was very difficult for him, and I was too busy at the time to recognize it. David continued to make fair grades, but he just had too much time on his hands. I was wrapped up in my new job, but I felt like I was failing as a father.

I attended a dinner or reception every night. And every weekend I had to go back to my district in Texas for meetings. My district was large. I flew to Amarillo one weekend and then traveled from Amarillo to ten counties. The next weekend I flew to Wichita Falls and then traveled from there to all the counties. The next weekend I flew to Lubbock and did the same thing, and the following weekend to Dallas. Some constituents complained because I was only able to make it to their town once a month. On Saturdays and Sundays, I attended events in the Thirteenth District.

My grandmother was now in her mid-eighties. I still talked to her every Sunday. She had been my strength and my sounding board for so long. She had always given me the best advice. She was my inspiration and my rock.

CHAPTER 24

The Lithuanian Dream

O ne night, during my first month in office, I was working late
when a tall man appeared at my office door. As soon as he
spoke, I knew he was from another country.

"Are you Mr. Sarpalius?" he asked. I said I was, and he introduced
himself as Dr. Vytautas Landsbergis from Lithuania.

I invited him in and offered him a seat. It was after 10:00 p.m., so
I was very curious as to why he was in my office at that hour of the
night. He told me that he was a music teacher at the University in Vilnius, Lithuania, and went on to say that the Sarpalius name was well
known across Lithuania. Apparently, my great uncle Peter Sarpalius
was a Lithuanian American music composer, and his music is popular
throughout his country. Dr. Landsbergis said he loved my uncle's music.

I told him about my background and explained that I knew very little
about my family history. He detailed my family's ancestry and told me
about my great-grandfather and his six sons.

"This is my first visit to the United States," he said. "I wanted to speak
to someone at the White House, but no one would see me. So I came to
the Capitol and searched the directory of congressmen. Of course, your
name, being Lithuanian, stood out to me." He smiled and adjusted his
glasses. "I am the head of a new political party in Lithuania, the Sajudis
Party. We need the United States to help us pressure the Soviet Union
to put the Sajudis Party on the ballot. I believe the Sajudis Party would
win most of the votes against the Communist Party. This would allow
Lithuania to declare its independence."

He leaned forward, and his eyes were bright with hope.

"If Lithuania can declare its independence and break away from the Soviet Union, then Estonia, Latvia, Georgia, and the Ukraine would follow too. I think other countries under Soviet rule would also follow our lead, and it would lead to the fall of Communism."

If anyone had been in my office that night in 1989 and heard this discussion, they would have thought Dr. Landsbergis was crazy. At first, I was kind of wondering that myself. But I liked him, I was fascinated by what he knew about my family, and I respected his dreams. I asked him how I could help.

"The Republic of Lithuania was annexed by the Soviet Union in 1940," he began to explain. "From June of that year to 1944, German troops occupied Lithuania. In those four years, they massacred more than a million Jews. Any person they could find that had any education or could read or write were loaded on trains and sent to Siberia to die. They are still finding mass graves to this day.

"In the summer of 1944, the Soviets reoccupied Lithuania, claiming it as a Soviet republic. The Soviet government deported about 350,000 Lithuanians to labor camps in Siberia as punishment for anticommunist beliefs or resisting Soviet rule.

"In 1949, the communist regime closed most of our churches, deported or imprisoned many priests, and persecuted people who possessed religious articles. In 1956, there were more deportations, followed by a great influx of Russians and Poles into Vilnius, our capital city. Consequently, Lithuania has been acknowledged by most nations as a Soviet republic." Here he paused for a moment and leaned in toward my desk. "However, the United States has never recognized Lithuania as part of the USSR. I need you to help me get the Sajudis Party on the ballot."

I stood up from behind my desk and shook his hand. I told him that I was new to Congress (if he only knew) and that I still had a lot to learn.

"I give you my word, Dr. Landsbergis. I will do whatever I can to help," I told him. "And with God's blessings, I pray that your dream will come true." I had found my purpose in Congress.

I could not sleep that night. All I could think about was Dr. Landsbergis, the issues in Lithuania, and everything he'd shared about my family background.

Dr. Landsbergis's timing was perfect. Both President Reagan and President Bush had established good relationships with Soviet president

Mikhail Gorbachev and had been pressuring him to provide more free-dom to the citizens of the Soviet Union.

At that time, Mikhail Gorbachev had also undertaken reform in the Soviet Union for restructuring of the political and economic system. Some of the people in the formerly independent nations were beginning to demonstrate for even more freedoms. CNN widely broadcast these demonstrations, which further fueled the fire for the people of the Soviet Union—the wanted values of freedom and a free enterprise system. It was becoming increasingly apparent that strict communism was not working. But Gorbachev hoped that his reform efforts would appease the people and the political undercurrents would subside.

The next day I called the Russian embassy and scheduled an appoint-ment. I met with Soviet officials at the Russian embassy. I knew my conversation was being taped. I asked how we could get the Sajudis Party on the ballot in Lithuania for their next election. "If the citizens of Lithuania were given the right to vote for more than one political party," I argued, "it would prove that the Soviet Union does not deny freedom to its members. The right to vote is the greatest form of free-dom. You would send a global message that communism is the choice of the people."

They stared at me and then had a sidebar conversation in Russian. I figured my time was up. They politely told me they would consider my recommendations. I was so naïve and felt stupid thinking that I could go over there and talk the Soviets into changing their election process.

One of the strongest Lithuanian communities in the United States is in Chicago. Congressman Dick Durbin is from Chicago, and his mother was an immigrant to the United States from Lithuania. Dr. Landsber-gis had also paid Dick a visit. Dick and I began giving speeches on the House floor supporting the addition of the Sajudis Party to the ballot in Lithuania.

Dick Durbin and I formed a coalition of congressmen to support the Lithuania movement. The members of our coalition included Mar-tin Frost from Texas, Chris Cox from California, George Miller from California, John Miller from Washington, John Tanner from Tennes-see, Steny Hoyer from Maryland, John Lewis from Georgia, Eliot Engel from New York, and Dennis Hertel from Michigan. Other members provided support as well.

Grandmother and me in the backyard. She was my rock. Courtesy of the Sarpalius family.

I phoned my grandmother and asked for her prayers and those of her prayer group. She encouraged me to continue to speak out on the issue.

I met with Speaker Wright and told him what we were trying to do. He was very supportive, and for the next several weeks, he gave speeches on the floor in support of Dr. Landsbergis and his Sajudis Party.

Our coalition passed a resolution asking the Soviet Union to place the Sajudis Party on the ballot. I met with embassy members from other countries asking them to do the same thing, and many countries did.

A few months later, in 1989, the Soviet Union finally agreed to place the Sajudis Party on the ballot in Lithuania. The elections would occur the following March in 1990.

~

My grandmother was now eighty-five years old. I need to visit her in Mississippi, so I flew down there. We spent a lot of time in her backyard. She had broken her right knee and was unable to bend her leg, so she had to use a cane. Her mind was still very sharp, but she was very frail. I was continually amazed by her strength. My time with her was so special, and she always gave me a fresh perspective.

When I returned from Mississippi, Senator Lloyd Bentsen from Texas, a good friend and mentor, invited me to lunch at his office in the Capitol. When I arrived, he asked me how things were going, and I told him I was doing fine.

"How is David doing?" he asked. "It must be a struggle trying to raise a boy in DC as a single parent while working in Congress."

I admitted that I was concerned about David, who would soon be a junior in high school. My constant travel had left little time to spend with him, and it had affected our relationship. He was a teenager and unhappy in DC.

"I don't have the money to send him to a private school."

"Plus you work long hours," Lloyd interjected.

"Exactly. And David doesn't want to travel with me on weekends."

"Have you given any thought to enrolling David in the Senate Page Program?" The program is available only to high school juniors. The students live in dorms near the Capitol, attend school at the Library of

Senator Lloyd Bentsen, a legend in Texas and a good friend. Courtesy of the Sarpalius family.

Congress, and work in the Capitol when the Senate is in session. It is an elite program, and thousands of kids from all over the US apply for it. Only senior members of the House or Senate can sponsor students.

"I talked to Congressman Brooks, the head of the program, but he said he didn't think it would look good for a member to have his son work as a page."

The senator looked at me. "Well, I would be honored to sponsor your son as a Senate page."

I was speechless.

The Senate Page Program was the best thing for David. I was always so grateful to Senator Bentsen. David did well and came to know several members of the US Senate. It was a blessing for both of us.

David finished the Senate Page Program and his junior year of high school in Washington, DC. He then returned to Amarillo, where he lived with Rick Smith and finished his senior year of high school at Tascosa High School.

~

Every day, Tricia and I reviewed my schedule and the various invitations to fundraisers and other congressional events. One day, she told me that I had received an invitation to play in an annual celebrity golf tournament to raise money for cancer research.

"I haven't played golf since I broke my back. The doctor told me I would never play again."

"This will be good for you," she said. "It will give you a chance to meet a lot of important people in the DC area."

I looked at her and shrugged. "OK, sign me up, and I'll get some lessons." The tournament was three weeks away, and I figured I could learn how to hit a ball by then. I bought a set of golf clubs at Sears, but I never found the time to practice.

The day before the tournament, I told Tricia I could not go through with it, but she and the rest of my team encouraged me to play anyway.

"There won't be many spectators, and it will be a good opportunity to learn the game," she said.

The next morning, on a Saturday, I drove to the Congressional Country Club in Bethesda, Maryland. The parking lot was already packed with media. I found a parking place, got my clubs, and followed the crowd to the course.

I kept thinking to myself, *What was Tricia thinking? What am I doing here?* There were hundreds of people there. I was going to embarrass myself. As I made my way to the registration table, it got worse. My partner was Leslie Nielsen, the famous actor and comedian, and the tournament would be televised on a national network. I wanted to turn and run.

I got into the golf cart, introduced myself, and explained to Leslie that I was new to this game and had never played in a tournament.

"I really shouldn't be here," I said.

He looked at me and laughed. "Sure," he said. "You politicians are alike." We laughed. He had no idea.

"I'm telling the truth! I'm afraid I'll hit someone with a golf ball," I said.

"Don't worry. We'll have fun," he said.

The first hole was a par three. Hundreds of people stood around the green. Leslie turned to me and said, "Grab your seven iron and follow me."

I followed him to the tee box, and an official introduced us to the crowd and the television audience. I was mortified. Leslie swept his hat off his head, waved at the crowd, teed up his ball, and wiggled his hips a little as he approached his ball, holding a three wood.

He swung the club, smacked the ball high in the air, and yelled, "Fore!" He had done it on my behalf. The crowd ran for the woods.

He turned to me, grinning. "Now move slow and hit it on the green." He winked as he walked by. "I cleared them off the green for you. I couldn't be seen with anyone with a wayward ball." My golf game was awful, but Leslie Nielson was a lot of fun.

~

I spent a wonderful Christmas with my grandmother in Mississippi while David went to visit Donna, who was now remarried and living in Montana. My grandmother was even more frail, but she still had her spirit. When I left to return to Washington, she gave me a tin full of her Christmas brownies. I ate one each day, cherishing each bite, just as I had done at Boys Ranch.

By the beginning of the next year, congressional support for Lithuania and the Baltic countries was building. The Lithuanian elections were in March 1990. I helped pass a resolution in support of open elections in Lithuania, which was sent to the Russian ambassador. My support for Dr. Landsbergis and the people of Lithuania had turned into a congressional movement to push for freedom through the Eastern bloc.

PART V

International Politics

CHAPTER 25

The Fall of the Soviet Union

I n January, I announced my intention to seek reelection, and state representative Dick Waterfield announced that he would run against me. Waterfield was a wealthy rancher from Canadian, Texas, who was into horse racing. One of his horses had run in the Kentucky Derby. Waterfield had the money to commit to the race. The Republicans in my district would do whatever they could to defeat me and return my seat to their party.

I was focused on the Lithuanian elections, which were being held in March. Several countries had agreed to observe the elections to make sure they were conducted fairly. President Bush sent Dick Durbin, Chris Cox, John Miller, and me to Vilnius, Lithuania, to represent the United States as official observers.

We flew to Berlin and were scheduled to fly into Vilnius the next day. When we got to our hotel in Berlin, the Soviets told us to give them our passports so they could give us a visa to enter the country.

That night Dr. Landsbergis called to report that representatives from most of the European countries had arrived, and they looked forward to seeing us. He was very excited and hopeful that his party would win so Lithuania could finally break free from the Soviet Union.

The next morning the Soviets did not return our passports and visas. The four of us were furious. Dick Durbin quickly called a press conference in our hotel lobby. The news was broadcast worldwide: the Soviets had taken passports from four US congressmen. The Soviets were

Flag that had been flown over the US Capitol and presented to President Landsbergis. Courtesy of the Sarpalius family.

denying the US congressmen their agreed-upon opportunity to observe the Lithuanian elections on behalf of the United States.

Dr. Landsbergis phoned again. "I am very disappointed you will not be here on Election Day, but the news about you and the other members is all over the newspapers in Lithuania. It is helping our cause."

"We're not going back to the States," I told him. "We plan to wait for the Soviets to return our documents. We still have every intention of going to Lithuania."

The following day, the Soviets returned our passports and allowed us to enter Lithuania but limited our time there to only eighteen hours. We arrived in Vilnius late that evening. Dr. Landsbergis and his delegation met us at the airport and took us to the Sajudis Party headquarters, which was located across the street from the Vilnius Cathedral. Crowds had gathered in the courtyard in front of the cathedral to celebrate the elections.

Dr. Landsbergis showed us the election results, which were written in pencil and taped on the wall beside the door. Dr. Landsbergis had been elected president of the new republic of Lithuania. There were forty-two seats in total, and the Sajudis Party had won thirty-six seats, leaving the Communists with only six seats.

The other congressmen and I held another press conference. Reporters from all over the world covered the event, asking us to comment on the Soviets withholding our passports, which denied us access to observe the Lithuanian elections. That had been the task, the very reason for coming here, and the Soviets knew that.

Dick Durbin, Chris Cox, John Miller, and I presented a US flag, which had flown over the US Capitol, to President Landsbergis to honor independence for Lithuania.

"This flag is a worldwide symbol of freedom," I told President Landsbergis, "and we, as members of Congress, are proud of your courage in declaring independence for your country."

Following the press conference, we went to the Vilnius Cathedral across the street. The crowd continued to sing and celebrate. The interior of the church looked like a construction site. Workers were erecting scaffolding, extending all the way to the ceiling, so that they could remove the pale-green paint on the walls and ceiling. The Soviets had used this cathedral as their Communist Party museum and warehouse. Now the Lithuanians were cleaning out their church.

We boarded a bus with the newly elected leaders of Lithuania for Kaunas, where we were to rescue Cardinal Vincentas Sladkevicius, the first cardinal appointed to Lithuania in three hundred years. The cardinal had been held in solitary confinement by the Soviets in a remote house since 1957, over a quarter of a century.

During the hour-long trip, we answered questions from the new Lithuanian leaders about how to establish and structure their government. Chris Cox gave them each a copy of the US Constitution, Bill of Rights, and Declaration of Independence, all translated into Lithuanian. History was being made, and it was exciting. We were also very fearful that the Soviets would send troops to Lithuania to retake it.

We arrived in Kaunas and met with Cardinal Sladkevicius. He was old and very feeble, and it was obvious that he had endured much suffering during his long lifetime. The Soviets had only released him because of our presence in Lithuania and because of our involvement in the liberation of the Lithuanian people.

We returned to the bus with the cardinal and were then informed that the Soviet army was headed to Lithuania with soldiers, tanks, and missiles. No one spoke. I asked President Landsbergis what he wanted from the United States, expecting him to say weapons, supplies, and reinforcements. He responded and said, "The only thing I want from the United

Dick Durbin, John Miller, Cardinal Vincentas Sladkevicius, Chris Cox, and me.
Courtesy of the Sarpalius family.

States is recognition. I want the United States to recognize Lithuania as a free and independent sovereign nation." He paused, then said, "We want to be able to carry our own Lithuanian flag in the Olympics."

Returning to Vilnius, we met with even more new governmental leaders at party headquarters. Huge crowds celebrated outside the church. About an hour later, we concluded our meeting and walked across the street to the cathedral.

Inside we made our way to the front pew with President Landsbergis and the other new leaders. While under Soviet rule, the Lithuanians had hidden all the artifacts, furnishings, treasures, and icons of the cathedral. Now the people were slowly returning these items to their church, including the preserved remains of a Lithuanian saint that had been hidden for more than fifty years.

The workers on the scaffolding had removed the paint from the walls and ceiling. And underneath was some of the most magnificent artwork we'd ever seen.

Cardinal Sladkevicius then entered the cathedral and said Mass for the first time in over a half a century. The Mass was celebrated in

Lithuanian and Latin. I could not understand a word, but it was one of the most moving experiences of my life. Everyone cried. These people had had no human rights, no freedom of religion, no freedom of speech, and no freedom to vote or even to congregate.

When our eighteen-hour visit was over, the Soviets returned to escort us to the airport. We promised President Landsbergis we would do whatever we could to help his new government.

"Perhaps you could visit the man who is building a movement in Moscow to eliminate communist rule," the president suggested. "His name is Boris Yeltsin."

As we boarded the plane, President Landsbergis hugged me and whispered in my ear, "God be with you, my friend. Thank you for all your help and for believing in me." Then he added, "We will make it. The Soviets will finally crumble. We will be free."

When we landed in Washington, several White House staffers met us at the airport gate. President Bush wanted to see us. We collected our luggage, climbed into the car, and headed straight for the White House. We were escorted into the Oval Office, where President Bush and Vice President Quayle welcomed us. There were probably ten other people crammed into the Oval Office with us: staff from the Department of State, White House, CIA, and Department of Defense. Two couches faced each other in front of a fireplace. Chris Cox and John Miller sat on one couch and Dick Durbin and I sat across from them. The president and vice president sat in chairs by the fireplace.

The president wanted to know everything about our trip and our thoughts about President Landsbergis. I described President Landsbergis's determination and passion for independence and freedom. President Bush asked a lot of questions, most importantly, "What does Lithuania expect from the United States?"

I told him that all they wanted from the United States was our recognition of Lithuania as a free and independent nation. "They want to carry their own flag in the Olympics."

President Bush was clear that he wanted to help, but he was also concerned about his relationship with Mikhail Gorbachev, the Soviet president. We discussed the president's concerns. He asked us what we would do if we were in his shoes.

Dick and I responded by explaining they'd elected enough members from the Sajudis Party to declare their independence. Many other countries were recognizing Lithuania as independent and that the United States should do the same. Chris and John stated that they would support the president's decision.

President Bush looked at us and said, "I can't afford to piss off Gorbachev."

I was infuriated. I had been so deeply moved by what I had seen in the last two days in Lithuania.

I responded to the president, "You might remind Gorbachev that the United States has never approved or recognized the occupation by the Soviets of Lithuania or any of the Baltic states. The Soviets are known to have slaughtered untold numbers of innocent people." Even though I understood the president's position, I knew his heart was on our side. Regardless, I could not stand by and let the United States do nothing after the Lithuanians had declared their independence. The battle was on.

Dick, Chris, John, and I began to give daily speeches on behalf of Lithuania. We built an even stronger coalition of members. Congressman Martin Frost, whose mother was also from Lithuania, was a great supporter and leader for this Lithuanian freedom movement.

On March 30, 1990, Estonia, following Lithuania's lead, held elections and declared its independence from the Soviet Union, though this was not recognized until the fall of the USSR in August 1991.

In January 1991, fifteen people were murdered when the Red Army, allegedly under a MVD (Ministry of Internal Affairs) faction, seized the television station in Lithuania, cutting off all outside communications. In Latvia, soldiers surrounded the parliament building, while the Soviet Black Berets killed five people in an attack on Latvia's ministry building.

In June 1991 Boris Yeltsin, the outspoken leader against communism and soon-to-be president of Russia, the largest of the Soviet republics, was elected to a new position as chairman of the Soviet Federative Socialist Republics. The old USSR was unraveling.

Dick Durbin invited me to accompany him to Chicago to speak at a rally in support of Lithuania. Chicago's large Lithuanian community made it an ideal location for a rally. By now, I had discovered that my great-grandfather and many of my relatives had settled in Chicago after they left Lithuania.

Chicago rally. Courtesy of the Sarpalius family.

Hundreds of people attended the rally and demanded freedom for Lithuania. A tall gentleman, Valdas Adamkus, introduced Dick and me to the crowd. We described our visit to Lithuania for the election, noting the strong determination of the Lithuanian people in their fight for freedom. We pledged our commitment as members of the US Congress to formally recognizing Lithuania as a free country.

Valdas Adamkus, who was born in Kaunas, Lithuania, had immigrated to the United States in 1949. In 1960, he graduated from the Illinois Institute of Technology with a degree in civil engineering. In the early seventies, Adamkus went to work for the newly established US Environmental Protection Agency, and in 1981, he was promoted to administrator of the agency.

His heart and soul were still in Lithuania. He was an outspoken leader for Lithuania's independence and helped motivate Chicago's Lithuanian community to undertake massive letter-writing campaigns to members of Congress and to President Bush. The Lithuanian Chicago rallies drew the country's attention to the Soviet sieges in Lithuania.

Meanwhile, we continued to apply pressure on President Bush. Our coalition of congressional members convinced the Helsinki Commission to visit the Baltic states. The Helsinki Commission, comprising about sixty countries, was created in 1976. The goal of the commission was to support human rights—freedom of speech, press, and assembly—in the former Soviet satellite states. Additionally, the commission served to monitor the transition to democracy, including free and fair elections. We mobilized everyone we could.

Following the Soviet killings in Lithuania and Latvia in January 1991, the Helsinki Commission invited a congressional delegation, led by Representative Steny Hoyer of Maryland, to visit the Baltic states. From February 9 to 15, 1991, thirteen members of Congress, the largest delegation to visit the Baltic states in fifty years, flew to meet with the newly elected leaders there.

We landed in Riga, Latvia, in the middle of a snowstorm. The plane stopped close to the terminal. Soviet KGB agents, not Latvian officials, boarded the plane. The Soviets wanted to make it clear that they were in control of the borders of the Baltic states. We waited on the plane. Finally, two buses arrived, and our Congressional delegation was escorted by Soviet soldiers, armed with rifles, onto one of the buses. All the other passengers boarded the other bus.

We were on a fact-finding mission, trying to learn as much as we could about the January Soviet invasions. The Baltic countries had no armies or any other way of defending themselves.

Our first meeting was with Anatolijs Gorbunovs, chairman of the new Supreme Council of Latvia. He told us his people were hungry and that food was scarce and expensive. I thought back on my homeless days, digging food out of trash cans and waiting for food that had been donated by local churches. Gorbunovs said he was encouraged by the fact that the farmers were now able to grow the crops they wanted to grow and were not forced to plant what the Soviet government told them to plant.

He told us about the murders of his people by Soviet soldiers. We asked him what we could do to help his new country. He requested that all humanitarian aid be sent directly to Riga and not through Moscow.

Our hotel was on the corner of a block, across the street from a public park. It was cold and dark. There were bullet holes everywhere in the hotel lobby, and broken mirrors hung on the walls. I asked one of the hotel clerks what had happened, and she said that the Soviet soldiers had killed some citizens in the lobby.

I could not sleep that night. I stared at the ceiling and wondered how we could possibly succeed against such odds. I prayed for strength. The next morning, I crawled out of bed, exhausted, and looked out the window. Soviet soldiers watched our building from across the street. I was so relieved when we checked out of that hotel.

We went to a rally in the same park where the Soviets had shot and killed citizens just weeks earlier. Hundreds of people waved signs protesting the presence of the Soviets. It was very cold, and snow covered the ground. Everyone wore long, dark coats and Russian fur hats. Our congressional delegation sat on a platform and took turns giving speeches to the crowd praising the courage and determination of the Latvian people. Soon after we began, several trucks approached the park, and Soviet soldiers jumped out. They pushed through the crowd and ordered everyone to leave. Latvian security guards quickly escorted us to our van. Soviet soldiers waved rifles and were trying to break up the demonstration.

We went directly to the airport and flew to Vilnius, Lithuania. A few government officials met us at the airport and escorted us to our hotel. President Landsbergis was at the parliament building. Several Soviet military units and tanks had been deployed from Afghanistan to Lithuania, including the Soviet Counterterrorist Alpha Group and the Red Army's Seventy-Sixth Air Assault Division.

When I later got back to DC, I met with Charlie Wilson and joked with him that he had forced the Soviets to leave Afghanistan and that instead they went to Lithuania. Now I needed to get them the hell out of Lithuania!

The Soviets had seized the National Defense Department building and the Press Building in Vilnius. Soviet paratroopers had seized the regional buildings of the National Defense Department in Alytus and Šiauliai. They had also destroyed the Vilnius railway station. They had taken over the TV tower and station, stopped all broadcasting, and killed several protesters at the tower. The only communication outside of Lithuania at that moment was a single phone line. There were photographs posted on the Wall of Freedom, surrounding the parliament building, of a student who had been run over by a Soviet tank. It was sickening.

Members of the new parliament drove us to the TV tower. Soviet tanks and soldiers surrounded the tower. The Soviets had drawn a line

Flowers on the spot where people were shot and died close to the TV tower. Courtesy of the Sarpalius family.

in the snow, and if anyone crossed that line, he or she was shot with no questions asked. There were flowers and lit candles placed in the snow to mark where a Soviet soldier had killed a Lithuanian. A man and woman with two young children were crying as they knelt in the snow by one of the candles.

I stood within two feet of a Soviet soldier and faced him on the other side of the line in the snow. He was probably about nineteen years old. We had no way to communicate, and he just stood there with his rifle facing me. I had no doubt that if I crossed that line, he would have shot me.

The officials then drove us to the parliament building, a three-story structure surrounded by twenty-foot-high and three-inch-thick concrete barricades. Soviet tanks surrounded the parliament building while Lithuanian armed guards manned the building's gates. Hundreds of people stood behind the concrete barricades or huddled around bonfires to keep warm. Taped to the wall were pictures of the citizens who had been killed and posters supporting the Lithuanian movement. They called it the Wall of Freedom.

The crowd cheered as we walked by.

The TV tower surrounded by Soviet soldiers. Courtesy of the Sarpalius family.

We walked around piles of sandbags to enter the building and climbed a flight of stairs also lined with sandbag barricades. Lithuanian citizens armed with hunting rifles cleared our path. We entered a large room, and President Landsbergis walked in and hugged me. He smiled and said, "Congressman Sarpalius, we are going to make it." Landsbergis asked us to have a seat at the table and briefed us on the standoff.

President Landsbergis recalled my work, efforts, and determination with the Russian embassy to allow the Sajudis Party on the ballot. He commended the work of Congressmen Dick Durbin, Chris Cox, and John Miller, and me on behalf of Lithuania.

"The morale of our people is high," he said. "There are at least a thousand people in the courtyard between the wall and the parliament building day and night, ready to defend this building against a Soviet attack."

We all sat at the large table wearing heavy winter coats. There was no electricity. I thought about when I used to stand on the corners in the Texas Panhandle to use the payphones in the dead of winter, when I was working for Speaker Bill Clayton—freezing my ass off. That is exactly how I felt sitting at that table in Vilnius, Lithuania.

Wall of Freedom surrounded by Soviet tanks. Courtesy of the Sarpalius family.

We all asked President Landsbergis questions. I asked him what he needed from the United States. President Landsbergis explained that his people had only a few hunting rifles for weapons. "But the world is watching. God is on our side," he said. "Congressman, all we want is the same freedom you have in the United States. Your country is a symbol of freedom worldwide. Every citizen in your country can choose an occupation and worship God at any time, in any place." Then he looked straight at me and said, "Most of the countries around the world have recognized Lithuania as an independent country. Why won't the president of the United States do the same?"

My colleagues and I looked at each other, but we did not respond. We were embarrassed because we knew he was right. Congress had passed resolutions in the House and Senate encouraging the president to recognize Lithuania, but the president did not want to upset Gorbachev. Landsbergis continued and said that if President Bush would agree to recognize Lithuania, the Soviet army would retreat, and Lithuania would be free. We assured President Landsbergis of our continued commitment to Lithuania. He thanked us for our help. We all held hands and prayed together.

President Vytautas Landsbergis and me. Courtesy of the Sarpalius family.

As we got ready to leave, President Landsbergis asked me if I would tour the rest of the parliament building with a sixteen-year-old boy while he stayed behind to talk with the other congressmen. I told him I would be honored. President Landsbergis then hugged me and once again whispered in my ear, "We are going to make it!"

"I am only one member of Congress, but as long as I am there," I replied, "I'll do whatever I can to help you."

I left with the boy, who spoke English very well. He led me upstairs, past more sandbags and men with rifles. Then we approached a door that opened to the rooftop of the building. The rooftop was covered with two-by-fours with nails driven through, points up.

"See?" The boy turned to me. "No Russian helicopter can land on top of this building."

Those nails could not prevent a helicopter from landing, but they would make it very difficult for any Soviet soldier to walk across the roof. I followed him back downstairs, around the barricades, and outside into the snow, where he showed me a pile of rocks that had been accumulated as weapons.

"Don't you understand that the Soviets have missiles and can blow up this building in an instant?" I asked.

He responded to me, "Oh, no, Mr. Congressman, you don't understand. Today we are a free people. We will live as a free people, or we will die as a free people."

I was speechless. This young boy and his people were ready to throw rocks at tanks. They were prepared to die for their freedom. I thought that if all the people fighting the Soviets had the same determination as this young boy, the Soviets didn't stand a chance. Then I took a deep breath and walked back inside with the boy.

The next morning, we flew to Estonia, toured the capital city of Talinn, and met with several leaders of the new government. Now that all the Baltic states had declared their independence, they had formed a pact to fight communist rule. Most countries had already recognized them as independent countries. The Estonian people also wanted recognition from the United States for the same reason as Lithuania. The new leaders in Estonia had the situation under control, and it did not appear that the Soviet threat was imminent in Estonia. The main concern was for Latvia and Lithuania.

~ CHAPTER 26 ~

Fighting the
Soviet Empire

A few years earlier, President Ronald Reagan had increased our nation's defense spending. The Soviet Union responded by building more ships, airplanes, submarines, and weapons of mass destruction. Following the fall of the Berlin Wall, there was not much commitment or loyalty to the Communist Party. The Soviets pulled out of the war in Afghanistan and moved those tanks to Lithuania. Pope John Paul II was from Poland, and he applied pressure because he knew the Soviets would not invade his homeland. The Soviets had endured several years of bad weather, resulting in significant crop failures. They were forced to turn to the United States for grain subsidies. The Russian government rationed food. They were hungry and desperate for change.

Our group of congressmen left Estonia for Moscow via Berlin on Aeroflot, the only airline that flew into Moscow. Safety was not a primary concern on Aeroflot Airline. We boarded an old, rickety airplane with no heat. All the passengers were bundled in heavy coats, wearing tall fur hats called *ushankas*. They carried brown paper bags of canned food and cigarettes that reminded me of the bags of food that we got from the Catholic Church's food banks in Houston at Christmastime. I could relate to their hunger.

All the passengers boarded the airplane and waited for the pilots and one flight attendant. It was snowing, freezing cold, and the wind blew strong around the plane. The two pilots finally walked onto the plane, entered the cabin, and cranked up the engines. The cabin filled with smoke. They turned off the engines, walked out of the cabin, and exited the plane. Forty-five minutes later, they returned and restarted the engines; finally, some heat. After we took off, the flight attendant served small cups of salt water. We all thought we would die on that flight; it was long. We finally landed in the city in the middle of a snowstorm. Officials met us at the airport and drove us to a hotel a few blocks from Red Square. It was very dark, there were very few streetlights and cars on the road, and all the buildings looked old, dark, and gray. There were no advertisements in any store windows or places of business—it was like this in the Baltic states as well. And it was so damn cold.

The next day we were escorted to the headquarters of the Russian Soviet Federated Socialist Republic. We sat in a large boardroom for a long time until a tall, gray-haired man along with two young, beautiful female interpreters joined us. We shook hands, and he said, "Welcome. My name is Boris Yeltsin."

We told Mr. Yeltsin that we had just visited Estonia, Latvia, and Lithuania. He asked a lot of questions about the Baltic states. He seemed genuinely committed to dismantling communism and the Soviet Empire. He expressed concern about the Soviet army's occupation of Lithuania.

"The Russian people are hungry," he said. "They want a free enter-prise system. I admire the United States. If the Baltic states can hold out a little longer, the momentum for independence will continue to grow." He confided that he and other spokesmen against the Soviet Union feared that they would be assassinated.

A few months later, the world watched Boris Yeltsin climb atop a Soviet tank as the Cold War came to an end. I met with Yeltsin several times over the next few years. He was a courageous leader.

The next day, as we headed back to the airport, we saw very long lines of people in heavy coats, in the freezing weather, standing in front of stores waiting to get food. They were starving. There were only a few small stores open because the people did not have the money to buy much. When the Soviet Empire collapsed, that all changed.

When we got to the airport, we waited for more than five hours for our plane to arrive. Finally, we boarded Aeroflot Airlines again. The pilots started the engines, and we had the same experience, all over

Meeting with President Boris Yeltsin. Courtesy of the Sarpalius family.

again: the cabin filled with smoke and the pilots turned off the engines. The pilots tried starting the engines again, and the smoke in the cabin became so dense that the oxygen masks in the plane dropped. I could not see the person in front of me. The pilots shut off the plane engines, walked out of the cabin, and exited the plane. They got in a car alongside the plane and drove off.

Congressman Dick Durbin was sitting next to me. We both thought we were going to freeze to death before we got off the plane. Finally, a bus arrived and took us back to the terminal. Five hours later, we boarded another Aeroflot plane and finally left Moscow for Berlin.

When we returned to the United States, our group continued its campaign for the Baltic states. I continued to visit the Russian embassy. Neither Lithuania nor Latvia had an army, so the Soviets continued to kill innocent, unarmed people who were fighting for their freedom.

I also hounded the Department of State and the White House and talked to anyone and everyone about the conditions in the Baltic states. The media was our friend. National newspapers, magazines, TV, and radio reported almost daily on the siege of Vilnius and the plight of the Baltic states; it became a worldwide story.

President Bush and me. Courtesy of the Sarpalius family.

On May 31, 1990, the Parliament of Moldavia was the first country to recognize Lithuania as a free and independent country. Moldavia was still part of the Soviet Union. Denmark, Croatia, Slovenia, and Latvia also recognized Lithuania. Other countries around the world began to follow in support of Lithuania.

The Vilnius massacre of January 13, 1991, validated the fact that Gorbachev had authorized attempts to overthrow the Lithuanian government. The slogan in Lithuania was "Freedom until our last drop of blood."

President Bush was under pressure to do something about the Baltic-Soviet standoff. Bush met with Mikhail Gorbachev in the White House.

On September 2, 1991, President Bush officially recognized Lithuania, and four days later, the Soviet Union finally recognized Lithuania. On September 17, 1991, Lithuania was welcomed as a member of the United Nations, along with Estonia and Latvia. Lithuania could now carry their own flag in the Olympics.

Years later, when President Bush and I were both out of office, we ran into each other at the airport, waiting to board a plane from Houston to Washington. The president saw me and motioned for me to join him by the window. He told me how much he admired me for standing firm in my efforts for the people of the Baltic states. He told me he had to do what he had to do. I understood. He said that he was glad I had applied the pressure to help Lithuania. I have always had tremendous respect for the president.

I phoned Grandmother and told her I was flying down to spend a few days with her in Mississippi. I knew her days were numbered. She was now confined to a wheelchair. I loved and respected her so much. I wheeled her around her backyard, and she pointed out all her flowers, many of which had been given to her by the Sunday school students she had taught for many years. She was always happiest in her flower garden. My brothers and I had many wonderful memories of Grandmother's small house and yard. She had always been a stabilizing influence in our lives.

CHAPTER 27

The First Lady
Comes to Boys Ranch

In 1990, I was in one of the toughest campaigns in my career. State Representative Dick Waterfield and the Republican Party were determined to unseat me. Waterfield had defeated former congressman Bob Price in the Republican primary by a landslide. He had a big ego and a lot of money.

Governor Bill Clements was doing everything he could to help Waterfield. He told the press that I didn't grow up at Boys Ranch and that I was a staff member's son. When the press called me about his remarks, I told them to call Boys Ranch. Dirty politics.

I managed my campaign the same as I always had: I carried signs in the back of my car and stapled them to poles, visited each town and business in my district as often as possible, and attended all the local sports events as often as possible.

One day a Dalhart newspaper reporter was in a local coffee shop, and one of the county deputies told the reporter he had seen Dick Waterfield's wife get out of her Lexus "dressed to the nines in her high heels" and tear down one of my signs off a utility pole. The reporter called Waterfield's wife to ask her why she had done that. She replied, "It was for safety." She said the signs were distracting the drivers on the highway. The reporter called to ask me what I thought about her comment. I responded that I was glad my campaign signs were getting so much attention and appreciated Mrs. Waterfield's help. The story was picked up by other newspapers, and it went statewide.

The main issues in this campaign were guns, abortion, jobs, and programs to benefit farmers and ranchers. Nobody in my district cared at all about Lithuania, the Soviet Union, or the Baltic states.

Two weeks before the election, someone dropped off an audiotape to radio and TV stations and newspaper offices. On it were several telephone conversations I'd had with a woman I had dated where I allegedly offered to find her a federal job. It was clear the tape had been spliced to combine several different conversations into one. I was single at the time. I immediately contacted the FBI. Someone had tapped my mobile phone. Some of those recordings involved federal business and constituent issues. The FBI got a copy of the tape and investigated.

I had chaired the Agriculture Subcommittee for eight years in the Texas Senate and served on the Agriculture Committee in the US Congress for four years at the time. I worked hard to help the Cattle Feeders Association. My district produced 28 percent of all the grain fed to cattle in the US. Over the years, I sponsored legislation that was very beneficial to them.

Waterfield was a rancher and raised cattle, and the Cattle Feeders Association, the largest cattle producer in the United States, decided to support him instead of me. They gave him thousands of dollars. I was not happy.

The Texas Cattle Feeders Association got a lot of criticism from many of their members. Paul Engler, who was one of my biggest supporters for years, withdrew his membership from the association. Every year, the Texas Cattle Feeders Associations would send a box of prime steaks to each member of the Texas delegation, but the Texas delegation refused to accept their steaks.

A week before the election, someone sent an unmarked envelope to my campaign headquarters. The blank envelope contained several revealing photographs of Dick Waterfield with his arms around a woman at a party, and it wasn't his wife. Members of my campaign team were ready to film a commercial using the picture that would put Waterfield away.

I told them no, that I'd think of a way to use the pictures, but I would not embarrass him publicly. Mudslinging and dirty politics had become commonplace in campaigns, particularly in the last three or four days before Election Day. I knew that was Waterfield's plan, but it wasn't mine. That is not how I was going to get elected.

In Wichita Falls, there was a African American preacher who was elected as a county commissioner. If he told the members of his church to vote for a specific candidate, they followed his lead. He invited me to attend his church services, so Aaron and I attended. The preacher had us sit in the first row. After a few great songs, he had me stand up and face the people, and he said some really nice things about me. Then he said to the crowd, "Now we all know how much money a US congressman makes, and we all know that our congressman will give as much as he can to support our church, so we can support him." A man approached me and held out the offering basket as every member watched. I pulled out my wallet and put everything I had in the basket.

Two live television debates were scheduled, one in Amarillo in prime time on Friday and the other in Wichita Falls the Monday night before the election. The polls showed me and Waterfield in a dead heat. I got to the television station in Amarillo an hour early. Waterfield and I had agreed to face off on the platform with the moderators in the middle. A TV camera was set up behind me facing Waterfield, and another behind Waterfield facing me.

We had to wear makeup on TV to prevent the glare of the bright lights and make us look better; I hated the makeup. As they applied my makeup, I mentally prepared myself for the one-hour debate. I walked from the makeup room toward the studio with my campaign staffer Robert Hinkle, a former employee at the television station. Robert had the damaging Waterfield photos in his pocket.

We had a plan. When Waterfield walked into the studio, with his wife behind him, Robert pulled the photographs out of his pocket and flashed them in front of Waterfield, so that only Waterfield got a good look. Then Robert quietly said, "If you want to play dirty, then we can get dirty too."

Waterfield looked like he might faint. He and I took our seats, and the debate started. When the camera zoomed to Waterfield, I reached inside my coat pocket and fidgeted, pretending that I had the photos in my pocket. He was a nervous wreck. He stuttered and lost focus. He began sweating profusely, and his makeup ran down his face.

The final debate on the Monday before Election Day was live from Wichita Falls. Waterfield and I stood next to each other on the platform. Just before the debate started, I turned to Dick and said, "Now it's time to explain your vote on House Bill 236." I had no idea what House Bill 236 was, but it threw Waterfield off balance. Throughout the debate, he thought I was going to challenge him on his vote on House Bill 236, and he was struggling with it; neither one of us recalled HB 236. My strategy was working. He started to sweat again and became very flustered. That debate ended in my favor.

On Election Day, once again I worked the voting places from sunup until sundown. My friends, family, and supporters gathered at a local Amarillo hotel, and once again Bobby tallied the election results on the chalkboard.

Waterfield had outspent me two to one, but I won. Waterfield had 62,996 votes; Sarpalius had 81,502 votes. That same night, my friend Chet Edwards also won his race. I was delighted that he and I would be working together again, this time in the US Congress.

After the election, I received a letter with no return address. Inside was an unsigned, handwritten apology for the mobile phone recordings. I gave the note to the FBI. About a week later, a young man in his early twenties confessed to recording my cell phone conversations and splicing them. The Republicans had paid him to follow me for several months.

~

I loved First Lady Barbara Bush and thought it would be special if she could visit Boys Ranch and talk to the kids. So I sent a letter to the White House. Several months went by with no reply. I figured she had more important things to do than fly to Amarillo and drive the thirty-six miles to the ranch.

One day, David and I were having lunch in the members' dining room, and President Bush walked in with Congressman Sonny Montgomery, a Democrat from Mississippi. When the president finished his lunch, he came over to our table and asked how I was doing. I told him fine and introduced David. The president graciously acknowledged him. Then he asked if there was anything he could do for me. I replied, "Well, I sent a request for Mrs. Bush to speak to the kids at Boys Ranch in Amarillo. But I haven't received an answer yet."

The president knew about my background and Boys Ranch. I told him it would mean a lot to the boys to have the First Lady visit. He nodded, smiled, and said, "I'll take care of it."

As soon as I returned to my office, Tricia said the White House was on hold. It was the office of the First Lady. They told me that Mrs. Bush would visit Boys Ranch, but due to security, I would be given only two days' notice of her arrival and could not disclose her visit to anyone until they had given me the OK, and the Secret Service had to visit the ranch in advance.

"I'd like to notify the ranch superintendent," I said, "so at least they can be prepared for her visit on such short notice."

The First Lady's office agreed to that and said that when all the details had been finalized, I could announce her visit to the press—within two days of her arrival.

I called Lamont Waldrip to tell him the First Lady might be coming to Boys Ranch and the Secret Service would contact him. A couple of months later, Lamont phoned to let me know the Secret Service had arrived at the ranch and spent a few days making plans for her visit. Just prior to her arrival, an advance team would fly into Amarillo to line up the First Lady's limo, vans, and cars that were specially equipped for protection.

I finally got a call from the White House with the go-ahead to announce her trip to the press. I was instructed to meet Air Force One at the Amarillo airport and ride with Mrs. Bush to Boys Ranch, where I would introduce her to the residents and staff at the ranch and then accompany her on a quick tour.

Joel Brandenberger, my press secretary, drafted the press release, and then we held a press conference announcing the visit, which would be closed to the public.

As soon as the news hit the press, the Republicans were in an uproar. State senator Teel Bivins, a Republican, and others called the White House and expressed their concerns about the First Lady's visit to Boys Ranch at the request of a Democrat. The White House phoned and told me that because of the concerns expressed by Republicans, I was to have no contact with the First Lady on her trip.

"This isn't an election year," I explained, "and my request for the First Lady's visit is merely to benefit the boys at Boys Ranch, not for myself."

It made no difference.

I flew to Amarillo and then drove to the ranch. I stood at the back of the auditorium when Mrs. Bush's motorcade arrived. The First Lady got out of the limo with Teel Bivins. The directors of Boys Ranch greeted her and escorted her into the auditorium. Boys Ranch was in my congressional district, and I was a graduate of Boys Ranch, but I was to have no contact with the First Lady.

I stood in the back of the auditorium, mad as hell, but also thrilled because I knew I had arranged for the First Lady to be here at my Boys Ranch. Teel Bivins introduced her. The media was everywhere. Mrs. Bush walked to the podium, and the audience stood and applauded.

Mrs. Bush thanked everyone, and then she said, "I want all of you to know I am here today because of your congressman, Bill Sarpalius." With that one comment, she had done what I could not do. Barbara Bush is a true lady and very gracious.

When she finished her speech, she got in her limo for a tour of the ranch. As I was walking to my car, ready to drive back to Amarillo, one of Mrs. Bush's staffers approached me and said that the First Lady wanted to see me before she left. I followed him to the visitor's center and went into the lobby.

A few minutes later, her limo pulled up in front of the center. I stepped outside, and she walked up to me and shook my hand. The picture taken of us together hit the newspapers the next day. She signed that photograph, and it still hangs on my wall.

President and Barbara Bush were very special to me—they were fellow Texans. And when people asked me who I voted for to be president in 1988, I was proud to tell them I had voted for George H. W. Bush.

～

In April 1992, Aaron and I were driving back from Dalhart after a speech at a local civic club, and Aaron answered a phone call. Aaron then gently told me that my grandmother had passed away that morning. I felt like my world had just ended. I had spoken to her the night before, and she sounded fine. My aunt Kat had taken Grandmother to see her doctor for a checkup. She was sitting on the edge of the examining table when her heart stopped. She was eighty-eight years old.

To: Congressman Bill Sarpalius - Thanks for showing me "your place" - Most warmly - Barbara Bush

First Lady Barbara Bush at Boys Ranch. Courtesy of the Sarpalius family.

I called Bobby and Karl to give them the news. Karl flew to Dallas to meet me, and we both caught a plane to Jackson, Mississippi.

I had known her health was failing and that she would face death soon, but losing my grandmother felt like losing my mother all over again. She meant so much to me. She was my rock and my anchor—the one person that I could trust and turn to for guidance. I will always cherish our Sunday-evening phone calls.

Bobby and his wife arrived, and we spent the day in Grandmother's backyard, reminiscing about her and Granddad and how important they had been to us and how much they had both influenced our lives.

At her funeral, her coffin was covered with beautiful pink azaleas from her own backyard. The church was packed with people who loved my grandmother. She had touched so many lives. Her friends told me how much I meant to her. My grandmother taught me a lot. She said that material things were not as important as helping those in need. She said that love is a gift you give, and if you give a lot, you will receive it back in kind, and that we must always be thankful for the things we take for granted—the ability to see, talk, and walk.

She told me and my brothers over the years that life itself was a gift from God and that when we finally stand before God, we will not be judged on what we accomplish for ourselves, but on what we have done in service to God and to others.

My grandmother had never learned to drive a car, but she never missed church on Sunday. I never heard her complain about anything. She was always focused on being a good wife, mother, and a faithful child of God. She lived a very simple life that was so full. I miss her.

CHAPTER 28

Voting for War

C asting a vote to send troops into war is historically one of the most dreaded decisions for an elected official. It was the one I faced when Iraqi troops invaded Kuwait. President Bush deployed US troops to Saudi Arabia in a mission called Operation Desert Storm. Twelve other countries sent naval forces, joining the United States and Saudi Arabia. Congress was given several classified briefings from the Pentagon, and it became pretty clear that we were going to war.

Several members of Congress gathered to fly to Saudi Arabia for more briefings and to meet with the troops. I was one of them. A car from the Pentagon picked me up at my condo to drive me to Andrews Air Force Base. The members and I boarded the same Boeing 707 jet that took President Kennedy to Dallas in 1963 and then brought his casket back to DC. The plane was light blue and white with the presidential seal on the sides. On the long flight to Dublin, Ireland, I sat in a high-backed leather chair that had a pipe holder bolted to the armrest that had been used by President Kennedy. On the back of the chair was a hat rest that had been used by Vice President Lyndon B. Johnson for his cowboy hat. It was on that plane that LBJ took the oath of office when he became our thirty-sixth president.

After a brief stop in Dublin to refuel, we flew on to Riyadh, Saudi Arabia, where we spent the night in one of King Salman's many palaces. My room was huge, with bright-red carpet and high ceilings. I lay in the bed, stared at the huge crystal chandelier, and thought, *This sure ain't Boys Ranch.* The next day we were taken to the US headquarters for

Desert Shield, where generals Colin Powell and Norman Schwarzkopf briefed us.

Their most disturbing report was the very real threat of the chemical weapons Saddam Hussein had at his disposal. He had used chemical agents on the Kurds in northern Iraq during a 1987–88 campaign known as Anfal. During that time, thousands of people were killed, thousands were left with severe skin and respiratory diseases and abnormal rates of cancer and birth defects, and the environment was destroyed.

There was a very good possibility that Hussein might use his chemical weapons on US troops, so our first action was to mount air strikes to knock out chemical plants or potential storage facilities for chemical weapons.

While we were in the Persian Gulf, we asked to visit our troops on the front lines. Our request was eventually granted, and a large helicopter, surrounded by other helicopters for protection, transported us to a base in the desert. We were in the air for a little over an hour.

I was sitting next to the gunner, who had his weapon pointing out the open door. He tapped me on the shoulder and pointed down to the desert to show me the base. I could not even make it out—it was camouflaged so well.

We went to the command center and met with several officers, who expressed their concerns about the potential use of chemical weapons—an invisible threat. Every soldier had a gas mask and wore protective gear.

We had lunch with the troops in a large tent, and I asked the commander if I might speak to the soldiers from Texas. He made the arrangements, and I met with ninety-four soldiers from my state. I passed around a large yellow legal tablet and asked each of the soldiers to write down his or her family's contact information, and I told them that I would contact their families when I returned to the States. I asked how they were doing and if there was anything they needed. They were most appreciative that I was going to call their loved ones.

On the plane back to Andrews Air Force Base, I thought about all those young soldiers and wondered how many of them would survive this war. The briefings indicated that the number of casualties could

Having lunch with brave soldiers in the middle of the desert. Courtesy of the Sarpalius family.

be very high. I couldn't sleep, thinking about voting to send many of those young men and women into war—and to their deaths.

When I got back to the States, I called everyone on the list. I talked to girlfriends, parents, and wives. As I called everyone on the list, I prayed they would never have a messenger arrive at their front door informing them that their loved one had been killed in action. Two of my Boys Ranch brothers had died in battle in the Vietnam War.

We had three days of speeches on the House floor, so all the members had a chance to voice their opinions and conclusions about the war. Almost everyone spoke in support of it. I cast my vote in support of the war to liberate Kuwait and prayed that all the intelligence information about the chemical weapons was wrong.

The world watched footage as we deployed our missiles and bombs. We were successful in decimating chemical plants, which saved the lives of many of our troops.

Following the liberation, I returned to Kuwait and met Colonel Mubarak Alenezi. Mubarak had a distinguished career as an officer of the Kuwait Ministry of Interior Affairs. During his twenty-four years of service, he served as chief liaison officer to numerous foreign embassies and military forces.

Mubarak told me of the atrocities he had seen when Iraq invaded Kuwait. Iraqi soldiers murdered family members in front of their children, raped young girls in front of their parents, and executed officers in the Kuwaiti army. Terrified, Mubarak finally put his wife and three children in his car and drove into the desert, leaving Kuwait. He told his family that if they were caught, he would shoot them all and then turn the gun on himself. He kept the gun in his lap as he drove. He was never caught, but many of his family members were murdered. Mubarak and I are still friends today.

We won that war, and President Bush's approval rating was at an all-time high, but we had not captured Saddam Hussein and had not removed him as a future threat. Years later, when his son, George W. Bush, was president, we captured Hussein, but the threat of terrorism continued to linger, and thousands of soldiers paid the price to protect our country.

One of the great accomplishments of President George H. W. Bush was the Strategic Arms Reduction Treaty (START), which was a giant step toward reducing nuclear weapons, and it had a huge impact on my Thirteenth District.

The largest employer in Amarillo was Pantex, a plant operated by the Department of Energy (DOE). Parts for nuclear weapons were manufactured at different plants across the US. All those parts were trucked to Pantex and assembled. Once assembled at Pantex, the nuclear weapons were then trucked across our nation in unmarked eighteen-wheelers surrounded by heavily armed, unmarked vans and cars for security. If Pantex quit assembling nuclear weapons, thousands of jobs would be lost. I had to figure out how to prevent that from happening. So I figured if we quit manufacturing nuclear weapons, then the plant was the perfect place to dismantle the weapons—that became my goal.

The DOE planned to close some plants and expand others. I knew this would be a long process, but Pantex needed to survive—and I needed to save those jobs.

The Pantex plant was very secure. Seven high-voltage fences surrounded the property, and most of the people who lived in the city had no idea what went on there. As a member of Congress, I had visited the plant several times.

I took the matter to the secretary of energy as well as the White House. I also spoke with one of the most powerful members of Congress, the chairman of the Energy and Commerce Committee, John Dingell of Michigan. John agreed to help me, and with his support and help, Pantex got the contract.

~

On January 3, 1993, I again took the oath of office in the House of Representatives chamber, with David by my side. He had been there for me for every swearing in. I was far more proud of him than he was of me.

A few days after his inauguration, President Clinton outlined his economic strategy in a closed-door session of the Democratic members of Congress. He planned to balance the federal budget, which I thought was ambitious. The economy was in shambles. Unemployment and the federal deficit were at an all-time high.

He told us he wanted to establish fiscal discipline, reduce interest rates, eliminate the budget deficit, and stimulate private-sector investments. He wanted to invest in the people through education, training, science, and research and reduce the number of welfare recipients by creating more jobs for people. He wanted to open more foreign markets so American workers could compete abroad, and he proposed raising the gasoline tax to use those funds to reduce the national debt.

President Clinton appointed Senator Bentsen as US treasurer and selected Leon Panetta as his chief of staff. Senator Bentsen was chairman of the Senate Finance Committee, and Leon Panetta was chairman of the House Budget Committee. Nobody understood the federal budget better than those two, and they were in charge of developing Clinton's economic plan.

CHAPTER 29

Losing What You Love

After Pantex's contract was up for dismantling the nuclear weapons, thousands of jobs were at stake. Because of our country's dependency on oil, there was a growing demand for alternative energy sources. Amarillo was perfect for wind and solar energy. As a state senator, I helped get funding for research on wind energy and ethanol. Over time, those energy sources had significantly expanded. This was a perfect opportunity to save jobs and create additional ones in the Texas Panhandle. A committee of business leaders was formed to build support for Pantex's expansion. Bill Gilland, who owned a successful car dealership, and Jim Simms, a successful businessman, served as cochairmen.

At that time, there was also research around a lightweight, long-lasting battery. There was much discussion about funding this research in a laboratory. I thought the best place to do this would be at Pantex. This would require expansion of the facility, which meant more jobs for the people of Amarillo and the surrounding towns.

Business leaders came together in support of the laboratory, and I arranged hearings in Amarillo with members of Congress and the Department of Energy. The hearing was held at the Amarillo Civic Center due to the number of people in attendance. I met with both President Clinton and Vice President Gore, gained their support, and passed resolutions to encourage the Department of Energy to place the laboratory in Amarillo.

It was critical to name the laboratory the "Pantex National Research Laboratory." That distinction was important because the "national" designation would secure funding of the facility for the long term.

President Clinton shakes my hand at his first state of the Union speech. Courtesy of the Sarpalius family.

Secretary of Energy Hazel O'Leary was generally opposed and not in favor of the project. She wanted it to be just a research laboratory under control of the Department of Energy, whereby they would control all the decision-making without having to ask for congressional approval.

I continued to work for the establishment of the Pantex National Research Laboratory, and eventually Congress approved the whole package. A press release was issued announcing that Secretary O'Leary and I would be making an announcement in Amarillo. Secretary O'Leary flew into Amarillo and reserved a suite at the hotel where the press conference would be held.

I arrived at the hotel about an hour before the press conference and called Secretary O'Leary to see if she needed anything. She said she wanted to talk to me in advance of the press conference. We met, and she told me that she was not in favor of the research laboratory and would not announce it as the "Pantex National Research Laboratory."

"Congress and the president understand that it is a *national* research laboratory," I reminded her.

"I am not going to announce that," she replied.

I picked up the phone and called the White House and explained the situation to President Clinton.

"Put her on the phone right now!" he demanded.

I held out the phone to the secretary and said, "The president wants to talk to you."

She made her case with the president and then handed the phone back to me.

"Call me back after the press conference," the president told me. "It will be called the Pantex National Research Laboratory."

The secretary and I headed toward the press conference with her staff trailing us, surrounded by media. We sat at the table together and the press conference began. The two of us explained the need to find alternate energy sources to oil and gas. We told the press that this laboratory was a long-term investment in the future.

The first question asked by a reporter was regarding the name of the laboratory. The secretary turned to me and said, "Congressman, what will be the name of the research laboratory?"

I proudly announced, "The Pantex National Research Laboratory."

Bill Gilland and Jim Simms, as cochairs of this committee, had spent two years working with me on this issue to build the support for it. It was a great opportunity for local economic growth and represented a significant investment in the Texas Panhandle. Pantex was already Amarillo's largest employer, and with the addition of the laboratory, the number of jobs would triple.

~

President Clinton and Vice President Gore, along with their cabinet members, traveled across the nation to promote Clinton's economic plan.

I was undecided on how I would vote on Clinton's economic plan. The pressure was on, and everyone knew it was going to be a close vote. US Treasury Secretary Lloyd Bentsen paid me a visit, along with his chief of staff, Dr. Michael Levy. They wanted me to vote for the plan. Senator Bentsen knew my district as well as anyone, and he told me it would be beneficial to the Thirteenth District. He also reminded me that he had always been there for me. That was true, and he had done so much to help me with my son.

"You know you could always count on me to help you," Secretary Bentsen said. "Now can I count on you to help us with your vote?"

Talk about pressure! I had to change the subject. I asked if he knew what the vote count was.

"Every Republican will vote no," he said, "so we need every Democrat we can get." He looked at me hard. "It is up to the Democrats to show leadership and change the direction this country is going. Can I count on your leadership?"

"This plan is not popular in my district," I said. "Voting in favor of it could cost me my next election."

"You can survive the election," he assured me, "and this is your chance to help this country. Can I count on your vote?"

I took a deep breath, nervous as hell, and responded, "I'm sorry, but I am still undecided. I need more time to think about it."

There was nobody I respected in government more than Lloyd Bentsen.

The vote was less than a week away; reporters called constantly asking about how I would vote. I told them I was undecided.

Bill White, the deputy secretary of energy and the future mayor of Houston, came to my office. He had been doing a lot to help me with the expansion of the Pantex National Research Laboratory. He knew this was a tough decision for me and that my vote in favor of it might cost me my election. We talked about how close the vote would be on this issue and how it would probably pass or fail by one or two votes.

My staff and I spent a lot of time analyzing the plan and discussing the issue. They too were getting calls from the press. I had never seen so much pressure on an issue.

Then I got a call from the White House. President Clinton and Vice President Gore wanted me to come to the White House for a visit. When I arrived, Senator Bentsen and Leon Panetta met me as I walked in the side door of the executive offices. Eight other Democratic members of Congress were gathered in the waiting room next to the Oval Office. We walked together into the Roosevelt Room and sat around a boardroom table. President Clinton and Vice President Gore walked in, shook our hands, and then sat at the head of the table.

The president began by outlining his plan and told us that he currently did not have the votes to pass his economic plan. He did not promise us anything but told us that if we did support the plan, we would finally be able to turn the country around together.

The night before the vote, I could not sleep. I missed talking to my grandmother.

The next day the debate started early in the morning and lasted all day until the night. After every member had a chance to express his or her thoughts about the plan, a motion was made, calling for a vote. Members had only fifteen minutes to slide his or her voting card into voting boxes. I waited to see how the vote was going. The process continued way past the fifteen minutes. As expected, every Republican voted against the plan. I kept my eye on the tally; waiting to see if my vote would be needed. I knew my political career was on the line.

I stayed in the members' lounge and watched the vote on TV. It flipped back and forth by one or two votes.

I walked into the House chamber and slid my voting card into the voting box. The total vote was tied. I pushed the green button, in favor. The bill passed by one vote.

When I got back to my office, I could see that my staff was concerned, but I knew I had done the right thing. The phone rang, and Tricia answered. It was the president. He thanked me for my vote and said he understood how difficult this was for me. He told me, "Bill, you did the right thing today, and I will never forget what you did for America. I'll do everything I can to help you in the next election."

I already had town hall meetings scheduled across the Texas Panhandle, and I was not looking forward to them—I knew they were not going to be pleasant.

The negative reaction from the people in my district was overwhelming. Everyone understood the need for a balanced budget and that the gasoline tax would be used to reduce the national debt. I explained that the gasoline tax would be eliminated once the federal budget had been balanced, but I still had tremendous difficulty in trying to convince my constituents that this was a good plan. My district was very large and rural, and people had to travel long distances between the towns. And there were a lot of farmers with heavy machinery and equipment—all of which required a lot of gasoline. The increase in taxes was significant to them. It was a hard sell.

Aaron and I drove to Plainview for another town hall meeting at the community center. The Republicans viewed this as a perfect opportunity to damage me. The press was everywhere, and the parking lot was full. I knew I was in trouble.

Inside, every seat was taken, and people lined the walls. The crowd was ready to challenge me. I gave my speech, explaining the need for change in our country. I outlined the provisions of the bill and the importance of reducing our national debt.

When I asked if there were any questions, that crowd let me have it. The people yelled and booed. The meeting got out of hand quickly, and I knew I was getting nowhere. I glanced at Aaron and let him know that we needed to be on our way. I gave some closing remarks, keeping it short. Cameras filmed me as I walked out of the room. I knew the news broadcasts that night would be terrible.

When we walked outside, Aaron told me that two supporters wanted to see me for just a moment. The men said they had just opened a new facility to help people with alcohol and drug problems, and they wanted me to see it. I was completely unfocused and was thinking about the disastrous town hall meeting and how I might recover from it. Aaron told me that we should go see the facility. We got in our mobile office and followed the men.

The facility was a new redbrick building. We walked inside, and several women greeted us. The two men provided a tour of the home. It had a large kitchen, a spacious living room, and a big fireplace. We also met several of the residents of the facility. It was all very nice, but I was still preoccupied by the events at the town hall meeting.

Outside in the backyard, I saw a woman sitting at a picnic table, smoking a cigarette. She looked very nervous. She reminded me of Honey. We went back inside, where about ten women sat on couches in front of the fireplace. The woman from the picnic table came in through the back door and settled on a couch. She looked like she didn't have much interest in life. One of the men began to introduce us to the residents.

I told the ladies how impressed I was with their new home. I learned that they were all single mothers with alcohol or drug addiction problems. Their children were either at school or with them in the home. I thought about Honey. I asked where they had gotten the money to build the home.

One of the men responded, "It was all paid for through a program called the Texas Commission on Alcohol and Drug Abuse."

I got a lump in my throat, felt like I was going to cry, and tried to regain my composure. I felt like I had been hit with a brick. I looked at those women and finally said, "Let me tell you the story of the Texas Commission on Alcohol and Drug Abuse"—and I told them about Honey and her struggles and how it had impacted our family.

When I finished, there was not a dry eye in the room, mine included. The ladies hugged me. Aaron and I drove back to Amarillo, and I told him that the day had begun as one my very worst but ended as one of the very best.

I had a town hall meeting scheduled in Amarillo. The press had done a number on me after the disaster in Plainview. I knew the Republicans would use Amarillo as another opportunity to knock me down. I had already received a few death threats, and the Amarillo Police Department agreed to provide protection to make sure the town hall meeting did not get out of hand. The police escorted me into the auditorium, which was filled with several hundred hostile people. I tried to explain my rationale behind my vote. I thought that I saw some folks nodding their heads in agreement, but nobody spoke up.

Kent York, a Baptist minister, stood to speak. He said, "We didn't send you to Washington to make intelligent decisions. We sent you to represent us." I let that sink in and did not say a word. I was trying to keep from laughing. The press got the minister's name, and that quote made it into every major newspaper in the United States, plus *Reader's Digest*. Members of Congress loved it.

I survived that town hall meeting, and as time passed, the economic plan produced what had been projected: more than 22.5 million jobs were created, the US had five consecutive years of real wage growth, overall unemployment dropped to its lowest level in more than thirty years, publicly held debt was reduced by $363 billion—the largest three-year pay-down in US history—and Americans benefitted from reduced interest payments on debt. The nation had a balanced budget.

After a few years of seniority, I became chairman of the US House Agriculture Subcommittee on General Farm Commodities. We had jurisdiction over all commodities such corn, wheat, rice, soybeans—almost every crop grown in the US. One of our most important pieces of work was drafting and negotiating the North American Free Trade Agreement (NAFTA). We spent months working out the terms of the agreement among the US, Canada, and Mexico. It was intense. We met one night at the White House with Secretary of Agriculture Mike Espy from Mississippi and representatives from Canada and Mexico. We were focused, working very late into the night, and President Clinton walked into the room wearing black sweatpants, a black sweater, and tennis shoes with a cup of coffee in hand. He asked about the status of the agreement. We told him we were close. He pulled out a chair, sat down and said, "Let's work it out." For the next two hours, we hammered out the final NAFTA agreement that removed trade and tariff barriers among the three countries.

~

Mac Thornberry was a young attorney with a struggling law practice in Amarillo. At the last moment, he decided to run against me. His parents were wealthy ranchers and had the funds to back him. The Republican Party began pumping a lot of money into his race. He began running TV ads stating that if he was elected, he would do everything possible in favor of limited terms in office and that he would support a constitutional amendment in support of a balanced budget. He ran what I thought were slanderous TV ads against me, telling voters that I was under investigation by the FBI and that I didn't grow up at Boys Ranch.

The Sunday before the election, pamphlets were placed on the windshields of cars throughout my district with pictures of dead babies, claiming that I was supporting abortion. I have always voted pro-life. I found myself in the dirtiest campaign ever.

On election night, my political career ended. I was not alone—fifty-four other Democrats across the nation lost their congressional seats. George W. Bush, a Republican, defeated the Democratic governor of Texas, Ann Richards. Jack Brooks from Texas, the longest-serving member of the House, was defeated, and Tom Foley, Speaker of the House, was defeated. Despite the significant economic growth generated by Clinton's plan, the president's popularity had declined along with the strength of the Democratic Party.

Mac Thornberry has been in office for more than twenty-five years. The budget has never been balanced since, and term limits have never been instated. The Pantex National Research Laboratory was never built

Last day in Congress. Courtesy of the Sarpalius family.

and was eventually abolished, costing Amarillo thousands of jobs. Reese Air Force Base in Lubbock was closed, eliminating more jobs, and funding for Sheppard Air Force Base in Wichita Falls was drastically reduced.

It hit me really hard the day after the election, but my first concern was for my staff. They had been so loyal to me, and we worked well together—and worked hard to serve the people of the Thirteenth District. Together, we had achieved so much. I felt lost—and had lost a job I truly loved.

CHAPTER 30

Grand Duke

djusting to life after Congress was not easy. I was barred from
lobbying for one year.

I called the president and ask him if there were any positions available within the Department of Agriculture, where I could
work for one year until I was able to lobby. He appointed me as an
undersecretary of US Department of Agriculture (USDA). Dan Glick-
man was appointed as the secretary of agriculture. Dan and I had
become friends after serving together for six years on the Agriculture
Committee. When my year was over, I resigned from the USDA and
started my own lobby firm, Advantage Associates.

My first client was St. Joseph Medical Center in Houston, Texas,
the very hospital where I had received care when I was a young boy with
polio. Over the years, Advantage Associates became Advantage Associates International, and we represented a wide range of clients, including foreign governments, health care and business associations, clients
contracting with the Department of Defense, and many others. I found
lobby work very rewarding, and it enabled me to maintain my political
connections.

~

I received a call from Wesley Masters's son, Wes Jr., who told me that his
dad needed me. I had not seen or heard from Wesley in years. Wes Jr.
told me his father was dying of cancer in a prison in Switzerland. I was
astounded. Wesley Masters was one of the most honest people I had ever

known. Wes Jr. brought me up to speed. Apparently, Wesley had been in Switzerland and, while at dinner, overheard a conversation between two men who were discussing anhydrous ammonia plants. He introduced himself to them and explained his business.

Ultimately the three had formed a partnership to build ammonia plants in Europe. Wesley was to design the plants, while the other two would raise the money. After they had raised several million dollars from investors and banks, one of the men took off with the money. Wesley and the other partner were sent to prison. He had been in the Swiss prison for almost two years, and he was up for his first parole hearing. Wes Jr. told me that only one person could testify on his father's behalf at the parole hearing in Switzerland. He asked me if I would be willing to testify. I told him I was on my way.

I flew to Geneva, Switzerland, and went straight to the courthouse. They put me in a small room and locked the door. I sat there by myself for what seemed like forever. Finally, the door on the other side was opened into the courtroom, and I saw Wesley wrapped in a blanket. As soon as he saw me, he started to cry. My heart sank. A clerk escorted me into the courtroom, and I stood in front of three judges, who all wore white wigs and black robes. No one spoke English. A clerk in a long black robe served as my interpreter.

The judges asked questions about my background and how long I had known Wesley. They asked if I thought Mr. Masters was a wealthy man. I responded that he was one of the richest men I knew. They looked surprised. I told them that Mr. Masters was not wealthy in the sense of owning material things; he was wealthy in that he had many friends, was unselfish, and had family who loved him very much. I told them about all the financial support that Wesley had provided over the years to his church, Texas Tech University, and other people in need and that he was one of the most generous people I had ever known. Wesley cried during my entire testimony. I did my best, through the interpreter, to answer their questions. The judges then told me to sit in the courtroom.

A minister who spoke English sat down next to me and translated what was being said in the courtroom. After about an hour, the judges recessed and left the chamber. When the judges left, I started to walk toward Wesley, but the clerk stopped me and told me I could not speak to him until after the hearing.

The minister and I went across the street to get something to eat. He told me Wesley had received no medication to treat his cancer and that if Wesley was not released, he would probably die in prison within a few months. He said Wesley was losing hope. We went back into the courtroom and waited for another hour.

The judges entered the courtroom. Wesley was still wrapped in that gray wool blanket. He was so weak and could hardly stand when the judges told him to approach the bench. The minister again translated for me as the judges said how much they appreciated my testimony and that if a former member of the US Congress was willing to travel halfway around the world to speak on behalf of his friend, then that friend must be a good man. They said that Wesley would be set free the next day.

As I hugged Wesley, we cried, and I told him that once we got him back to Amarillo, I was going to buy him a big T-bone steak. Then we were going to make sure he started treatment right away. He thanked me over and over again for coming. I told him that he would have done the same for me. I told him that when I was still at Boys Ranch, I had asked God to use me to help other people. And then I said, "He led me to you, Wes." I owed Wesley Masters a hell of a lot more than that. I went outside, borrowed a phone, called his son, and told him his father was coming home. Wes Jr. began to cry and thanked me for all my help.

～

In 1998, I received an invitation to the Lithuanian embassy in Washington. President Valdas Adamkus, the gentleman from the Chicago rally in support of the Lithuanian freedom movement, was going to be there. Adamkus had returned to Lithuania and been elected president after President Landsbergis's term expired. President Adamkus was a great leader, helping that new nation prosper and gain the respect of countries around the world.

I got to the embassy and stood in line to greet President Adamkus. Then I saw President Lansdbergis. Tricia and Debbie from my staff were also there in addition to John Tanner, member of Congress from Tennessee, and his wife, Betty Ann. John Tanner is a dear friend to this day. Several other members of Congress were there as well.

Grand Duke award presented to me by President Valdas Adamkus and Ambassador Stasys Sakalauskas from Lithuania. Courtesy of the Sarpalius family.

I hurried over to Landsbergis and hugged him. We reminisced about when he had come to my office that night many years earlier. We talked about how neither one of us were in office and how difficult it was to not be actively involved in political decisions. It was so good to see him and visit with him.

The ambassador welcomed everyone, and President Adamkus made opening remarks. Then to my surprise, he invited me to join him on the platform. The president said some very nice things about my efforts in helping the Lithuanian people in their fight for freedom. He told the crowd about President Landsbergis's visit to my office that night in 1989 and the vision that he had shared with me. He acknowledged the members of Congress who had worked tirelessly to help the tiny Baltic states gain their freedom from the Soviet Union.

Then President Adamkus opened a leather case containing a large gold-and-silver medal attached to a ribbon. He placed the ribbon around my neck and told me and the crowd that this was the highest award and recognition that Lithuania could give to a noncitizen. I was now the official Grand Duke of Lithuania! I was speechless. It was a totally unexpected and incredible honor.

Debbie Miller, me, Betty Ann and Congressman John Tanner, and Tricia Wilson. Courtesy of the Sarpalius family.

After the award ceremony, John, Betty Ann, Debbie, Tricia, and I went to dinner at a restaurant in DC. We talked about freedom and what it meant to us and for countries like the Baltic states. With the fall of the Soviet Empire, Moscow had become a thriving city.

The world had certainly changed since I left Boys Ranch in 1969.

~

Later that same year, Boys Ranch invited me to speak at the church service honoring Cal Farley thirty years after his death. I flew to Amarillo, and a white station wagon picked me up at the airport. The wagon's doors had the familiar Boys Ranch logo painted in black—a cowboy riding a bucking horse with another boy behind him holding onto the cowboy's shirttail—and "Cal Farley's Boys Ranch" beneath the logo.

Once again, it was snowing on our ride to the ranch. As I gazed out the window, I recalled that same drive the day after Christmas, thirty-seven years earlier. Bobby, Karl, and I didn't know it then, but we were on our way to a place that would change our lives forever, for the better. Boys Ranch gave us a chance.

I thought of the extraordinary changes in my life, in my family, and in my world since I first passed through the gates of Boys Ranch. And

The grave site of Cal and Mimi Farley in front of Tascosa Courthouse. Courtesy of the Sarpalius family.

as we entered the gates, I began to notice many other changes that had been made there as well. The old white chapel, where Cal Farley had died, was gone. A beautiful new chapel had been built in its place a little farther back on the property. A stunning life-sized bronze statue of Cal Farley had been erected near his and Mimi's graves in front of the old

Rick Smith, Aaron Alejandro, and me. We all grew up at Boys Ranch and became friends for life. Courtesy of the Sarpalius family.

stone Tascosa Courthouse. The dorms that once held thirty-six boys were remodeled to hold four to eight kids and resembled a home instead of a dorm. Boys Ranch had changed, and all for the good. Everything I had ever accomplished, I owe to Cal Farley and his Boys Ranch.

We pulled up in front of the beautiful new Boys Ranch Chapel, built out of Colorado red stone. Cal would have been proud of it. More than five hundred children and two hundred staffers filled the chapel. The pastor walked to the podium to introduce me.

He said, "Please welcome a graduate of Boys Ranch, a former FFA state president, a former teacher here at Boys Ranch, a state senator, a US Congressman, and now the Grand Duke of Lithuania, Bill Sarpalius."

As I stood behind the podium and looked out at the crowd, with hundreds of boys, girls, and staff of every race, I choked back tears and began: "I want to tell you about a man named Cal Farley and what his Boys Ranch did for me, about how my life changed thirty years ago."

I was back home—back where it had all started.

Epilogue

M y brothers, Bobby and Karl, mean the world to me. We have
traveled an incredible journey together.

Bobby earned an associate degree from Amarillo Col-
lege, a bachelor's degree from Hardin-Simmons, and master's and doctorate degrees from Southwestern Baptist Theological Seminary. He
was a pastor for twenty years. After he left the ministry, he worked in
the defense industry for eighteen years. He then went to work as the
executive director of the Cal Farley's Boys Ranch Alumni Association
and served in dual roles for the ranch in supporting alumni activities. Bobby has three grown children. He and his wife, Cindy, live in
Arlington, Texas.

Karl earned a bachelor's degree in communications from California State University and a master's degree from Golden Gate Baptist
Theological Seminary. He also became a minister and served for nearly
forty years, including time spent as the chaplain at Boys Ranch. After
he retired from the ministry, he became a very successful photographer
(http://www.luv2shootu.com). He and his wife, Debbie, live in the San
Francisco area and have two grown sons.

My son, David, has been my greatest blessing. David earned a bachelor's degree in business administration from West Texas A&M in 2001.
He worked for United Parcel Service (UPS) and retired after twenty-
two years of service. He and his longtime girlfriend, Ann, live in Amarillo, Texas. David is a now a licensed landscape irrigator. Additionally,
he and Ann specialize in house remodeling.

David's daughter and my only grandchild, Katy, lives in Austin,
Texas, and is pursuing her own dreams. She is twenty-five years old.

Me, my brother Karl, my son David, and my brother Bobby. Courtesy of the Sarpalius family.

Gene and Tommy Sue Peggram are retired and still live in Amarillo, Texas.

Guy Finstad became the executive director of the Vocational Agricultural Teachers Association of Texas. Guy and Geneva Finstad are now enjoying retirement in Cranfills Gap, Texas.

Wesley Masters died in October 2015. He was seventy-seven years old. Wesley lived almost twenty more years after he was released from prison in Switzerland.

For the past eighteen years, Aaron Alejandro has served as the executive director of the Texas FFA Foundation. He continues to travel the state of Texas promoting the Texas FFA. Aaron and his family live in Wichita Falls, Texas.

President Vytautas Landsbergis still resides in Lithuania. He is eighty-five years old.

Lieutenant Governor Bill Hobby lives in Houston, Texas. He is eighty-six years old.

In 2004, I married my best friend, Jenny Barnett, from Lake Charles, Louisiana. She is my true inspiration. Jenny is a finance executive in the health care industry. Jenny and I split our time between the eastern shore of Maryland and Texas.

Cal Farley's Boys Ranch still stands strong today under the leadership of President Dan Adams and his board, who have successfully led the organization for more than thirteen years. Under Dan's leadership, the organization has improved significantly. Cal Farley's Boys Ranch is not the same Boys Ranch of fifty years ago. The mission of

My son, David, and my granddaughter, Katy. Courtesy of the Sarpalius family.

Cal Farley remains strong to this day. Thousands of lives have been changed for the better because of Cal Farley—his dream, dedication, and unyielding commitment to helping others. I would not have had the chance to travel my incredible journey if not for Cal Farley's Boys Ranch. I am one of many who is proud to call Boys Ranch home. My brother's family and I have continued to support the ranch over the years. The Boys Ranch rodeo is still held every Labor Day weekend. Jenny and I try to attend as often as possible. In 2017, our 1967 Boys Ranch graduating class celebrated our fifty-year reunion in Amarillo, Texas, over the Labor Day weekend so that we could attend the rodeo.

In 2017, Jenny and I donated all my legislative memorabilia to Boys Ranch. The ranch re-created my "legislative" office in my honor in the old Tascosa Courthouse building.

In March 2019, Cal Farley's Boys Ranch will celebrate its eightieth anniversary.

My wife, Jenny. Courtesy of the Sarpalius family.

INDEX

Page numbers in *italics* refer to figures.